The SUPERINTENDENT'S FIELDBOOK

The SUPERINTENDENT'S FIELDBOOK

A GUIDE FOR LEADERS OF LEARNING

NELDA CAMBRON-MCCABE ~ LUVERN L. CUNNINGHAM

JAMES HARVEY ~ ROBERT H. KOFF

A Joint Publication

CORWIN PRESS
A Sage Publications Company
Thousand Oaks, California

Illustrations by Greg LaFever.

For information:

Corwin Press
A Sage Publications Company
2455 Teller Road
Thousand Oaks, California 91320
www.corwinpress.com

Sage Publications Ltd.
1 Oliver's Yard
55 City Road
London EC1Y 1SP
United Kingdom

Sage Publications India Pvt. Ltd.
B-42, Panchsheel Enclave
Post Box 4109
New Delhi 110 017 India

Printed in the United States of America

Library of Congress Cataloging-in-Publication Data

The superintendent's fieldbook: A guide for leaders of learning/Nelda Cambron-McCabe . . . [et al.].
    p. cm.
Includes bibliographical references and index.
ISBN 1-4129-0610-5 (cloth)—ISBN 1-4129-0611-3 (pbk.)
    1. School districts—United States—Administration—Handbooks, manuals, etc.
2. School superintendents—United States—Handbooks, manuals, etc.
I. Cambron-McCabe, Nelda H.
LB2817.3.S86 2005
371.2'011—dc22

       05   06   07   10   9   8   7   6   5   4   3   2

Acquisitions Editor:	Robert D. Clouse
Editorial Assistant:	Candice L. Ling
Production Editor:	Melanie Birdsall
Copy Editor:	Sally M. Scott
Typesetter:	C&M Digitals (P) Ltd.
Proofreader:	Scott Oney
Indexer:	Julie Grayson
Cover Designer:	Michael Dubowe

Contents

Acknowledgments

The four of us have many people we want to thank. Of course, we appreciate Corwin Press for its foresight in agreeing to publish this fieldbook when it was little more than a concept in our minds. We also want to acknowledge the many individuals who developed papers and vignettes for the fieldbook. Authors are identified at the beginning of their contribution and are listed with their affiliation in Appendix C. Throughout the text, you will find artwork that illustrates our ideas, including a dynamic jigsaw-triangle outlining the seven commonplaces of school reform and how they fit together. The triangle recurs as an icon throughout the text to help orient you to where we are in discussing the commonplaces. We thank illustrator Greg LaFever of Oxford, Ohio, for this artwork. His talent and skill helped bring our ideas to life.

Above all, we want to thank the 200 members of the Forum for the American School Superintendent for the many ways in which they improved our understanding of life on the front lines. Some succeeded in what they were trying to do; some did not. We learned from them all. These superintendents were tireless public servants working year after year, often thanklessly, to improve the quality of life for the children and families in their communities. This fieldbook is dedicated to them.

This fieldbook would never have seen the light of day without generous financial support from the Danforth Foundation, St. Louis, Missouri. Danforth supported the Forum for the American School Superintendent for a decade, and then provided a grant to Miami University, in Oxford, Ohio, to finance development of the fieldbook. The authors want to acknowledge their deep debt of gratitude to Danforth and its leadership.

Corwin Reviewers

Corwin Press gratefully acknowledges the contributions of the following individuals:

Randel Beaver
Superintendent
Archer City Independent
    School District
Archer City, TX

Benjamin O. Canada
Associate Executive Director
District Services
Texas Association of School Boards
Austin, TX

Chris Christensen
Superintendent of Schools
Deubrook Area Schools
White, SD

Brenda S. Dietrich
Superintendent of Schools
Auburn-Washburn Unified School
    District #437
Topeka, KS

James Halley
Superintendent
North Kingstown School Department
North Kingstown, RI

Douglas Hesbol
Superintendent/Principal
Thomasboro Grade School
    District #130
Thomasboro, IL

Beverly Kreeger
Principal
Clermont Elementary School
Quarryville, PA

Dan Lawson
Superintendent
Tullahoma City Schools
Tullahoma, TN

Gina Marx
Assistant Superintendent
Augusta Unified School District #402
Augusta, KS

Gary P. McCartney
Superintendent
Parkland School District
Allentown, PA

Bob Moore
Superintendent
Oklahoma City Public Schools
Oklahoma City, OK

Ulrich C. Reitzug
Professor, Department Chair
University of North Carolina
Greensboro, NC

Gina Segobiano
Superintendent/Principal
Signal Hill School District #181
Belleville, IL

Glenn Sewell
Superintendent/Principal
Wheatland Union High School District
Wheatland, CA

Dennis Siegmann
Principal
Bristol Central High School
Bristol, CT

Howard W. Smith
Superintendent of Schools
Public Schools of the Tarrytowns
Tarrytown, NY

Fred A. Wall
Superintendent
Roaring Fork School District
Glenwood Springs, CO

About the Authors

 **Nelda Cambron-McCabe** is a professor in the Department of Educational Leadership, Miami University, Ohio. She was an advisory board member and a coordinator of the Danforth Foundation's Forum for the American School Superintendent. She recently coauthored *Public School Law: Teachers' and Students' Rights*, 5th ed. (2004) and *Schools That Learn* (2000).

 **Luvern L. Cunningham**, Ed. D. from the University of Oregon, has served in administrative and teaching roles from K–12 through graduate school for more than four decades. A member of the Danforth Forum advisory board, his specialties are educational leadership, the school superintendency, educational governance, inter-institutional collaboration, and inter-professional education and practice. He has served in professorships at the University of Chicago, the University of Minnesota, and Ohio State University. For several years, he served as Dean of the College of Education, Ohio State University.

 **James Harvey**, Senior Fellow at the Center on Reinventing Public Education at the University of Washington's Evans School, was a member of the Danforth Forum's advisory board. Earlier in his career he served in the Carter administration and was on the staff of the Education and Labor Committee of the U.S. House of Representatives. He helped write *A Nation at Risk* (1983) and coauthored *A Legacy*

of Learning with David Kearns, former CEO of the Xerox Corporation (2000).

 **Robert H. Koff** directs the Center for Advanced Learning at Washington University, St. Louis. He previously served as Senior Vice President of the Danforth Foundation; was Dean of the School of Education, State University of New York at Albany; and was a professor of education at Stanford University. He served on a number of state and national advisory bodies at the invitations of New York Governor Cuomo and President Carter and provided editorial advice to such journals as the *Journal of Educational Psychology.*

Part I
Orientation

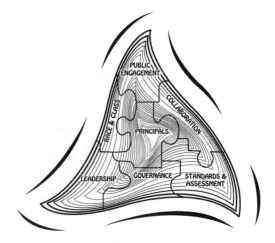

A s a school leader, you have a lot to do and little time to spare. Why should you spend any of it on another book about school leadership? Because the world is changing. You won't be able to get by with yesterday's ideas. Many of the lessons in this book can make a difference in children's lives . . . and some of them may save your career. This orientation introduces you to how that world is changing and what it means for the schools you lead.

1. Preface

So, you're sitting at the school superintendent's desk or you aspire to be behind it. Congratulations. It's a wonderful profession. Your career choice is a sign of your commitment to young people and your community. It's a good feeling, isn't it? Your family is proud of you. Your neighbors look up to you. But what are you going to do if any of the following scenarios unfolds?

• Directed by your board to bring student achievement up to national norms, you've created a national profile for your leadership. But the price has been high. Contention with principals and the teachers' union has alarmed and divided the board. And this morning your finance director insists on a private meeting, during which he drops a bombshell. The district is facing an immediate $40 million budget hole, a consequence, apparently, of the old computer system's inability to work with the new financial program. Your job's on the line.

- The telephone rings as you return from lunch with the union president. It's the local reporter who's been questioning district spending on technology. Today, he has a new issue. Some parents at one of your elementary schools are picketing the school about a library exhibit on the family. It seems the exhibit includes pictures of gay couples and their children. What do you say?

- Asked to make a presentation to the local business community about student achievement, you turn to your research director for data. What you learn is alarming. As you work through the numbers with her, it becomes apparent that respectable districtwide averages disguise an alarming achievement gap. The correlation between student performance and family income is almost perfect. Students from upper-income families (most of them white) perform very well on standardized tests; those from low-income families (many of them minority) are at the bottom of the educational pecking order. You can bury this information in your presentation to the business community, but can you live with yourself?

- While taking advantage of a professional-development opportunity that takes you out of town, you receive a call from your deputy. A crisis in the high school has erupted. Without a hearing, the principal suspended six boys for climbing onto the school roof to hang a banner as part of a Homecoming stunt. The father of one of the boys filed a lawsuit just as the local newspaper reported that the principal was inappropriately involved with a cheerleader. How do you respond?

There's nothing theoretical about any of these scenarios. Working with almost 200 superintendents in the past 10 years, the authors of this volume have heard variations on each of them. And each of these developments cost someone a job. We could cite dozens of similar examples. The truth is that the high-minded pursuit of what's best for children often runs into the rough realities of budget catastrophes, interest-group politics, human folly, and the residue and by-products of the nation's racial past. School superintendents have to be prepared to confront and deal with these challenges.

That's why this book is important. As a potential or current superintendent, you must understand that what you do not know can kill you professionally. The world is changing. Your world as an educator is changing with it. Where once school superintendents could be content to define themselves as managers, today they must understand that they are leaders of learning who are simultaneously public figures.

This fieldbook can help you cope with challenges such as those we have described. It can't guarantee success. Nothing can. But it might help you avoid major blunders. It is called a "fieldbook" because it draws on the stories and accumulated experience of nearly 200 school leaders—members of the Danforth Foundation's Forum for the American School Superintendent—as they struggled with the problems of leading today's schools. (See Appendix A for list of Danforth Forum members.)

In an effort to improve learning, these superintendents examined the latest research on brain development and tried to understand how it applies to early childhood programs. They worried about how to respond to public demands for higher standards and new assessments. They fretted about how to defend a system in which they believed while the broader environment insisted that the system justify its own existence. They explored district governance with their boards and unions. And they wrestled with the challenges of race and class in the United States, the great fault lines in our national life. Although four of us developed what you read here, in a very real sense these superintendents wrote this fieldbook. You'll find their stories and the lessons of their experience here.

Who This Book Is For

We have developed *The Superintendent's Fieldbook: A Guide for Leaders of Learning* with several audiences in mind:

• School superintendents in districts of all kinds (urban, rural, and suburban) who want to ratchet up their effectiveness will find this text a valuable resource. If you're a superintendent, this is the book you need as you struggle with the demanding leadership responsibilities of your position.

• Teachers, administrators, and deputy superintendents who are interested in moving into the superintendent's chair will gain a sense of the job's challenges. Experience is a great teacher. One definition of experience is "learning by making mistakes." Most of the school leadership mistakes that can be made have been made by the authors and contributors of this volume. Learn from them, without the pain.

• Principals interested in enhancing their own leadership will find a lot to use in this fieldbook. Here you can explore school-level issues of leadership, public engagement, collaboration, and how to create better learning environments.

• School board members and union leaders worried about the sheer amount of public abuse that schools absorb can use this volume to move beyond today's sterile dialogue about governance. Some of what you find here may call into question how your district functions, but the exercises will offer positive ways to move forward.

• Schools and colleges of education preparing potential administrators will find this a useful text. Each of the authors of this volume is affiliated with a major university, and we understand the importance of improving professional preparation. This *Superintendent's Fieldbook* can support preparation programs by buttressing theory with practical insights and hands-on experience.

• Government officials and philanthropists interested in improving pre- and in-service professional administrator development can use this book as a guide. Too frequently, government and private funders find themselves trying to improve professional development without knowing exactly what to do. This volume provides some insights.

Although developed, in brief, for current and aspiring school superintendents, this fieldbook has much to offer a variety of school leaders and institutions of higher education.

Overview

So, what is essential in a school leader? What should a fieldbook addressed to leaders incorporate? Do you need to be able to teach everything from the alphabet to calculus, trigonometry, and quantum physics? What about the budget? Perhaps you need to know how to design the spreadsheet that develops it. How about technology? Surely that's important in a new century. Should you be double-checking building wiring schematics?

Of course you shouldn't be doing any of those things. There aren't enough hours in the day, and you probably couldn't do most of them, anyway. (Well, all right, you could teach quantum physics. But the rest of that stuff is hard.) As superintendent, your job is to lead a district in which each of these tasks, among many others, is performed with a degree of excellence. You don't have to actually do them, but you do have to see that they're done. Those tasks define the superintendency of the previous century; this fieldbook helps you look ahead to the challenges of the new millennium.

The Superintendent's Fieldbook is divided into ten major "parts." These parts are laid out as follows:

I. *Orientation.* This is made up of a brief overview of how demands on school leaders are changing today, and an introduction to what we call the "commonplaces" of leadership. The rest of the fieldbook is organized around these commonplaces.

The commonplaces begin with the major elements that you need to worry about in terms of leading your organization—leadership itself and governance. Under leadership, we pay a lot of attention to metaphors of organization—images you carry around in your head that shape your understanding of leadership.

Next, the commonplaces drill down into the educational system to explore standards and assessment, race and class in our schools, and the imperative to develop school principals. The three final commonplaces step back and examine the system through a broader lens. They explore collaboration with other agencies of government and how to engage your community and its citizens productively. The last part asks what all of this means. How do the commonplaces of learning interact with the "images of organization" you have in your head to shape your leadership style.

II. *Leadership.* Here you'll learn how to think about your organization and how to distinguish between merely technical problems and "adaptive" challenges requiring deep-rooted institutional change. It's in this part that we introduce you to one of the central framing ideas of this fieldbook, the idea of "images of organization."

III. *Governance.* Do the ins-and-outs and headaches of dealing with school boards and unions bedevil you? Here you can find some answers. This part suggests that you need to understand not only how you think about your organization but also how your board and union members think about it as well. After all, you have your images; they have theirs.

IV. *Standards and Assessment.* With new demands for accountability and the No Child Left Behind legislation, it's a brave new world out there for school leaders. This part helps you make sense out of it.

V. *Race and Class.* These are the great fault lines in American life. They can also be a "third rail" that school leaders touch at their peril. Part V provides some ideas about how to approach this third rail and how to begin to close the achievement gap.

VI. *School Principals.* It's a truism, but still accurate, that schools are only as good as their principals. Here you'll find some exciting ideas about how to turn principals from building managers into leaders of learning.

VII. *Collaboration.* Think you can do it all by yourself? Think again. Who are your allies? What about the child protective services office? The employment security and public assistance offices? Medicaid and well-baby screening? This section touches on the many agencies concerned with child welfare in the United States and suggests some ways you can partner with them, particularly around early care and learning.

VIII. *Public Engagement.* You don't want to be the leader who turns around and finds no one behind her. Nor do you want to be the poor guy scurrying to get in front of the parade. School leaders, like most public officials, once thought of public engagement as public relations. It was enough to persuade the public to go along with the established policy. That no longer works. Today's public insists on helping develop that policy. This part suggests a new concept of "public engagement," one that encourages citizens to help create a shared vision of the future.

IX. *So What?* Here, the fieldbook pulls it all together, linking organizational images with the commonplaces to show how the combination can encourage certain kinds of behavior within your district. Are you curious about why your last district insisted on the party line while your new district promotes a lot of open discussion? Did your last district empower teachers and encourage a thousand flowers to bloom, while your new one specifies curriculum and assessment techniques in exquisite detail? The explanation probably lies in the different images that these districts hold of themselves. No matter what kind of school system you lead, or aspire to lead, you'll find it here.

X. *Appendices.* The final part is made up of appendices, primarily brief descriptions of the contributors to this volume and a description of the Danforth Forum.

Within each of these major sections, you will find a discussion of what these issues involve, along with vignettes describing what the issues look like on the ground. The districts discussed cover densely populated urban areas on the East and West coasts, sparsely populated local education agencies in the Southern and Plains states, and everything in between. You'll also find something else here: tools you can use in your district to get a better handle on these challenges. Most of the time, the tools are exercises to use with administrators, teachers, citizens, and parents in your district. Sometimes they're a series of questions to ask yourself. However structured, the tools are valuable exercises. Finally, each part concludes with "questions for reflective practice," a series of provocative questions designed to encourage you and your colleagues to think deeply about what you are doing.

How to Use the Fieldbook

If you're like most of us in education, you will be inclined to think you should start *The Superintendent's Fieldbook* on page one and continue until you reach the end. If you want to do that, by all means be our guest, but that's not what most people will find useful. A fieldbook is more like a reference manual than a textbook. Our inspiration came from Peter Senge's pioneering "fifth discipline" work and the fieldbooks associated with it. A fieldbook is something you should use as you need it. You will probably find that dipping in and out of the material as your needs change is the most profitable use of this fieldbook.

Some morning your challenge may be explaining student test results at a local community forum. You're likely to want to look at Parts IV (Standards and Assessment) and V (Race and Class), while ignoring the rest. The following week, you may find yourself with a major public relations crisis on your hands. Here, you're likely to find Parts II (Leadership) and VIII (Public Engagement) more immediately useful.

You may find the fieldbook useful as a guide to a series of seminars you might want to offer in your district. It benefits you little to possess a fine theoretical understanding of governance and organizational images if your board, administrators, or teachers don't know what you're talking about. The fieldbook and the exercises incorporated into it can help develop your understanding of the leadership team with which you work.

2. Introduction

Leading Learning in New Times

It's been hard to turn anywhere in recent years without hearing about American schools and the challenges they face. Presidents and members of Congress scrutinize American schools. Governors and legislators develop plans to improve them. Business leaders complain about them. Blue-ribbon commissions issue proclamations about them. And parents and other citizens worry about them. The energy behind school reform in recent decades is unprecedented in its depth, scope, intensity, and duration.

If you get nothing else from this book, understand this: your world as an educator has changed. It will never again be the same. You may have heard that before, in an intellectual sense. You're already saying, "Yes, I know that." But this book will help you understand these changes so that you can cope with them. What does it mean to lead schools in which the majority of students are children of color while the majority of teachers are white? How do you lead when citizens and local officials insist you do more with less and when national policies encourage private consumption at the expense of public investment?

Parallels to the current ferment in education can be found in few periods of our national history. The late nineteenth century, when Horace Mann and his colleagues invented the idea of public schools, comes to mind. A few years in the 1960s, as President Lyndon B. Johnson struggled to create the "Great Society," might qualify.

For sheer intensity and sustained interest in schools, however, the last two decades are nearly without equal. In 1983, the National Commission on Excellence in Education produced *A Nation at Risk*, with its stern warning of "a rising tide of mediocrity" in American life and American schools. By 1989,

For a more complete summary of education policy developments in the past 20 years, and the general nature of the argument in support of standards-based reform, see David T. Kearns and James Harvey, A Legacy of Learning: Your Stake in Standards and New Kinds of Public Schools (Washington, DC: Brookings Institution, 2000).

President George H. W. Bush had helped develop six National Educational Goals. Throughout the 1990s, states struggled to develop "aligned" educational systems, in which curriculum, assessment, and teacher training would be lined up with state standards. Much of this effort culminated in 2002 with the enactment of No Child Left Behind, legislation advanced by President George W. Bush to increase accountability, close the achievement gap, and open public schools to competition from private tutors and schools. (See Figure 1.1 for a primer on this legislation.) Nearly 20 years of intense focus on schools promise to transform how Americans define public education. These developments present you, as a school superintendent, with formidable leadership challenges. You can't afford to take them lightly.

These educational developments have been matched by equally powerful demographic changes. In most of the

| **Figure 1.1** | Did You Know? A Primer on No Child Left Behind |

On January 8, 2002, President Bush signed into law the No Child Left Behind Act, a comprehensive reauthorization of the Elementary and Secondary Education Act of 1965. (You can find the exact text of the law at *www.ed.gov/policy/elsec/leg/esea02/index.html*). Among the key provisions of the new statute:

Accountability

- States create standards for what children should know and learn for all grades. Standards must be developed in math and reading immediately, and for science by the 2005–2006 school year.
- With standards in place, states must test every student's progress toward those standards. Beginning in the 2002–2003 school year, schools must administer tests at least once in each of three grade spans: grades 3–5, grades 6–9, and grades 10–12 in all schools, starting with math and reading. Science is to be added in each of the three grade spans in 2007–2008.
- By 2005–2006, every student, in each grade from 3 to 8, is to be tested annually in math and reading.
- Each state, school district, and school is now expected to make adequate yearly progress toward meeting state standards, judged by sorting test results for students who are economically disadvantaged, are from racial or ethnic minority groups, have disabilities, or have limited English proficiency.
- School and district performance are publicly reported in district and state report cards that include individual school results.
- Within 12 years all students, from all subgroups, must perform at a proficient level under their state standards.
- If a school is found to be in need of improvement, it is to receive technical assistance and develop a two-year turn-around plan. Every student in such a school has the option of transferring.
- Schools not making adequate yearly progress for three consecutive years must continue to offer school choice and provide supplemental educational services to children, which parents will choose.
- Schools failing to make adequate progress for four consecutive years may also be required to replace staff and implement new curriculum.
- After five years, such schools will be identified for restructuring, which might involve staff firing, state takeover, private management, or conversion to charter status.

Proven Education Methods

- Beginning in 2002, millions of dollars were distributed to states for the president's Reading First plan, with the money tied to programs that use scientifically proven ways of teaching children to read.
- In addition, Early Reading First will help develop language and reading skills for preschool children, from low-income families.

Choice

- Starting in the 2002–2003 school year, parents with a child enrolled in a school identified as in need of improvement could transfer their child to a better-performing public school or public charter school.
- Parents with children in a school identified as in need of improvement are able to use federal education funds for "supplemental education services." Those services include tutoring, after-school services, and summer school programs.
- Starting in 2002, hundreds of millions of federal dollars could be used to establish and fund charter schools.

nation's major urban areas, minority students make up a majority of public school enrollment. And the face of minority America is changing. When President Johnson set out to create the Great Society, the term "minority" primarily referred to African Americans. As the nation enters fully into the twenty-first century, however, Hispanic and Latino Americans make up the largest minority population in the United States. Meanwhile, the number and proportion of Asian Americans is increasing rapidly.

In fact, it won't be long before white students are a minority in public schools. Indeed, sometime within the next two generations, assuming current trends and birth rates continue, white Americans will become a minority in the United States. We mention these developments not because they change our fundamental understanding of what the United States wants from its schools, but because they will profoundly change how we understand who we are. In fact, it's no exaggeration to say that you, as a school leader, will encounter sooner than most the effects of the changing face of America. Schools are a sort of "early indicator system" for the challenges communities encounter as their populations change. You need to be prepared for this.

As school superintendent, you also need to alert your community to the economic correlates of emerging demographic and educational realities (see Figure 1.2). If current trends are permitted to develop without thoughtful policy responses, the social structure in the United States will begin to resemble that of a Third World country. Despite its great riches, this will become a society in which a relatively small layer of wealthy and well-educated citizens (mostly white) enjoy all the blessings of American prosperity, while a large population of poor and badly educated citizens (mostly minority) struggle to make ends meet. This is not the America most of us want to bequeath to our children. The moral dimension of your work is the task of passing on to future generations the ideal of the United States as a beacon of hope in a world of want and oppression.

A compelling case for new ways of organizing and governing public schools while engaging community interest can be found in Paul T. Hill, Christine Campbell, and James Harvey, It Takes a City: Getting Serious About Urban School Reform *(Washington, DC: Brookings Institution, 2000).*

Troubled? Don't be. As one former superintendent put it, "leaders make their own good days." Franklin D. Roosevelt, he said, never "had a good day." Laid low by polio as a young man, President Roosevelt took office during the Great Depression and was then forced to lead the nation in a great global war, involving unprecedented carnage and loss of life around the world. He died before that

Figure 1.2   Changing U.S. Demographics, 2000–2070

Projections, US Population by Race/Ethnicity, 2070

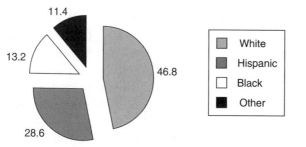

☐	White
■	Hispanic
☐	Black
■	Other

SOURCE: U.S. Bureau of the Census

war ended. Yet Roosevelt is universally remembered as the supreme optimist, the "Happy Warrior." As a leader, you'll have to make your own good days.

Which reminds us, the challenges are still piling up. The business community has imposed new concepts of management and markets on schools. Corporate titans have argued that the private sector needs to find some way into the schools to shake things up. Charter schools. Home schooling. Vouchers. All of these approaches owe something to the ethic of competition and the market.

As if the difficulties of dealing with a climate of public skepticism and changing demographics were not sufficient, you may be expected to respond with a financial hand tied behind your back. The 1990s were a bit of an anomaly for public finance. A burgeoning economy and an ebullient stock market promised rivers of cash for public services, including education. Unhappily, that period has ended, at least in the short run. As our schools move more fully into the twenty-first century, communities are casting a skeptical eye on municipal finances and requests for new levies. Even foundations are piling on. Once content to fund school efforts uncritically, they now show an increasing tendency to withhold awards when unhappy with progress. Many of these pressures are most acute in low-income rural and urban communities, precisely the places you are likely to wind up as a new superintendent (rural) or a savvy, experienced hand (urban). Aren't you glad you got into this line of work?

It now turns out that an unusual idea has developed. It holds that people who were never trained to do the work of leading schools are better equipped to lead them than those who were. The thinking is that "leadership" is what is required, not competence in leading schools. The argument is that leaders who were trained in traditional school administration have demonstrably failed, leaving the field open to others. Many large urban systems have instead experimented with nontraditional leaders whom they have plucked out of the ranks of the military, law, and business, and even from the ranks of former professional basketball players and nonprofit managers.

This is a very interesting phenomenon that intimately involves you. In effect, it makes the following argument: because school superintendents have to be school experts, leaders, solid managers, and savvy public officials, effective superintendents can be found in any of these four labor pools. The implications of this view for institutions preparing superintendents, and for the competition you will encounter as you seek a superintendent's position, are intriguing. This view of the world argues that, to succeed as a superintendent, the training you are likely to need may be found just as easily in schools of government, public affairs, business administration, and communications as in traditional schools of education.

And, in fact, in many ways the experience of the Danforth Forum corroborates that insight. The professional development provided to superintendents during the 10 years the Danforth Forum existed drew from many sources. It called on Harvard's John F. Kennedy School of Government, the University of Pittsburgh's Learning Research and Development Center, and the University of Pennsylvania's Annenberg School of Communications, among others. Even a former CEO of the Xerox Corporation, David T. Kearns, and a university president, Lattie Coor of Arizona State University, offered their insights.

Because, you see, "leadership" is a large concept, one that is sketched out on a very big canvas by many prominent thinkers. It is only in understanding these concepts that you can develop a theory of action to guide your life—and your decisions—as a school leader. The next section in this first part breaks down this large concept into seven bite-sized nuggets. It introduces you to the bedrock organizing principle of this fieldbook—the seven "commonplaces" of school leadership. The remaining parts of the fieldbook develop each of these commonplaces in turn.

3. The "Commonplaces" of School Leadership

It's very easy for educators to get bogged down in complex theory. They can quickly lose sight of the practical issues involved in educating large numbers of students. In the 1960s and 1970s, the University of Chicago's Joseph J. Schwab warned teachers and administrators in uncompromising terms of the dangers of overreliance on theory. By its very nature, he wrote, theory "does not and cannot take account of all the matters which are crucial to questions of what, who, and how to teach. . . . [T]heories cannot be applied . . . to the solution of problems concerning . . . real individuals, small groups, or real institutions."

See Joseph J. Schwab, Science, Curriculum and Liberal Education: Selected Essays, ed. Jan Westbury (Chicago: University of Chicago Press, 1978).

In place of arcane and complex theory, Schwab argued that an adequate theory of instruction could rest on four relatively straightforward "commonplaces": curriculum, teaching, learning, and community. These were Schwab's stakes in the ground. With them, educators could understand what they were doing. Without them, theory had little meaning.

If those are the commonplaces of instruction, what are the stakes in the ground for leadership today? What skills do you have to command as a school leader to do what you were hired to do? What are the "commonplaces" of school leadership today?

We believe there are seven, as shown in Figure 1.3. Although we call them the "commonplaces of leadership," there is nothing simple about them. They are, however, stakes in the ground. You cannot be fully effective as a superintendent unless you master them. To develop them completely will require a very deep, clinical exposure to these ideas. It will take a lot of work. In fact, you might just need to unlearn a lot of what you've learned at great cost in dollars and time. What we describe here will sometimes contradict what you were taught in your formal preparation.

These seven concepts grew out of a major investment in a broad conceptual sweep of the state of public affairs in the United States. Over 10 years, with our colleagues in the Forum, we asked internationally renowned experts on public opinion (such as pollster Daniel Yankelovich of Public Agenda and Dean Kathleen Hall Jamieson of the Annenberg School for Communication at the University of Pennsylvania) to share with us their insights into how the public comes to judgment. We sought the advice of Harvard University's Ronald Heifetz, Martin Linsky, and Marc Roberts about the nature of leadership amid economic,

Figure 1.3   The Commonplaces of School Leadership

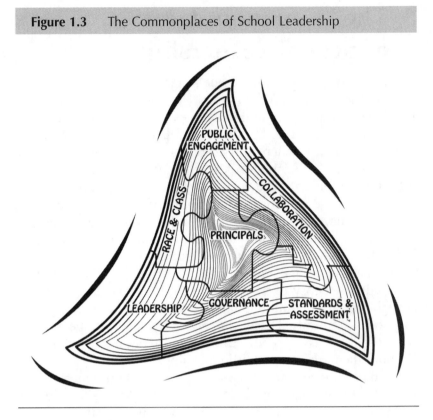

demographic, social, and political change. We studied learning organizations with Lauren Resnick of the Learning Research and Development Center at the University of Pittsburgh and with Peter Senge's colleagues Charlotte Roberts and Nelda Cambron-McCabe. From author Lizbeth Schorr we extended our knowledge of what's involved in preschool development. All of this was rounded off by the personal stories of about 200 school superintendents.

From this activity, we learned that seven issues are rapidly becoming the "commonplaces" of the world of the modern school superintendent:

• You must *lead*. You will be expected to lead your school system, not simply manage its operations. The existing governance system and relations with unions may orient you around making sure the buses run on time, but you have to find a way to reshape governance and union-management relations so that the entire district focuses on learning. This volume will highlight the difference between adaptive and technical leadership and will provide you with some advice on how to manage different issues as they ripen.

- You must lead within a *governance* structure that is hardly ideal. In some ways, you have an impossible job. You are simultaneously an educator, manager, budget-maker, public servant, politician, community leader, and local preacher. In each of these roles, you are subject to second-guessing by everyone around you, including the board to which you report and the teachers (and their union) you nominally supervise. You must find a way to work with your board and your unions.

- You must understand *standards and assessment.* You may have to become a data-driven field scientist to boost student achievement. You will need an expert grasp of what is required of you from federal and state officials in terms of standards—and how those standards are gauged by emerging assessments. These new developments carry with them powerful implications for your community, requiring you to demonstrate a confident grasp of data and analysis that has never before been expected of any public official. This book will provide you with practical advice on how and where to begin—whether you are the only professional in the central office or you oversee an office with hundreds of professionals.

- You must worry about *race and class* in your district and set out to close the achievement gap. Of all the imperatives, this one may be the most challenging, opening up all of the sores and wounds of the nation's racial past, while requiring of you a level of patience and dedication that will try most people's souls. In this volume, you will find tools for holding difficult conversations and advice from others who have gone before you.

- It goes without saying that you must develop your schools' *principals.* You will succeed or fail as a leader based on the quality of the leaders you put in place in schools. It's simple. Good schools require good principals. This book provides lessons from the field.

- You will have to learn how to *collaborate.* It is no longer sufficient to oversee a school system that worries about children from kindergarten through grade twelve and from 8:00 in the morning until 3:00 in the afternoon, 180 days a year. You have to worry about your students when they're not in school, persuading the community it needs to invest in them, while fending off those who think you should stick to your knitting. The fieldbook has some suggestions to offer and some compelling stories to tell.

- You must *engage your community*. The days of superintendents arriving with a mandate and imposing it on the community are over. You will have to work with your community to create a shared sense of what the community wants to accomplish through its schools. This fieldbook can show you how.

These seven "commonplaces," then, frame the rest of this fieldbook. Our position is straightforward. These issues are the stakes in the ground framing leadership for twenty-first-century schools. They are the heart of the matter. You must also, obviously, be doing a lot of other things; if you are not intimately engaged in these seven, however, it is hard to know how you can succeed.

Think about that. What is more important to you as a superintendent (or potential superintendent) than leading your district, making governance work, understanding standards and assessment, worrying about race and class, developing school principals, collaborating with other community agencies, and engaging your community? Simply to ask the question is to answer it. If your priorities are elsewhere, there is a very good chance you're wasting your time.

Part II
Leading
Your Schools

LEADERSHIP

W hat will it take to lead your schools? How can you transform education in your district as you face the daunting obstacles that make the superintendency what one recent study called "an impossible job"? This part launches you on a learning journey in which you encounter the first of our seven "commonplaces"—leadership itself.

1. Orientation

Leadership Theory
for the Theoretically Challenged

James Harvey
Robert H. Koff

In imitation of innumerable "how-to" books for "dummies," we were tempted to call this chapter "Leadership Theory for Dummies." But that threatens to be offensive in a way that "DOS for Dummies" never was. Outside the arcane and specialized world of technology, people don't mind admitting their ignorance about computer programming. But you're expected to understand the basics of your own motivation. You can't afford to acknowledge ignorance here. Most people, however, won't hold it against you if you have little interest in theory. In fact, some will take that as a good sign and consider you a better person for it.

The previous section reminded you of the macro-challenges facing educators everywhere today. This section explores what these developments mean for you as a leader.

Robert Starratt gives you insight into cultivating meaning and community in Centering Educational Administration *(Mahwah, NJ: Lawrence Erlbaum, 2003).*

For the "theoretically challenged," therefore, we want to give you enough information to understand that, as German psychologist Kurt Lewin put it, there's "nothing as practical as a good theory."

The first big theory we want to put before you is the notion that your image of the organization you are leading profoundly influences how you understand your role. (In turn, how others imagine your organization powerfully influences how they understand what they expect from you.) You're going to hear a lot about "images of organization."

Then, leaning heavily on the work of Ron Heifetz of Harvard University, we introduce you to the distinction between "adaptive" and "technical" challenges. You know how to develop a bus schedule or budget. That's technical work. But how do you help your community understand the role of its schools in economic development? Or why changing demographics in the district are important? That's adaptive work.

One way to think about how to advance these important issues is by turning your district into a "learning organization," one that assesses its own progress. Here we rely on Peter Senge's "fifth discipline" work as applied to schools by several of his coauthors and colleagues. This work gives you some sense of what's involved in transforming your district so that everyone— from you and your senior staff to your bus drivers and maintenance people—is focused on learning.

We conclude with questions to encourage you to reflect on your practice. Most people aren't asking these questions. You can't afford to ignore them.

2. Thinking About Your Organization

Forget most of what you think you know about organizational behavior. Put it out of your mind. Much of it bears little relationship to reality. Like many of us, your view of your organization is shaped by mental metaphors defining what you think a school district should be. Do you envision your district as a well-honed machine? Or is it a comfortable and forgiving family and culture? Perhaps it's more akin to a political coalition?

In this section, you will learn about different metaphors and how they shape your understanding of your role and your conception of responsibility. We will also introduce you to the first tool you can apply in leading your district.

A. Images of Organization

Nelda Cambron-McCabe
James Harvey

Ronald A. Heifetz's Leadership Without Easy Answers (Cambridge, MA: Belknap Press of Harvard University Press, 1994) is a powerful description of the difference between adaptive and technical leadership and what is involved with both.

See Gareth Morgan's Images of Organization: The Executive Edition (San Francisco: Berrett-Koehler Publishers, 1998) for a compelling description of mental images at work in organizational development.

It was the late 1990s, and Peter Negroni, the superintendent in Springfield, Massachusetts, knew he was in trouble. He and the school board were at each other's throats. The board was divided and couldn't see things his way. He sensed that it was just a matter of time before he and the district came to a parting of the ways.

Then a simple question at a Danforth seminar opened his eyes to new possibilities. The question transformed his relationship with the board and the district. "What do the board members have to lose in this transaction?" asked Ron Heifetz of the John F. Kennedy School of Government. The question got Negroni's attention, because he had begun to look at board questions as ill-motivated meddling. He'd been looking at the challenges of dealing with the board largely from his own perspective and that of students and parents, rather than from the board members' point of view.

Once he began to take the question seriously, he was able to reinvigorate his leadership of the district—and to open himself and the district to a new vision of the superintendent as a leader of learning. His responsibility now extended beyond making sure the buses ran on time to creating what he consciously thought of as a "learning organization" in which the district itself became a living, breathing organism. (See section 3E, "'Lone Ranger' to Lead Learner," for a detailed description of Negroni's journey.)

Professor Gareth Morgan of York University in Toronto, Canada, has written compellingly about the images most of us carry in our heads about the nature of organizations and institutions. His work is as applicable to schools, churches, and the nonprofit world as it is to corporations and government agencies.

All organizational (and management) theory, Morgan writes, is derived from images or metaphors that help us understand organizational situations in powerful, yet incomplete, ways. These metaphors are compelling. They extend our insight, help us manage complexity, and assist us in visualizing the similarities between a reality we face and an ideal of some kind in our mind's eye. Paradoxically, of course, these images also distort our perceptions by encouraging us to ignore differences between the reality we face and the ideal we cling to. As Morgan puts it, "ways of seeing become ways of not seeing" as well.

See Figure 2.8, the "Ladder of Inference," as a way of working with these images within an organization.

Images and metaphors also permit different observers to view the same situation through different lenses. If central office personnel see the district as a "structure," they will find plenty of structural elements to worry about. If they think of it as a living, breathing organism, as Negroni began to see Springfield, the task of finding ways to nourish the organism takes on new urgency. In a sense, images become self-fulfilling prophecies. That can be dangerous, but there's nothing wrong with this tendency as long as we recognize it.

Morgan describes several metaphors that guide how most of us understand the organizations with which we are involved. These include

• The organization as *machine*—a mechanistic metaphor of the organization as something made up of interlocking parts that must be made to mesh and work together smoothly.

• The organization as *organism*—a metaphor in which the needs of the organization and its environment are emphasized, along with consideration of how organizations grow, develop, adapt, and decline.

• The organization as a *brain*—a metaphor emphasizing information processing, intelligence, learning, and the possibility of developing intelligent learning organizations.

• Organizations as *cultures*—a metaphor emphasizing values, beliefs, norms, rituals, and patterns of shared meaning.

• Organizations as *political entities* or systems of government—a metaphor in which politics, power relationships, and conflict tell the major story.

• The organization as a *psychic prison*—a metaphor where people become trapped in their own beliefs about the nature and shape of the organization.

• The organization as a site of *flux and transformation*—this metaphor involves several models, one of which, drawing on theories of chaos and complexity, insists that order can emerge from disorder in complex, even chaotic, systems.

• Organizations as *instruments of domination*—this final metaphor emphasizes the exploitative aspects in some elements of organizational life.

These metaphors resonate powerfully with much of the dialogue about organizational life and school administration. For every practical educator and business leader who wishes that somehow schools' diverse interests could be made to work together more harmoniously (the organization as machine), there can be found another assuring the world that order emerges from chaos (the organization as flux). For every idealist who is intent on advancing them concept of schools as living organisms, you will find a self-styled realist insisting that they are political entities in which power and district politics are the predominant forms of engagement. And visionaries intent on creating schools as learning organizations are more than matched by cynics emphasizing that they are power-driven entities, political institutions capable of exploitation.

Here's the beauty of these metaphors. These images give you a chance to understand how you view your organization, as well as an insight into how others view it. Imagine that you're trying to shake up the existing order of things while leading a central office wedded to the concept of the district as a machine. You probably won't make much progress unless you help central office employees reframe their thinking. One place to start is with the image of the organization your people hold in their heads.

You don't have to think of these images as mutually exclusive. In fact, they're not (as you can see in Table 2.1). It's easy to see how an organization might be dominated by a machine metaphor, supported by secondary images of the organization as a brain (emphasizing data systems) and as a political entity (in which the machine's goals are determined at the top). Conversely, a dominant metaphor might be the district as an organism, with supporting story lines emphasizing culture (beliefs and values) and flux and transformation (order emerging from disorder).

Nothing really prepares you for this job. I was 22 years in one system, coming up through the ranks to an associate superintendent. I thought I was ready. . . . The difference to being second in command and the superintendent is so vast and so unexplainable because of the political context of the job.

Linda Murray,
Superintendent,
San Jose Unified
School District,
California

Table 2.1   Imagining Your School District

Image	Nature	Strengths/Weaknesses
Inherited Images		
Machine	Goals and objectives predominate; rational structure; organizational charts; people interchangeable within the system.	Works well where machines work well/Creates a sort of mindless bureaucracy.
Political System	Management as political process; identify different styles of government; view politicization as near inevitable and accept conflict as normal; study power and learn how to use to best advantage.	Puts power and conflict center stage while emphasizing the interest-based nature of organization/Breeds more politics and can understate gross inequalities in power and influence.
Psychic Prison	Psychic forces encourage or block innovation; frozen mindsets and unconscious forces make people resist change; irrational things take on power and significance; people imprisoned by their own way of thinking.	Challenges basic assumptions, puts the "irrational" in new perspective, and encourages the management of tension/Focus on unconscious may deflect attention from other forces of control.
Instrument of Domination	Power dominates organizational activity; workaholism, occupational accidents, and social and mental stress common; exploitation of employees and customers taken for granted.	Indicates that rationality can be mode of domination and brings ethical concerns to forefront/Metaphor is so extreme it can polarize discussion.
Emerging Images		
Culture	Organization as unique mini-society; organization reflects people; accept idea that some cultures are uniform, others fragmented.	Emphasizes symbolic significance and interdependence of management and labor in everything/Can manipulate and ignore some dimensions of culture.
Organism	Focus on open systems; organizational health, life cycles, and development considered important; adapting to environment encouraged; relationships of species to ecology explored.	Contributes to organizational development/Easily becomes ideology and overstates cohesion in most organizations.
Brain	Examine organizational intelligence; interest in learning organizations; use technology to decentralize and distribute intelligence.	Recognizes importance of paradox and provides clear guidelines for learning organizations/May be naïve if conflicts arise over learning and realities of power.
Flux and Transformation	Try to understand fundamental nature of change; look "around the corner"; analyze systemic forces encouraging change; try to encourage organization to shift from one pattern of operation to another.	Leaders get powerful new perspective on role in encouraging change/May imply that leaders and managers just have to "go along for the ride" and are powerless to do much about change.

SOURCE: Adapted from Gareth Morgan, *Images of Organization: The Executive Edition* (San Francisco: Berrett-Koehler Publishers, 1998).

There's no rule that requires you to have a simplistic image of your district. Your metaphors need to be as complex as the district you lead.

Although Morgan did not characterize his metaphors in this way, you may find it helpful to visualize models of inherited structures of school administration and models of emerging practice. Under inherited images, we find the district described as a machine, a political system, a psychic prison, and even, unlikely as it seems, an instrument of domination. Each of these can be thought of as distinct and different. What would they look like in your school district? In combination, if these images came to dominate school administration, we can predict that most educators would not like what they would see. These images imply a return to the schools of the 1950s, confrontational union-management relations, and the revival of the nineteenth-century emphasis on corporal punishment and stamping out difference. (Some minority leaders would argue that current urban schools, with their tolerance for minority failure, act, in fact, as instruments of oppression for minority students. On the basis of that argument, some of these leaders argue for greater choice for minority students, including vouchers to help them attend private schools.)

The emerging images, perhaps because they are complex and still developing, are more difficult to describe completely. The image of the organization as a culture is a familiar one. All organizations are characterized by their own culture. Emerging cultural images call on you to build organizations that reflect the diverse values and history of the people within them. In this emerging arena, a growing literature has developed that describes organizations as learning institutions. Much of this literature was developed in *The Fifth Discipline,* by Peter Senge, and subsequently applied to schools by Senge, Nelda Cambron-McCabe, and their colleagues in *Schools That Learn.* Morgan's work pushes our understanding of learning organizations further. Now we are asked to visualize schools as organisms (emphasizing mutual interdependence among systems), as brains (in which intelligence and control are distributed across the system), and as sites of flux and transformation (emphasizing self-renewal). It was possibilities such as these that reenergized Peter Negroni in Springfield.

The reality is that, as you shape your view of your district based on the metaphors and images you bring to it, you also shape and form what you think your job as super-intendent actually is (see Table 2.2).

Peter M. Senge, The Fifth Discipline: The Art and Practice of the Learning Organization *(New York: Doubleday, 1990).*

Peter Senge, Nelda Cambron-McCabe, Timothy Lucas, Bryan Smith, Janis Dutton, and Art Kleiner, Schools That Learn: A Fifth Discipline Fieldbook for Educators, Parents, and Everyone Who Cares About Education *(New York: Doubleday, 2000).*

Table 2.2 Acting Out Your Metaphor

The Image	What It Looks Like in Your District	How You Act
Inherited Images		
Machine	Detailed rules and regulations govern school operation and curriculum; emphasis on control, accountability, and uniform outcomes; separation of planning and design of teaching from classroom delivery.	You are either a mechanic or an organization man or woman. You supervise, monitor, oversee, and enforce rules; you see individuals as replaceable; you subordinate individual interests to organizational goals; you focus on uniform "products."
Political System	Competing interests in school and community dominate decision making; interests, conflicts, and power continuously assessed; power relationships always under consideration.	You are a politician. You build coalitions among stakeholders to support schools; you use formal power of position to structure agenda; you think that knowledge is power and use information as a political tool.
Psychic Prison	District is trapped in old ways of thinking; blind spots obscure new ideas and pedagogies; district unable to think past current school structures.	You bully people. You use rules to reinforce the status quo; to you, boundaries are a big deal. You encourage "groupthink" so that the district fails to see other options.
Instrument of Domination	Inequality in educational opportunities and resources among schools and students is taken for granted. School sites are "battlegrounds" rather than teams or collaboratives. Labor-management strife is rampant, and educators' work is "deskilled" or made teacher proof.	You dominate people. You believe in managerially rational decisions without concern for unintended consequences; you reproduce privilege and advantage of certain groups; and you emphasize organizational efficiency and effectiveness at expense of individual needs of students and teachers.
Emerging Images		
Culture	Schools may be defined by social processes, images, symbols, and rituals. Or evidence of the competitive spirit of American society may be reflected in schools, which are encouraged to be different or to compete with each other for resources.	You are the superintendent as bard. You lead by developing shared meaning. You shape stories, legends, and myths to create culture. You encourage organizational change through cultural change, and you tend to worry about the symbolic significance of every aspect of schools.
Organism	Schools and their environment are viewed as mutually dependent and interactive. The district seeks alignment of interrelated subsystems and collaboration with other community interests.	You are a gardener. You scan the environment for changing conditions. You structure leadership for continuous adaptation and worry about the "fit" between the schools you lead and your community
Brain	Intelligence and control are distributed throughout the system. Flexible, resilient, and inventive systems valued. An integrated information web exists across schools so that leadership can be diffused; schools are guided by core values that shape behavior.	You are a teacher, learner, and problem solver. Through inquiry, you encourage a "learning to learn" orientation in schools. You engage in "double-loop" learning—questioning assumptions and appropriateness of existing norms. You imagine and anticipate new futures, and you uncover forces/structures beneath recurring problems.
Flux and Transformation	Educational chaos theory is at work. Schools self-create and self-renew from chaos. Small changes can lead to massive system change (the famous image of a butterfly flapping its wings in Tokyo and precipitating a downpour in New York); meaning and purpose serve as primary points of reference; the key role of relationships and participation in creating the reality of schools is emphasized.	You organize anarchy. You shape and create new contexts to encourage self-organization. You use minimum specifications to create contexts. You nurture emerging context for change rather than controlling change, and you direct attention to "attractors" that pull systems into new forms rather than directing attention to how to resist change. You highlight the tensions between reality and aspirations.

If your district is a machine, what does that imply for you as superintendent? You may not like the answer (although your school board and local political leaders might). When the district is a machine, you as superintendent are expected to attend to it. Your job is that of a high-level mechanic, expected to grease the wheels, maintain the parts, and make sure the machinery functions the way it was designed. But your functions change dramatically if you select a different metaphor. Take the image of the district as an organism. Now your task is more akin to that of a gardener or even a scientist. Most of your energy will be devoted to caring for this organism's environment and worrying about how to feed and nourish it.

Take some time to think about the images you hold and the metaphors you like to use. As a school leader, what's the image of your district that comes to mind? The answer to that question defines how you see your role.

What, then, is a school district about in terms of the metaphors that might describe it? Several different possibilities offer themselves. Business leaders (and many analysts) are quite fond of the machine metaphor. At conferences of one kind or another, including school conferences, they are likely to produce displays of an organization represented by an enormous arrow pointing in a specific direction (see Figure 2.1). This huge arrow holds many smaller arrows that point chaotically to different points on the compass, and even in reverse.

You're likely to be told that this unsatisfactory state of affairs represents your school district. The big arrow represents the

Figure 2.1   Organization as Culture

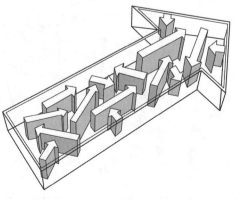

central goal of the district, almost invariably described as achievement or student learning. The smaller chaotic arrows represent the different tendencies within your district, possibly the focus of teachers on conditions of employment and your board's interest in its perquisites of office. Whatever the smaller arrows represent, they are a distraction from the Main Thing the district is supposed to be worrying about. Ideally, the small arrows should be aligned to support the central orientation of the district.

You should note that the system described here is completely self-contained. The assumptions on which this is built hold that a single goal defines the district's many purposes and that there is no interchange of any kind with the larger world. As superintendent in this world, you preside over an entity that is unable to deal with external constituents. They, in turn, are unable to deliver a message to you. (As the poet said: "Oh, wilderness were paradise, enow.")

Inevitably, in this presentation, a new image appears (see Figure 2.2). In the new image, all the arrows within the holding bin are neatly aligned in the central direction. This is still an isolated and self-contained organization. It does not interact with the outside world. The larger community has no way of influencing what goes on inside the system. When this desirable state of affairs has been attained, however, everything in your district will be attuned seamlessly to the pursuit of higher student achievement. Theoretically compelling, this image represents a bit of a dream world. It leaves no room for the zeal with which adults in your community may insist on athletic

Figure 2.2   The Aligned Machine

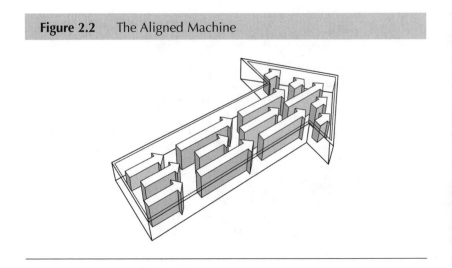

championships or the fascination of students with members of the opposite sex. It allows no time for students' emotional, social, or personal growth. In fact, when push comes to shove, this arrow will create pressures to cut music, arts, and drama (and even whether children have recess) in the search for higher test scores.

The litany of alignment is familiar. In fact, it has been encoded in federal law under the administrations of presidents Bill Clinton and George W. Bush. Standards are to be developed to establish the learning goals (central direction) of the system. Then curriculum, assessment, and teacher professional development are to be aligned with those standards. Regular assessment of student learning is intended to keep your district on track toward the standards, creating a district that hums with machinelike precision in pursuit of a learning nirvana, which, under the provisions of No Child Left Behind, is to be achieved in 12 years.

What is rarely put explicitly on the table in this discussion is that alignment threatens to turn the American tradition of school governance on its head. At its root, the alignment vision suspects that local citizens can't be trusted to oversee their own schools.

Figure 2.3 depicts the new policy context that is driving alignment. To implement demands for accountability, decisions about school goals are being moved as far from the classroom as possible. Federal legislation directs what states have to do in order to receive federal funds; states, in turn, transmit those pressures to local school districts. You, as superintendent, then transfer these pressures to your principals, teachers, students, and families.

With respect to schools, things probably are not that simple. Alignment might be a wonderful way to organize a plant that produces ball bearings, but it is hard to understand its relationship to what an institution of learning in a free society should look like. The United States is a place that celebrates differences, not conformity. Local autonomy and personal independence are greatly prized in this society. Freedom from the "heavy hand of government" is a cornerstone of American economic thinking. Yet you, as superintendent, are like the Soviet farmer with an unrealistic production schedule. The principal difference is that, unlike the farmer in the former Soviet Union, who was given five years, you've been handed a 12-year plan.

Another image can be conceived, as shown in Figure 2.4. This image also defines high student achievement as the dominant goal. It doesn't pretend that performance isn't important. But

Figure 2.3   The Accountability Policy Context

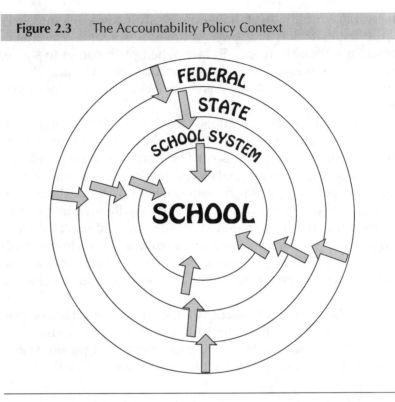

this image also takes Gareth Morgan's metaphor of the brain and its learning organization orientation to heart. Although this image also conceives of schools and districts as places with fairly well-defined boundaries, it assumes that the membrane separating the schools from the community (and the larger policy arena) is permeable. This figure does not ignore the economic or social imperatives governing schools. It embeds schools in a policy context that respects community and family sensibilities. It asks that the educational vision for the nation's school systems be developed out of the core values and the shared meanings and relationships that define community in a free society.

Something else stands out in Figure 2.4. Impulses from within the school and district can find an outlet in the family and community—just as pressures from the policy context, the community, and the family can be transferred to the schools. This image says, "The district's schools are in and of the community. They are your schools. Together we will work out how we expect them to educate your children to the highest possible standards.

Figure 2.4   The Learning Organization

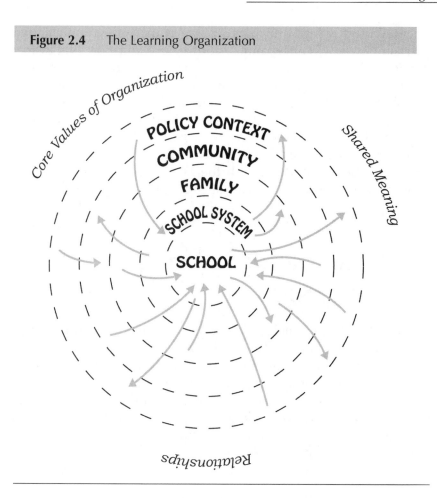

Like friends and family, we will have disagreements. Differences of opinion are to be expected on occasion. But we will respect those difference as, together, we pursue what is best for our children."

Take another look at Figure 1.3. The figure illustrates what alignment looks like when learning respects the contributions of family, school, and community. The triangle of seven common-places still focuses on leaving no child behind. What it does not do is pretend that high achievement for all can be guaranteed solely through standards and assessment, not even when substantial funds are provided. Instead, the triangle vibrates with the tension that is inevitably involved when the many complex variables involved with human learning—what we call the seven commonplaces—are being successfully nurtured, encouraged, and balanced.

When you lead a district capable of managing that creative tension, you will be leading a learning organization. Not everything will go smoothly. There will be days when you wonder why you bothered getting out of bed. Your tolerance for ambiguity will be stretched to the limit. But you will produce more real learning by creating and leading this kind of risk-taking learning organization than your colleague in the next county who is directing an aligned machine ever will.

This fieldbook deals with the task of describing what you need to be able to do to create such a learning organization.

3. Encouraging Adaptive Leadership

Ronald A. Heifetz helped revolutionize thinking about leadership when he published *Leadership Without Easy Answers* in 1994. He and his team from Harvard University's John F. Kennedy School of Government are greatly in demand all over the world as they help governments, corporations, and nonprofit entities explore their leadership challenges. Heifetz spent quite a bit of time with us over several years talking about the implications of his work for school leaders.

A. Principles of Adaptive Leadership

James Harvey
Nelda Cambron-McCabe

> *Ron Heifetz emphasizes a practical philosophy of leadership—*
> *"an orienting set of questions and options for confronting the*
> *hardest of problems without getting killed, badly wounded, or*
> *pushed aside." Aspiring and newly appointed superintendents,*
> *as well as seasoned veterans, will find his distinction between*
> *adaptive and technical issues right on the mark. This distinc-*
> *tion will help you understand why some aspects of your work*
> *are so intractable.*

"Why are leaders attacked?" is a question very much on Ron Heifetz's mind. "Why are reputations destroyed? Why is it that sometimes national leaders are, literally, assassinated?"

"The complicated academic answer," he suggests, "is that the link between authority and leadership is broken and that some members of the 'tribe' expect complex problems to be solved with technical fixes. The simple answer is that leaders are attacked because what they are asking of us represents a loss—a loss of respect, an important value, a competence, or a privilege. The leader may understand that a gain lies over the hill, but the people being asked to follow can't see over the hill."

And, Heifetz cautions, "Leadership in this context involves the hard work of holding people together and resisting the demands for quick answers." In this situation, the best that you as a school superintendent can do is to ask the right questions, provide information, and frame the issues. "Giving the work back to the people" is what Heifetz calls it. It can be a difficult thing to do, particularly in times of distress, because the greater the crisis, the more desperately we look to authority figures for the "right" answer.

Adaptive and Technical Leadership

"When you think about leadership issues," advises Heifetz, "be aware of key distinctions between technical and adaptive problems." The classic error in both human and animal societies is to treat adaptive problems as if they were merely technical.

The biggest leadership challenges revolve around adaptive problems—new threats, different forces, changes in the environment, shifts in the earth's axis. A leadership challenge is that most people are reluctant to change and want every problem treated as a technical issue that can be solved quickly by those in authority. As a superintendent, according to Heifetz, your leadership challenge "is to confront the 'tribe' with the gap between its aspirations and current reality." For example, we talk about all children achieving at high levels in our school districts. Disaggregated data, however, paint a very different picture of achievement. Progress on a problem such as this requires both the school and community to learn. It also often demands changes in people's attitudes, values, and behavior.

Leaders are expected to provide five things for their followers, according to Heifetz. Like mature silverbacks in gorilla colonies, leaders are expected to provide *direction*, so that the group knows where it is headed; *protection*, so that

Ronald A. Heifetz's Leadership Without Easy Answers *provides the theoretical framework for taking up adaptive work in your school district.* Leadership on the Line: Staying Alive Through the Dangers of Leading *(Boston: Harvard Business School Press, 2002), written by Heifetz and Marty Linsky, leads you through the practical aspects of doing this difficult but meaningful work.*

Heifetz warns us, "If you have an adaptive problem that you treat as a technical issue, it will take longer to solve than if you confronted it as an adaptive problem from the start."

the group can protect itself from attacks; *orientation*, because people do not like to be confused about what their role is; *conflict resolution*, so that equilibrium can be maintained; and *norms*, because people have to understand what is involved with being a member of a particular community.

All of these things can be provided in both adaptive and technical areas, but they are much more difficult in an adaptive environment. Why is that? Because in adaptive situations the leader cannot do the community's work. The community has to do it. As leader, you must turn the work back to the community. In effect, you have to say: "I cannot solve these problems for you. You have to solve them yourself."

Strike a Bargain With the Public

All leaders need to understand the basic bargain under which they are granted authority. The bargain in all authority relationships, according to Heifetz, is something like the following: "I will give you power in exchange for a service that I expect you to provide."

"The real service they want you to provide," Heifetz continues, "is to take the load off their shoulders and come back with answers." That is obviously a reasonable enough bargain around technical issues, no matter how complex. If the questions citizens want answered involve topics such as "How much mathematics and foreign language does my daughter need to go to college?" educators can provide a ready answer. If board members need analysis of data on student performance in individual schools, staff can provide information, often overnight.

But if questions revolve around values and attitudes, around norms of adolescent sexuality, or around desegregating or closing schools, the bargain becomes much more complicated. These more complicated issues are almost always adaptive challenges.

> *It is not a matter of developing a cadre of better-trained people to become superintendents. It is a question of developing new conceptions of the possibilities of schooling and then asking about the role of the district CEO and other actors within this conception.*
>
> Pete Mesa,
> Superintendent,
> Oakland, California

Demonstrate Competence
Dramatically on Technical Issues

If you are telling your board, or your community, that "you can no longer protect them from tough realities," you need some kind of permission to do that, to keep stress levels high, but productive, warns Heifetz. You can't do that if the board or community lacks trust in you.

Heifetz suggests that you gain permission through your technical work. "To obtain the permission you need on the adaptive side, you have to be successful with the technical work first. Like the silverback in the gorilla community, you have to find the water hole." Nobody will trust you if you can't find the water hole, or if you blow a hole in the budget. "But having found the water hole (or solved a financial crisis) you will be able to challenge people, because you already have built some trust. And, you can always say: 'Look, I got the bond passed. I renovated the buildings under budget. You can trust me on this, too.'"

"Try to sequence the issues," is Heifetz's advice. "First, provide some dramatic demonstration of competence in a technical area. Then try to sequence the adaptive issues so that those that are ripe for resolution come to the fore first. That can be hard, but your key problem is how to be strategic in challenging your own supporters so that you can give them the work at a rate they can stand."

One way superintendents might try to pull this off, he suggests, is to avoid the urge to take credit or blame for everything that happens in the district. Distributing and sequencing victories and losses among various constituencies is good practice and good politics. Such an effort means that the superintendent avoids being a continual, visible lightning rod; equally important, it forces other members of the community to do the work of learning that is required in adaptive situations.

Get on the Balcony

Think of the dances you once had time to attend. Sometimes, Heifetz notes, you were on the dance floor in the thick of the action; occasionally you took a break, perhaps on a balcony. The balcony is a good place for public officials to find themselves. On the dance floor you are so preoccupied with keeping time to the music and avoiding other dancers that you never see the whole picture. Heifetz advises the following: leave the floor and go up to the balcony periodically. Observe the patterns on the floor. Watch who dances with whom, what kind of music brings out which dancers, and how different people keep time. Do the partners change as the steps become more complicated? The point is to leave the immediate environment occasionally in order to gain a better sense of the overall scene (see section 3B).

Heroic Suicide or Staying Alive?

How do you develop some strategies for staying alive? "Heroic suicide is not the answer," says Heifetz. Telling everyone else they are wrong, even if they are, is not effective leadership. "Trying to do it alone will not work. How do you survive?" Heifetz lays out a menu of strategies:

- *Don't exercise leadership alone.* Leaders cannot get from the balcony to the dance floor and back again quickly enough. They need partners of two kinds. First, they need allies among the different factions to kindle constructive conflict in each faction. Then they need confidantes who can serve as a reality check.

- *Externalize the conflict.* Don't make yourself the issue. If people get the impression that the conflict is between you and everyone else, you are dead. Identify the conflict and give it back to its owners.

- *Listen.* Listen to outsiders. Listen to insiders. Listen to yourself. You conduct electricity from many sources and are a barometer of distress in the system. Your confidante can help you with this.

- *Distinguish between your role and yourself.* Remember: "It's not personal." Your emotional health depends on understanding that the attacks on you are rarely personal. People become upset at what you ask them to do, but that is rarely directed at you as an individual, no matter how much it feels that way.

- *Distinguish between a purpose and a "sense of purpose."* People die spiritually because they spend a lot of time on one purpose, which they either achieve or are denied. Regenerate a sense of purpose in life outside of professional obligations.

- *Find a sanctuary.* Leaders must find a daily or weekly time to think and regroup, and they must be disciplined about finding that time. Just as leaders have to plan on being swept up in the music, so, too, do they have to plan to get away from it—whether in social activities, houses of worship, exercising, or enjoying dinner with friends.

- *Give the work back.* Find ways to keep reminding people that you cannot do the work for them. In this task, you'll find yourself continually dealing with "work avoidance"—staff and others who insist it's too hard, it's not necessary, you're not to be trusted, you should be ignored. Deal with the avoidance, don't become caught up in it yourself, and insist that the work move forward.

Will these strategies guarantee success? Perhaps not, but without them it may be difficult to take up the formidable challenges of leading schools without "getting killed, badly wounded, or pushed aside."

B. Questions for Getting on the Balcony

Identifying the Adaptive Challenge

- What's causing the distress?
- What internal contradictions does the distress represent?
- What are the histories of these contradictions?
- What perspectives and interests have I and others come to represent to various segments of the community that are now in conflict?
- In what ways are we in the organization or working group mirroring the problem dynamics in the community?

Regulating Distress

- What are the characteristic responses of the community to disequilibrium—to confusion about future direction, the presence of an external threat, disorientation in regard to role relationships, internal conflict, or the breaking up of norms?
- When in the past has the distress appeared to reach a breaking point—where the social system began to engage in self-destructive behavior, like civil war or political assassination?
- What actions by senior authorities traditionally have restored equilibrium? What mechanisms to regulate distress are currently within my control, given my authority?

Directing Disciplined Attention to the Issues

- What are the work and work avoidance patterns particular to this community?

- What does the current pattern of work avoidance indicate about the nature and difficulty of the present adaptive challenge and the various work issues that it comprises?
- What clues do the authority figures provide?
- Which of these issues are ripe? What are the options for tackling the ripe issues, or for ripening an issue that has not fastened in people's minds?

Giving the Work Back to People

- What changes in whose values, beliefs, or behaviors would allow progress on these issues?
- What are the losses involved?
- Given my role, how am I likely to be drawn into work avoidance?

SOURCE: Adapted from Ronald A. Heifetz, *Leadership Without Easy Answers* (Cambridge, MA: Belknap Press of Harvard University Press, 1994), pp. 254–263.

C. A Tool for the Balcony: The Transition Conversation

Nelda Cambron-McCabe
Luvern L. Cunningham

An enduring ordeal in school systems is the rapid-fire turnover of leadership at the top. How can we be more deliberative in these frequent transitions? Rosa Smith proposed the creation of a Transition Conversation to support her move to the superintendency of the Columbus Public Schools in Ohio. Here's how this powerful process for reflecting "out loud" about issues, questions, and leadership worked.

The Transition Conversation process detailed here is one example of support for individuals taking on new leadership positions. This tool provides a powerful process for incoming superintendents to gain an in-depth, systemic perspective on the challenges, opportunities, and barriers they face.

What Is It?

The Transition Conversation consists of a small group of 10 to 15 people convened by the superintendent for an intensive two-day session prior to the superintendent's entry into a school district.

The session focuses on an assessment of the community and its environment and an exploration of leadership strategies that will promote the educational well-being of children. It provides the new superintendent a chance to join other committed and experienced school leaders in examining the history of the system, the present performance of the school district, and its projected social, political, and economic trends. In other words, it allows one to "stand on the balcony" and gain a wider perspective on people and events.

> *Peter Senge's colleague Art Kleiner argues that, in every organization, there is a group of key people "who really matter." To lead, you must understand who that core group is. See Art Kleiner,* Who Really Matters: The Core Group Theory of Power, Privilege, and Success *(New York: Doubleday, 2003).*

Topics and Participants

Prior to the selection of specific participants, it is helpful for you (as the new superintendent) to think about questions such as the following:

- What do I know about this district?
- What issues does this community and its district have in common with other systems?
- What interferes with student achievement in the school system?
- What issues need attention immediately?
- Does the district face any unique problems?
- What will success look like in this system?
- What has created the greatest turmoil for previous superintendents?

Table 2.3

Participants:	10–15
Time:	2 days
Who:	Superintendents and others with extensive knowledge and experience in similar school districts
Where:	Preferably a site away from the district
When:	Prior to beginning the position

Identify the top four or five issues that require the greatest deliberation. Next, identify potential school leaders who can inform your thinking around these issues. These may be individuals who are in similar leadership positions or superintendents who have confronted particular issues and possess a certain expertise.

Depending on your context, several "insiders" may be invited into one or more sessions, but keep in mind that you want an independent assessment, not a restatement of local conventional wisdom. This is a conversation, not a strategic-planning process where you should reach out to all segments of the school community.

Structuring the Conversation

You should think carefully about how to get the most out of the Transition Conversation. You can take it a step at a time.

Setting the Stage. Begin your deliberations with a "perspectives" session. Typically, this will require a full morning to explore the historic context of the school district and community; the current state of the school system and its programs, staff, and students; and the community's expectations of the new superintendent. Individuals who are knowledgeable about the school system and community should be invited to speak about this context. You want to know the answers to the following questions:

- What does the community expect the new superintendent to do?
- What is the most critical issue confronting the school district? Who is at the table? Who must be brought into the deliberations?
- What is the public's opinion of the schools? How well are the schools doing? What's working? What's not working?
- How do the business and educational communities work together?
- What is the relationship between the media and local schools?
- What is unique about the politics of this community?
- How can we engage the public in the educational conversation about students' learning?

What you want here are brief, concise presentations, not extended speeches and posturing with numerous charts and graphs. Focus most of the time on asking questions and engaging in interaction with your transition advisers.

Engaging the Issues. Set aside the afternoon for considering the issues raised in the morning. Ask two or three of the superintendents in the group to facilitate this conversation by beginning with what they heard, what they did not hear, how it fits in the larger local context, and what it means for your leadership.

A number of questions can be explored during this period. Here, you want to consider the following:

- What are the critical questions in the school district? In the community?
- Which issues need attention immediately?
- Which issues require adaptive work? (see 3B)
- How does the work facing this school system compare with that in similar school districts?
- How have other superintendents thought about these questions and issues?
- What are the forces at play behind the systemic structures? (see 3A, 3B and 4B)

This conversation can open your thinking to a wide range of perspectives and important arenas for inquiry. You will see the system through new eyes and different experiences.

Reflecting on Leadership Strategies. Focus the second day on how to accomplish the work that you must do as the new district leader. This is where you bring the collective learning of the group to bear on your work. What lessons did they learn from their transitions? What would they do differently next time? What do they think you are likely to miss in the beginning months? What parallels do they see between your school district and theirs?

You may want to situate your conversation within several explicit frameworks. (Peter Senge's work on fifth discipline principles, Ron Heifetz's analyses of adaptive leadership, and Gareth Morgan's insights about organizational images can all be helpful.) Try to get yourself out of the mindset of today's crisis and into a framework of exploring what lies behind the crises.

As you move into the final conversations, ask the group to reflect on the context and a set of questions such as the following:

- Where and how do I begin?
- How do I get across to the community and schools what I stand for?
- How do I involve others in getting the work done?
- What mistakes can I avoid?

Follow Up. Don't drop this ball after you take on your new role. Try to reconvene your group at least once during the following year. If it's not convenient for you to get together with them at professional meetings, go to the trouble and expense of scheduling a special meeting. This debriefing can be invaluable as you plan for subsequent years.

D. Looking Back on the Transition Conversation

Rosa Smith

In retrospect, I am amazed that I did not make more mistakes as I entered my first superintendency in Beloit, Wisconsin. I came into the position with a strong philosophy about teaching and learning, a respect for other people's children, and extensive experience. But I had not asked myself enough strategic questions. Most important, I had not engaged other superintendents around the issues of entry and leading with "the end in mind."

As I took on a new superintendency in Columbus, Ohio, I wanted to be better prepared to tackle the challenges of this bigger and more complex district.

Transition Conversation

Columbus, the nation's sixteenth-largest school district, is an urban district with complicated issues, all demanding attention. I asked a group of respected, experienced colleagues to meet with me to think about this transition. I posed the question, "How does one think about entering and leading in this environment . . . with the end in mind?" By "end," I didn't mean my exit, but the purposes or ends of public education.

Twelve people joined me for this "thinking out loud" experience. They were about equally divided between experts and analysts and active and former superintendents. The first morning of the one-and-one-half-day session began with gaining multiple perspectives on Columbus and the Columbus Public Schools. Within this context, the afternoon session focused on three conversations framed by the work of Ron Heifetz and Peter Senge: (1) What are the adaptive and technical issues? (2) What are the critical questions? (3) What are the implications for leadership? The next morning, two facilitators synthesized the rich conversations of the previous day and led the group through a reflection process.

This conversation really became my "balcony time"—a time to reflect, observe, and gain perspective on the events and patterns surrounding us. The questions dealt with focus, linkages, collaboration, vision, the school board, and the union.

One key issue became avoiding sending the signal that the new superintendent was solely responsible for children's progress. The point became how to reinforce the message that this was everyone's work. Probably, the central and most pivotal point concerned the imperative to articulate my vision for children clearly and consistently.

I tried not to let issues around reorganization, union relationships, school board disagreements, and the like define the situation. The group emphasized that "*How* becomes easier when the *what* has been established."

Reflections on the Conversation

The conversation shaped my entry into Columbus in very positive ways. The group urged me to define unequivocally who I was and what I was about. I started with an initial presentation to the Chamber of Commerce in early September. I told the Chamber, and everyone else, on what grounds they would be able to judge me—increasing student achievement; operating more efficiently and effectively; and increasing hope, trust, and confidence. Those three goals were based on studying the school district and what I learned in the conversation.

The impact of this one stance cannot be minimized. Those goals became the primary goals for the school district. That was very significant. When I arrived, the school system had an ambitious plan, which contained 117 wonderful things. Nobody could get her arms around a district talking about so many things. I worked with the school board to help them understand that the three broad goals encompassed everything they really wanted in the expansive plan.

In addition to articulating my goals, I left the Transition Conversation armed with a great deal of information to help me understand the city I was going to—its experiences, challenges, and opportunities. The process gave me a chance to gain that perspective from people I trusted. I didn't have to worry about their agenda or what they wanted. They wanted me to succeed. Without the transition work, my assumptions would have been different, and I would have made more protocol errors than I did.

One of Heifetz's rules was critical. He says: "Don't take it personally." This is an important point about seeing the difference between oneself and one's role. A leader must understand that attacks are a response to the role she plays and the stance she represents. It is difficult in the face of emotional attacks, but I keep in mind that it is really not about me. It's about what I am trying to do. People attack because they believe a lot is at stake and they have a lot to lose.

I believe every superintendent moving into a new school district, whether they're seasoned and mature or green and inexperienced, should go through a similar exercise. The better you're able to frame the questions, the more helpful the process is going to be. As I look back on my experience, I know that I didn't ask all the right questions. I didn't ask enough questions. And sometimes I didn't understand the answers. For example, I wasn't prepared for the tension surrounding desegregation in Columbus. Desegregation was mentioned, but I didn't probe. Even I, an African American woman, thought it was an issue in the past tense. I was wrong. Around race and class, the politics in Columbus were still raw when I arrived. I should have understood that at the outset.

Was the Transition Conversation useful? Absolutely. Would I do it again? I did. When I left Columbus to assume the role of president of the Schott Foundation, I included in my contract the opportunity for transition conversations by establishing a President's Advisory Council. The PAC met twice during my first year to give me advice about my new work.

E. "Lone Ranger" to Lead Learner: One Superintendent's Journey

Peter Negroni

In 1989, Peter Negroni, formerly a principal and superintendent in the New York City system, took on the superintendency of the small, economically struggling city of Springfield, Massachusetts, about 80 miles west of Boston. Negroni was committed to the idea that all children could learn. He came in with a mandate to make a difference. But things weren't so simple. He had to learn to develop not just relationships and humility, but also a learning orientation that was more personal and respectful. The four phases described here represent a developmental path that few "reforming" superintendents can avoid—if they want their reforms to survive their tenure.

When I retired in 2001 as superintendent of the public school system in Springfield, Massachusetts, a leading national newspaper put the advertisement for my successor in the wrong place. They listed it under "S" for superintendent rather than "E" for education. Applications from managers of buildings and grounds came pouring in. Well-meaning applicants paraded their experience overseeing water heaters, cleaning buildings, and collecting rents.

It was comical but not really amusing. The mistake reflected an unsettling trend in school administration. For the past several decades, superintendents and principals have become increasingly focused on the machinery and structures of education and on driving up test scores. These issues are more easily comprehended by the public than the messy and often-hidden work of teaching and learning.

An earlier version of Negroni's experience was published in Senge, Cambron-McCabe, Lucas, Smith, Dutton, and Kleiner, Schools That Learn, *pp. 425–432.*

In today's environment, successful leadership is animated by the will to educate all children to high standards. Such leadership depends, first and foremost, on the example set by the district superintendent. This requires a radical change in the superintendency itself. We cannot manage systems if that means we neglect teaching and learning, leaving the business of instruction to others. We cannot lead learning if we leave the core of instruction unquestioned, unexamined, and essentially mysterious. If we truly intend to educate all students to high standards, then superintendents must become lead teachers again.

The Superintendent's Journey

Most superintendents come to their position after moving up steadily through the teaching and administrative ranks. They are unprepared for the leadership role that faces them. Their careers in the classroom are usually distant memories; their leadership training usually occurred on the fly. An effective superintendent has to relearn what it means to be an educator.

I know this from my own experience. When I became superintendent in Springfield, the system was desperately in need of educational leadership. The staff was insular. There was no overall curriculum. Schools were set up with haphazard grade levels; some elementary schools were K–4, while others were K–6. Some youngsters had to go to as many as four different schools before starting high school.

Most critically, Springfield had very rapidly changed from a basically white and black community to an increasingly Hispanic city. Many civic leaders, including school leaders, had not acknowledged that change. Our high school dropout rate was 51% and showed no signs of improving. I came to the district with an overriding personal goal of changing this static, inbred system.

As I look back, I realize that I had embarked on a journey that sometimes quite literally kills people. If one takes on this position as I did—with conventional ideas about the kind of leadership required—he or she might be lucky to last three years. I was fortunate. As I tried to "make change happen," I was confronted by the community in a way that forced me to make some painful but essential discoveries. If my experience is typical, successful superintendents go through a four-part journey. They go from being Lone Rangers to being Lead Learners.

Part One: The Lone Ranger

Many new superintendents coming into a district are tempted to do it all. Often, they bring a lot of experience from other systems, but they're not familiar with the new environment and they're typically alone. Even if they bring trusted colleagues with them, the colleagues are also new to the district. The new superintendent is tempted to act like the Lone Ranger. I know I was.

Convinced that I knew what was wrong with the system, I also assumed I knew how to fix it.

Convinced that I knew what was wrong with the system, I also assumed I knew how to fix it. Instead of trying to build relationships with the union or the board, I worked around them. Most of the time, I felt that I was way ahead of them. I could change things on my own. And I could change them to suit my preferences.

Take my word for it: you can enjoy some exciting successes as a Lone Ranger. Early on, I managed to develop a clearly defined set of district standards and assessments. I adjusted all the schools into a coherent K–5 elementary, 6–8 middle, and 9–12 high school structure. Beyond that, I committed to build some badly needed new schools, in the process breaking a political deadlock that had blocked all new school construction. And I took on Springfield as a racist city, opining that if we wanted to create conditions where all children could learn, we would need to do plenty of work on ourselves first.

But they were three brutal years. I found myself confronting people on an ongoing basis. At public meetings, I would dress down school committee members who didn't agree with me. I would yell: "Well, if you don't see it my way, I can go somewhere else." I knew I might be riding for a fall, but I didn't know how to slow down.

I now realize I needed to learn three lessons during this phase of the journey. They should be part of the developmental roadmap for any superintendent. First, I had to articulate the goals more effectively, not just what I wanted to achieve but the motivation behind my goals. Second, I needed to learn how to engage people in genuine dialogue. My version of "public engagement" was really a vehicle for pushing people to buy into the changes that I had already agreed to. Third, I needed to search beneath the surface of the discrimination problem to discover its root cause. It wasn't rooted in racism; it was rooted in a dearth of quality educational alternatives and people's anxiety about the future.

A "Lone Ranger" cannot implement the necessary changes. Implementation requires something else—a deeper, stronger web of relationships, on which the superintendent and everyone else can rely.

> *. . . the critical issue wasn't getting the union members to recognize* me. *I had to learn to recognize* them.

Part Two: Reexamining Relationships

In my fourth year, I started to realize that I would never be able to accomplish lasting change by being a loner. Yet I still saw myself as the central character in Springfield's story. Everyone else was a minor character.

I recognized that I couldn't go it alone after two crises hit at virtually the same time. The first had to do with teachers' contract negotiations. I still didn't understand that the critical issue wasn't getting the union members to recognize *me*. I had to learn to recognize *them*. This became abundantly clear when the membership voted the contract down. Even the union representatives were shocked. After the vote, they sat down with me and we agreed that the rejection of the contract was a signal that we were all out of touch.

I also needed to pay more attention to relationships with the school committee. I'd established a reputation as an arrogant stranger from New York. In my fifth year, I cemented this reputation by restructuring the central office—eliminating all of the positions that existed and saving a lot of money. Soon, a candidate for the school committee ran on a platform based on throwing me out of office—and won. Some people in the school system regarded me as a symbol, not of the solutions that would save the system but of the problems that had to be eradicated.

Soon after, I talked with Harvard's Ron Heifetz about these stresses in Springfield. He asked what the people who supported the candidate had to lose. He pointed out that the candidate who had triumphed had received 18,000 votes. "Who does she represent?" he asked. "Once you find out what she stands for, you may find out that you represent the same principles."

Typically, my first response was, "Here is a woman with an axe to grind. I'm right and she's wrong." Then, as I began to listen more closely, I realized that Heifetz had offered me a genuine insight. My opponent wasn't anti-school. She didn't oppose high achievement. On the contrary, she cared deeply about the students. She wasn't an opponent at all; she represented a point of view that could be incorporated into the drive for excellence.

I began to change. I made new attempts to get parents genuinely involved, trying to make sure I really heard and was willing to be persuaded by them and wasn't just trying to make them feel good. I made dramatic adjustments in the way I negotiated with the union. Instead of sitting down at the table with the goal of winning, I sat down with the goal of letting the union win as well. My approach to the school committee began to shift. Instead of giving half-hour presentations about what I wanted to do next, I began to solicit its opinion about the best way to proceed.

Part Three: Coaching Instruction

My role began to evolve quite naturally from that of boss to that of coach. I began to create opportunities for others to reflect and act together. This meant trying things on their own and accepting the occasional failure. Rather than micromanaging, I helped principals, staff, and teachers find their own way.

A good coach raises awareness by asking questions. The best place to start that questioning and creating of opportunities is the classroom. And the best topics revolve around core matters of teaching and learning. My visits, and the nature of the visits, sent a powerful message to the entire system. This is what matters, my visits said. My job is to coach improvement. So I started to visit classrooms and never stopped. By this phase, I was making 150 classroom visits a year.

These school visits became learning experiences, a much more intensive process than simply visiting classrooms as a critical observer. The most tangible aspect was the "Walkthroughs" (see Part VI). In every classroom I visited, I looked for evidence that the children were learning something. I saw it in the ways they dealt with the teacher, in the work they produced, and in their interactions with their classmates.

Some teachers reacted badly to my visits. They questioned how I dared come into their classroom and interrupt their lesson. I always explained that the point was not to judge teachers but to open up conversations with them about how to meet students' learning needs.

I encouraged principals to do the same with teachers at their schools. To support and model this, at the beginning of the year three or four central office administrators and I conducted 46 school visits in 46 days, with the principals of each school alongside us. Then the administrators and all 46 principals met to summarize what we had seen.

In the beginning, nobody would critique anything at our meetings. But people grew more capable of identifying issues and areas for improvement, without shutting down discussion. Principals also began to realize that some of their assumptions about who was a good teacher and who wasn't were cockeyed. I recall one principal saying, "I've always called that teacher my best because I don't see many kids from his classes for discipline." But of course the academic growth of the students was what was important, not the teacher's ability to make life easy for the principal.

A few years ago, I made a presentation about these developments to superintendents in Texas. They were fascinated to discover that a superintendent of a 28,000-student district with 46 campuses could spend almost every day in schools. Yet I know they had trouble believing me. They asked how I did it. I told them I delegated everything else. It was more important for me to be in the schools. The staff would tell callers: "He's visiting schools. That's what he's supposed to be doing." At last, I had stopped managing the machinery and was focused on our core enterprise.

> *Texas superintendents were fascinated to discover that a superintendent of a 28,000-student district with 46 campuses could spend almost every day in schools. I know they had trouble believing me.*

Part Four: Coaching Community

Once you get principals and teachers to sustain their own dialogue, engage critically in their own growth and development, and delegate the management of machinery, what should you be doing? In this final phase of the journey, which overlaps with Part Three, you turn from coaching classrooms to coaching the community.

We all know that what we do in schools is only part of what educates children in our communities. In 2003, a new Commission on Children at Risk confirmed what I knew in my gut. For students to be successful in schools, they need to be supported by what this commission called an "authoritative community"—one that respects the students and that the students can respect.

While my initial efforts at community engagement in Springfield yielded few real-world results, it set a precedent and pattern upon which to build. We continued to structure a series of interactions whereby we could examine, make explicit—and change, when needed—the views of education held in the community. We engaged parents, businesses, religious groups, and social service agencies so that we could all define an explicit covenant with one another. That covenant, which was most visible in our curriculum, then could drive our common enterprise.

A genuine personal transformation takes place for many superintendents as they go through this final phase. They move from being advocates—experts with answers to convey—to conveners of dialogue, in which the right answer might emerge from anyone in the room. In this phase, the superintendent stops managing the machinery altogether and takes the lead in establishing opportunities for people to experiment, innovate, and stretch themselves and the school system.

Part of me still holds on to the view that I internalized for most of my life, that I should give focus and direction to the people who report to me. Tell them what to do and they should do it. You may feel that way too. But my experience convinces me that genuine leadership means enhancing the opportunity for people to think, act, grow, and develop on their own. It is a journey from discovering personal motivations to engaging one's colleagues and then the larger community. It is a journey you must be willing to make if you want to advance equitable student learning.

4. Creating Your Learning Organization

As leaders, we play a crucial role in selecting the melody, setting the tempo, establishing the key, and inviting the players. But that is all we can do. The music comes from something we cannot direct, from a unified whole created among the players—a relational holism that transcends separateness.

Margaret J. Wheatley, *Leadership and the New Science* (San Francisco: Berrett-Koehler, 1994), p. 44

Adaptive work as described by Ron Heifetz is difficult and demanding. One useful way to proceed is by applying to schools the principles of the "five disciplines" developed by business guru Peter Senge and his colleagues. Senge's seminal work, *The Fifth Discipline*, can help you do adaptive work by creating a "learning organization." This is where you are going to start seeing the connections between the leadership challenges of adaptive work and many of the major elements of the emerging images described by Gareth Morgan—the organization as a culture, a brain, an organism, and something subject to flux and transformation.

Our guide for this journey is Senge's colleague Charlotte Roberts. She introduces us to a new language involving five disciplines, diamonds, ladders of inference, and what lies submerged beneath the iceberg's surface. The rules here aren't as hard and fast as they are in Management 101, but they'll help you a lot more.

A. The Five Disciplines

James Harvey
Nelda Cambron-McCabe

What does it mean to help people do their jobs better? Or, in terms of reconceptualizing leadership, what is a learning community? Why do schools, of all places, not appear to be effective learning organizations?

These are some of the questions Charlotte Roberts, coauthor of *The Fifth Discipline Fieldbook* (1994), likes to explore. In doing so, she applies the lessons of organizational leadership writ large to the challenges of leadership for learning. Roberts believes that the ability to be a self-learning, self-regulating organization will be what will characterize successful organizations of all kinds in the future—public and private, profit and nonprofit.

Peter Senge, Art Kleiner, Charlotte Roberts, Richard Ross, and Bryan Smith, The Fifth Discipline Fieldbook *(New York: Doubleday, 1994).*

"Learning is really about developing the capacity for thinking and interacting with others," she says. A learning organization is an institution that worries about developing its "collective intelligence" so that it can create its own future, according to Roberts. It does so by concentrating on perceived reality, both the reality you perceive and the reality others see.

"In terms of perceiving reality, think of a diamond," says Roberts. "It has many facets. But most of us see only one facet—the one reflecting our view of the world. As leaders, you need to understand how others view the world. Can you imagine the deeper perspective you would gain if you could see all facets of the diamond? Do you know how others perceive reality? Yuppies without children? People upset about property taxes? Students who have dropped out of school?"

The Five Disciplines

Five cross-cutting, personal, and interpersonal disciplines lie at the heart of creating a learning organization. These ideas promise great potential for improving learning in schools:

Personal Mastery. The focus of this work is on clarifying personal vision and aspirations within the context of current reality. Individual learning, says Roberts, is the foundation for organizational learning. Individuals must have a clear view of current reality and an explicit sense of what is important to them. Continually contrasting the vision against current reality can produce positive creative tension to help achieve what's important. Personal mastery that makes a meaningful difference arises from ongoing individual reflection that is supported, nurtured, and modeled by organizational leaders.

Shared Vision. We know. You already have one. It's in a folder. But shared vision here is not a document—it's a continuing conversation. The central aspect is common agreement about values, an agreement that forms a collective sense of identity and purpose. With sustained attention and dialogue, the vision grows deeper, ever more complex and more useful.

Roberts warns that leadership is not about "getting your hands on a formula and applying it." Leadership is about creating a vision with others, designing an organization to achieve that vision, and then thinking and interacting with others to make it happen. The old vision in the folder is an internal one. It emphasizes the traditional elements of the school community— the superintendent, principals, teachers, students, parents, and school board. The new vision is much more likely to be all-encompassing, viewing schools and their needs in the context of other local problems including health, housing, employment, economic development, and environmental concerns.

Mental Models. Like Morgan, Roberts finds it useful to talk about mental images of how things work. "Think of mental models as a giant jukebox" containing compact discs, Roberts urges. "Most of us have a model of what a good parent is. To recall that model, we select the right CD. Models apply across the board. Who's a good teacher? We pick a CD. What's a good school? We pick a CD. Really, all of these models are a set of abstractions based on experience. We have to understand that if I think one thing and you think another, it does not mean one of us is right and the other is wrong. It simply means we have different mental models."

Effective tools for surfacing assumptions behind mental models include the ladder of inference and balancing inquiry and advocacy (see the tools in 4D).

An important part of creating learning communities is coming to terms with these different mental models. We must inquire into the invisible assumptions that shape our thinking. What do you mean when you say "all children will learn at high levels"? Do you mean "all," or do you mean "most"? Or do you mean "some, most of the time"? How high is high? You may be operating with one set of definitions while your board and different parent groups are operating with others. Failure to surface these different mental models can lead to all kinds of confusion as people talk past each other.

Team Learning. Team learning is the coursework that nobody offers. It's the ability to think and learn together. Most leaders in business and elsewhere probably have an average IQ of 130, says Roberts, but "put them together on a team, and the group IQ drops to 68."

Team learning is a tricky concept. "For team learning to occur," says Roberts, "individuals must suspend their assumptions. It doesn't happen without practice." Unfortunately, many people believe they already use this discipline because they work within numerous groups. Team learning, however, requires deeper conversations and more complex strategies. In the effort to develop team learning, you as an educator have an advantage. Your normal work environment provides a great practice space for applying the skills of dialogue, surfacing mental models, and using inquiry.

See tools for using dialogue and surfacing mental models, Section 4E.

Systems Thinking. "This is the ability to see the whole and its parts, and how the parts interact to create what is in front of us right now," according to Roberts.

Systems thinking opens up powerful new avenues for leadership in all kinds of organizations. "Systems thinking," says Roberts, "replaces reductionist approaches with holistic concepts. In place of thinking that is separate, competitive, and apart from others, systems thinking encourages cooperative and collaborative thinking. Systems thinking replaces discrete, functional approaches to problem solving with 'seamless' approaches."

Peter Senge talks about systems thinking as a "shift of mind." Instead of looking at events for cause and effect, we seek out the interrelationships and the deeper patterns behind the events. The iceberg metaphor illustrates this shift of mind; we look for patterns, forces at play, and ultimately the mental models that limit our thinking (see 4B).

Creating truly engaged learning organizations is a tall order, Roberts acknowledges, but don't be intimidated. She quotes Nelson Mandela: "As we let our own light shine, we unconsciously give other people permission to do the same. As we are liberated from our own fear, our presence automatically liberates others."

B. Systems Thinking Tool: Using the Iceberg

Gary Wegenke

The purpose of this exercise is to identify and reflect on a school problem using four levels of questions that create the foundation for a systems thinking process. This exercise provides a way for all members of a group to share their perspectives and data that may reveal system barriers. Failure to pursue these interrelationships leaves us merely acting on the "tip of the iceberg" (see Figure 2.5). In this exercise you are challenged to worry about events, patterns, systemic structures, and mental models.

Our deepest fear is not that we are inadequate. Our deepest fear is that we are powerful beyond measure. It is our light, not our darkness, that most frightens us. We ask ourselves, who am I to be brilliant, gorgeous, talented and fabulous? Actually, who are you not to be? You are a child of God! Your playing small doesn't serve the world. There's nothing enlightened about shrinking so that other people won't feel insecure around you. We were born to make manifest the glory of God that is within us. It's not just in some of us; it is in everyone. And as we let our own light shine, we unconsciously give other people permission to do the same. As we are liberated from our own fear, our presence automatically liberates others.

Nelson Mandela (1994 Inaugural Speech)

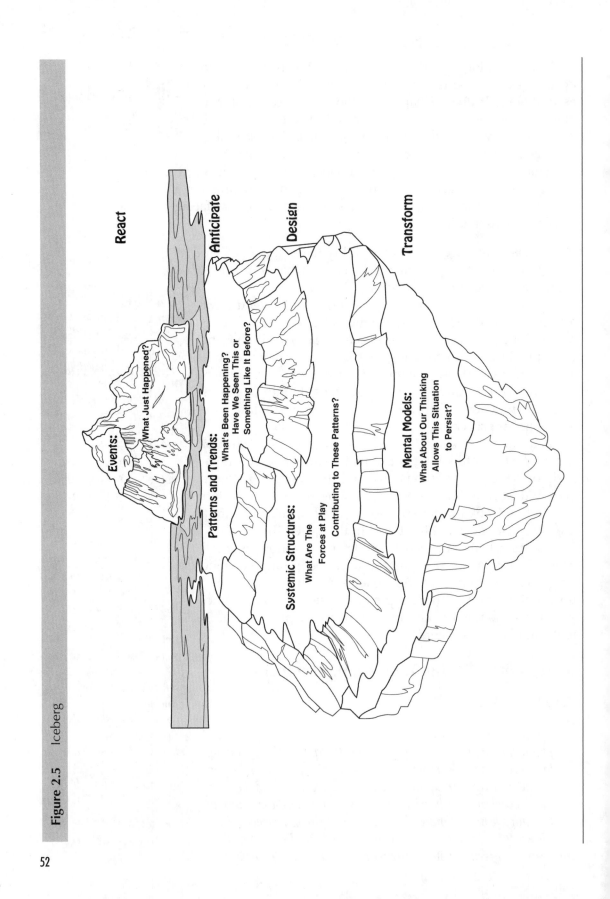

Figure 2.5 Iceberg

React

Anticipate

Design

Transform

Events:
What Just Happened?

Patterns and Trends:
What's Been Happening?
Have We Seen This or
Something Like It Before?

Systemic Structures:
What Are The
Forces at Play
Contributing to These Patterns?

Mental Models:
What About Our Thinking
Allows This Situation
to Persist?

Step 1: Events

Identify a problem in your school district, school, or classroom that has been ongoing for weeks, months, or possibly years.

Reflect on the events (and their details) that have caused the problem to persist. How have you and others responded to these events? What have you done or what have others done collectively to manage the events in an effort to resolve the problem? Are you reacting to the event in an effort to seek causes and determine effects?

From a systems perspective, schools are complex organizations intertwined with multiple constituencies. Seldom do events represent an isolated issue. Yet, often events are treated as separate problems leading to searches for "quick fixes." Typically, this means looking for some action that has been used to manage this event, or something like it, in the past. Questioning revolves around items such as the following: Who is responsible? Were procedures followed? How do we prevent this from happening again?

Take the problem of the achievement gap. As an example, the Heartland School District superintendent realizes that forthcoming state data reveal significant achievement differences by race, ethnicity, and income. What should the district's leadership do in the face of this information? One approach would be to convene some kind of ongoing districtwide consideration of what the data mean and how to respond. Such a discussion might reveal that board cutbacks in teacher aides and professional development had severely affected schools in the poorest part of town.

Another approach would be to treat the release of the data as an event, something to be survived and pushed out of the public consciousness as rapidly as possible. Adopting this second approach practically guarantees that, at least in the short run, Heartland will do nothing about the achievement gap.

In fact, Heartland went for the "quick fix" of managing the release of the state data. When the superintendent tried to discuss systemic causes for the achievement gap, the school board president quickly squashed the discussion, noting the board's plans to consider a resolution expanding the number of days devoted to test preparation.

Step 2: Patterns and Trends

Explore the event or problem you identified in Step 1 at a deeper level. What's been happening? Have you been here or some place similar before? Chart the data and/or events over recent years. Do patterns or trends emerge? This analysis moves a group from simply reacting to individual events to being able to predict what may happen.

Heartland, predictably, was hammered in the local newspapers. It took a step back and recouped its public affairs losses. School leaders knew that budget reductions and cuts in programs and services were not new. They graphed the patterns and trends over the prior 10 years and discovered a budget that had been driven by increases or decreases in state and local revenue rather than a set of clear priorities. Reductions in revenue had narrowed educational options just as the student population grew and schools became more crowded and diverse. Adding student achievement to the graph revealed a widening gap between high- and low-achieving students. These multiple, complex events had developed slowly over the decade, unnoticed and little remarked. A significant change in school board members and three new superintendents during the decade had little impact on budget trends or educational programming.

For the most part, Heartland officials had been in a reactive mode, responding quickly to budget developments by attempting to maintain current initiatives or minimizing the impact of financial cuts. School leaders and concerned community members could now begin to break the cycle by engaging in a communitywide dialogue to develop a shared set of goals.

Step 3: Systemic Structures

As you consider the patterns and trends you identified in Step 2, what forces, internal and external to the school district, are contributing to these patterns and trends? What permits them to continue? What structures must be changed in the school district to shift these patterns?

Senge and his colleagues, in *Schools That Learn*, note that "behind each pattern of behavior is a systemic structure—a set of unrelated factors that interact, even though they may be widely separated in time and place, and even though their relationships may be difficult to recognize." The structures are hard to see because they represent the way we've "always done things." You have to identify and root out these systemic problems.

As the Heartland school board and superintendent explored the issues before them, they recognized the influence of multiple interest groups in the budgeting process. They realized that the "squeaky wheel got the grease." Parents of upper-income children argued for gifted and talented programs. The "Heartland Volunteers" testified in favor of athletic programs. And the teachers' union lobbied for seniority as the sole criterion for making staff reductions. The board began asking itself: "How do different interest groups in the community influence events?" "Who is ultimately responsible for managing conflicting positions taken by these interest groups?" "Who's supposed to do the right thing for *all* students?" Finally, the board has asked the key question—that is, who is doing the right thing, and doing it for all students?

The Heartland board was beginning to understand that closing the achievement gap meant realigning current program priorities based on student needs. Doing things right in terms of budget adjustments (a technical response) isn't always enough. It's more important to do the right thing (an adaptive response).

Step 4: Mental Models

Examine the structures you identified in Step 3. What is it about your thinking and others' thinking that allows these structures to persist? What shifts in attitudes, beliefs, and behaviors must occur to change these forces and structures?

The mental models we hold of our organizations influence structures and interactions within the system. Too often, these images remain hidden and obscure. To transform a system, they must be brought to the surface and examined. Skills of reflection and inquiry are central to unearthing mental models.

Tools in Sections 4C and 4D can support your efforts to surface mental models.

Different mental models probably explain why individuals registering concern about Heartland's budget offer conflicting perspectives. People have their own beliefs about what's important. They fail to see how their positions may be detrimental to the general welfare of all students.

Like the Heartland school board and superintendent, you can use the "iceberg model" to begin engaging in systems thinking. Insights can be gained regarding the multiple problems and events associated with budget balancing, the student achievement gap, and responses to special interest groups. Initially, you may use the "iceberg model" in a linear fashion, following it step by step. However, just as problems are not discrete and linear, neither is the model. With experience, you will find that the process is nonlinear as you move back and forth among the various steps, and you will discover that your iceberg is only one in "a sea of icebergs."

C. Tools: Creating Shared Vision in a Learning Organization

Les Omotani

> *A compelling vision of your desired future can be the magnet that pulls you toward your hopes and dreams. West Des Moines Community Schools symbolize the power of a common vision to change a school district and its community. Superintendent Les Omotani shares the ideas and tools that guided their transformation.*

By most standards, our district's schools would be deemed highly successful. Yet, in the early 1990s, we began to raise questions about how we could be more vibrant for all learners. After much deliberation, we knew that we had to move from a traditional, strategic-planning process to a way of learning and developing that was more systemic. We needed to become a learning community.

We embarked on a learning journey to acquire the skills to function as a learning organization. The journey involved not just the school system but the broader community itself. We invited national experts to coach us as we pursued deeper learning and then the development of our shared vision.

A set of basic understandings guided the creation of our vision:

"What wants to happen here?" is an essential question. Tension in the system indicates that the difference between aspirations and current reality is under stress. Creatively channeled, this tension can be directed toward helping group purpose evolve.

- It's not what the vision is but what the vision does that matters most!
- Personal visions precede a shared vision.
- Organizations do not learn, but rather individuals within the system learn, develop, and grow.
- Learning communities develop from commitment rather than compliance with power and authority.
- Systems achieve balance by adhering to natural laws.
- As the community goes, so go the schools.
- As the schools go, so goes the community.
- The effort to close the gap between the present state and our desired future begins with honest conversations about our current reality.

The more than 900 members of the West Des Moines community asked four fundamental questions: What do we want to create? What needs to go away? What do we want to conserve and improve? And, what wants to happen here?

From our dialogue sessions, we created a shared vision statement. As you attempt to create your own vision statement, you may find our process for holding "shared vision conversations" useful (see Figure 2.6).

Shared visioning is a process, not a static statement. With that understanding in mind, here is the vision statement we produced:

The West Des Moines Community School District will be a caring community of learners that knows and lifts every child. We will inspire joy in learning. Our schools will excel at preparing each student for his or her life journey.

The power of this initiative is not the statement it produced but the process that created it. At this point, it's tempting to declare the process complete. The hard work is just beginning, however. Identifying, developing, and implementing strategies for closing the gap between our current reality and our desired future is the real work. Remember: "It's not what the vision is but what the vision does that matters most!"

> *The lessons we learned in our almost decade-long process may be helpful as you embark on your journey (see Figure 2.7).*

D. Tools: Ladders, Advocacy, Inquiry, Blinking Words, and How to Use Them

Mary Leiker

Charlotte Roberts gave this Michigan superintendent the "ladder of inference" and other tools to help her district understand what was happening around it. Mary Leiker, superintendent in Kentwood, Michigan, describes what she learned and how she used these tools.

Figure 2.6   Format for Shared Vision Conversations

1. Distribute the shared vision statement to all participants.

   - Explain the process used to develop this vision.
   - Explain the revision steps and the status of the statement.

2. Explain that it is an overarching picture of the future (no, it isn't comprehensive) for us to build toward collectively (and, yes, there will be many other things to focus on as well).

3. Ask participants to read and think about the statement (five minutes are usually adequate for this stage).

4. Ask participants to turn the page over and paraphrase the statement—ask them to share what they think it means in their own words to someone else (do this with a partner or small group).

5. Ask participants to state what they think our current reality is in terms of realizing the vision: What parts of it are we currently doing well? What parts are we not doing? What are the gaps between current reality and the vision? (This can be done by taking the statement as a whole or by breaking it into parts for individual conversations. This step may take several meetings.)

6. After identifying the gaps between current reality and the vision for the future, you can discuss how to reduce the gaps both individually and collectively by asking, "How can you (we) contribute to closing the gap between current reality and our vision for the future?"

Figure 2.7   Lessons Learned About Leading Shared Visioning

- A philosophy of servant-leadership is necessary. Lots of patience is required to sustain the development of the learning community. The creation of a shared vision requires that individuals first develop personal visions and then be encouraged to share their hopes and dreams with others. This takes time.
- You must "dance" with those who challenge your core beliefs and values. Rather than giving in to the urge to push back against those who think differently than you, seize the opportunity to embrace them.
- Understand that most people find comfort in identifying problems and problem solving rather than thinking about the future they might create. They prefer the permanence of a brass plaque on the wall, assuring the world that the problem has been overcome, to the reality that the challenge still exists.
- Thinking about and sharing personal visions is a prerequisite for developing a shared vision. It does take precious time that is difficult to find with teachers, school staffs, students, and community members. But it is obligatory to do the work.
- Honestly describing current reality is difficult for everyone. Caveat: When the learning community engages in honest conversation, the collective perception of the current reality seems to get a lot worse than the original assessment. At this point, it may be tempting to pull back on the vision to reduce the gap rather than face the challenging work ahead. Don't give in to that temptation.
- When developing a shared vision with a school district, it is important to have widespread input and to identify the common threads. Look for meaning behind the words. Listen to people's stories of how it is and how they dream it might be. This takes time.
- The right words do matter. Certain phrases can catch the imagination of people and stay with them over time.
- Taking time to build a solid learning community ensures that the vision statement does not seem phony or contrived or become a point of derision.
- It takes courage to lead a learning process.

The ladder of inference (see Figure 2.8), together with several related tools, helped me improve the interaction in our administrative team and with and among school board members. I see the ladder as a way of breaking apart and slowing down my thinking and opinion formation as well as the thinking of others. Typically, we reach hundreds of conclusions each day and act on those without thinking about how we reached those conclusions.

The ladder of inference can force us to make our thinking visible to ourselves and others. An action that seems to occur instantaneously actually begins with the data we observe. From that data pool, we select certain information, add our own personal meanings, make assumptions based on those meanings, draw conclusions, and take action. Because of our own unique experiences and our beliefs about the world, you and I can see the same event and describe the outcome quite differently.

When we reach an impasse, "backing down the ladder" provides a mechanism for us to learn together. Because we've run up the ladder so often with our built-in assumptions, individually we reach similar conclusions each time. We fall into a mental habit, which can easily become a prejudice. Working with the ladder (on our own or with others) helps us take off the blinders. Making our thinking visible enables us to bring our best ideas to every issue.

Figure 2.8   The Ladder of Inference

Tools to Enhance Our Learning

The ladder of inference can be used by a team to build collective intelligence. Four skills associated with this tool can strengthen its use in your practice: advocacy, inquiry, blinking words, and "and" rather than "but."

Advocacy. Advocacy is the ability to articulate the data, assumptions, and conclusions embedded in one's opinions and recommendations and to invite others to question and refine the thinking.

A detailed description of the ladder of inference can be found in Senge, Cambron-McCabe, Lucas, Smith, Dutton, and Kleiner, Schools That Learn *(2000).*

Most of us are quite expert in advocating our point of view. It is expected of us. It has served us well as school leaders. But there's a difference between advocacy and high-quality advocacy. High-quality advocacy has two parts. First, I must be explicit about my thinking. That is, I need to start at the bottom of the ladder by telling you the data I'm using, how I've interpreted that data, what assumptions I'm making about the data, what conclusions I'm drawing, and why I'm recommending a specific action. When I start at the bottom of the ladder and go up step by step as clearly as I possibly can, you'll understand why I think the way I do. You haven't asked, but I've told you where I got an idea. That's the first part of high-quality advocacy.

The second part is inviting you into my thinking to make it better. Are these the data you would select? Are my assumptions on target? Does my logic make sense? What am I missing? I must be clear with others that I want a real critique. I'm not asking them to tell me how wonderful my thinking is. If what I really want is inclusive, open thinking, I've got to say, "Come on, have at it. What do you think?" Then (the difficult part for those of us who know it all), I need to listen intently, ask questions, and reflect on my own thinking.

Inquiry. Inquiry is the ability to use powerful questions to draw out another's conclusions, assumptions, and data without provoking defensiveness.

If I really believe there's collective intelligence and that you know things I don't, wouldn't it be helpful if I asked you questions about your thinking? That is the essence of inquiry. How often do people raise genuine questions in your meetings? In my administrative team meetings, I attempt to model inquiry and encourage other administrators to practice it. Questions that I use to prompt learning and reflection include these: What led you to that conclusion? Could you share the assumptions behind your proposal? What do the data mean to you? How does your recommendation connect with others on the table?

Inquiry, then, is asking questions so that other people can expose their thinking, thus giving you a deeper understanding of it. This is not to say that you're going to agree with their thinking; it merely provides you with a glimpse of the data they selected and the assumptions they drew from it. More than likely, they relied on different data or different aspects of the data than you did or made quite different assumptions about it. Inquiry enables us to begin collective learning.

A helpful distinction for me is that advocacy "sells" while inquiry "seeks." When administrators and board members understand the difference, they begin to help each other and the organization develop a deeper consciousness.

Blinking Words. Check out words, phrases, and tones that are rich in meaning and have several possible interpretations.

It's amazing how often we assume we know what a person means. Some words may specifically signal the need for inquiry. These "blinking words" are any words that are complex in meaning or interpretations. When I'm unsure as to how you are using a word, I need to ask for elaboration. Failure to establish a shared understanding of the word leaves us open to significant frustration and overall poor understanding. Our work is saturated with blinking words—"excellence," "learning," "leadership," "quality," and "high standards," to name only a few. When you hear a blinking word, simply follow up: Help me understand how you are using the word "success," or what do you mean by "success"?

"And" Rather Than "But." Using "and" rather than "but" can improve your advocacy and inquiry practice. "And" builds on another person's contribution, while "but" erases that voice.

Have you noticed the frequency with which someone in a conversation follows up another person's comments with the word "but"? This happens even if the new comments are not at odds with the point that was just made. The consequence, however, is rejection of the other person's remark. If I really accept your point of view and want to add something else, then the word I use is "and." Its use carries a strong message: Here's what I heard you say, and I want to add this point, too. Avoid the use of "but" unless you do mean "but."

Using the Tools

When I attempt to understand my own thinking, I start with the ladder of inference. If our administrative team or the school board is going to take up a particular issue, I try to become clear on the data I'm using, its interpretation, the underlying assumptions I've made, the conclusions I've reached, and my proposed recommendations. Then, when we're together, I check to see if I'm practicing high-quality advocacy. Am I articulating my point of view and inviting others into my thinking? While I'm advocating a particular line of action, am I asking good questions of others? Do I practice a style of inquiry that permits me to understand the thinking of others and to deepen our overall thinking? Do I encourage people with "and," or do I dismiss them with "but"? These tools can improve learning at every level of our school systems—from the classroom to the board.

E. Dialogue: Suspending the Elephant Over the Table

Barbara Omotani

Sharon Smith from Heartland High excitedly laid out her ideas about how the school might become more student centered by embracing the diverse learning styles of students. It all seemed so logical to her. It would enable alignment of the school's vision (a place where all students achieve at high standards) with what actually takes place in the classroom. Her enthusiastic description of classrooms where students would understand a world of interdependencies rather than memorizing facts and looking for the right answers met a brick wall. Her teammates' response boiled down to, "We could never do that. It would never work here." With that, the conversation was quickly diverted to something that *would* work.

Sharon was frustrated. No one even tried to understand this teacher's contribution, leaving her feeling her ideas were not worthy of consideration. She sat silently as the meeting continued.

Dialogue: Creating a Common Understanding

Linda Lambert, in her work with constructivist leadership, notes that leaders' primary role is leading conversations. A leader "opens, rather than occupies, space." Linda Lambert and colleagues, The Constructivist Leader, 2d ed. *(New York: Teachers College Press, 2002), p. 64.*

Surely you remember the old story about the six blind men and the elephant. Each identified the animal as something different, depending on where he touched—a wall (touching the side); a rope (grabbing the tail), or a tree (feeling a leg). Dialogue is a way to suspend the elephant over the table so that everyone can get a good look at it and describe what they see to everyone else.

It is critical to understand that dialogue is a conversation with the center, not the sides. Rather than participants taking sides, it encourages thoughtful consideration of all diverse perspectives and views. These perspectives go to the "center of the table" for deliberation and understanding. With dialogue, individuals release the need to defend/justify their mental models. The purpose is learning.

If Sharon's teammates had engaged in dialogue, they would have listened carefully and asked questions to understand Sharon's thinking. They would have considered her ideas to be valid and worthy of further conversation. The group would have attempted to determine what Sharon might be seeing that others were missing.

Dialogue requires willingness to come up with the best idea, not necessarily *my* idea. Individuals come to the deliberation open to others' opinions. The conversation takes on a different quality: time flies; everyone speaks to the center of the group; it's hard to remember who said what; there's a sense of working together to create something rather than to win; and individuals leave the conversation thinking in new ways.

Necessary Conditions for Dialogue

As you begin your work in dialogue, pay attention to the conditions identified here. Each condition requires new skills that all of us have to acquire and practice if we are to engage productively in learning conversations.

Suspend Judgment. It's easy to judge someone else's ideas as being good or bad, right or wrong. In dialogue, however, judgments must be set aside. Suspension of judgment is realizing that we are about to judge—then making a purposeful effort to hear what another is saying. This critical ability to silence the critic in your attic is especially important when the other person's thinking differs from yours. Peter Senge reminds us that suspending judgment does not mean giving up our convictions. Rather, it means bringing them forward and exploring them from new angles in an attempt to understand why we hold them.

> *A concise description of dialogue and ways to make conversations more effective can be found in Senge, Cambron-McCabe, Lucas, Smith, Dutton, and Kleiner,* Schools That Learn *(2000).*

Listen. When most of us say we're listening, we're really just "waiting to talk." Genuine listening is more than that. Listening to hear what others mean drastically changes group dynamics. Listening in a dialogue session is truly hearing and seeing the larger picture of what everyone is saying. It is listening with the intent of discovering others' mental models.

> *A "talking stone" can be used as a technique to encourage listening. The individual holding the stone talks; everyone else listens and cannot add ideas until receiving the stone.*

Reflect. Reflection is thinking in silence before judging or making a decision. It is pausing between thoughts and actions, consciously slowing down conversations to avoid jumping to premature conclusions. Taking time to reflect enables us to observe the various parts of a conversation and to see connections among them. A place to start your reflection is to ask: How are the ideas connected? What does this mean for our work?

Surface Assumptions. Mental models arise from the assumptions we carry around in our heads. Making progress toward a common vision depends on surfacing and examining underlying assumptions that get in the way of realizing the vision. Often, we are completely unaware of underlying assumptions. Even if conscious of them, we may refuse to explore them because it is uncomfortable to expose and confront differences within a group. Dialogue provides a safe space to share these assumptions and understand their source and impact on the organization.

Inquire. Inquiry involves two dimensions. First, we invite others to critique our thinking: "I've laid out my reasoning here. What do you think?" "What am I not seeing?" Second, we seek to understand others' thinking: "Can you help me to understand your position?" "Can you tell me more?" Inquiry requires an open mind. You need to be curious about all possible sides of the elephant.

Recognizing Dialogue in Your Schools

Learning dialogue skills can alter interactions within your district and the community. But how do you recognize dialogue? If you see the following characteristics, you have established a strong foundation for team learning to happen:

- Individuals are asking questions, truly listening, and respecting diverse opinions.
- Individuals are taking responsibility for the whole.
- Individuals are taking ownership of the organization and their role in it.
- You see increased understanding, respect, and trust in interactions; less conflict and competition exist.
- "Quick fixes" are avoided.
- Reflection is evident in group actions.
- You don't see people jumping to conclusions or making snap judgments.
- Conversation is purposely slowed.
- Individuals are not silenced.
- Individuals identify and build on common themes.

You will find great conversation-starter ideas in Margaret Wheatley, Turning to One Another: Simple Conversations to Restore Hope to the Future *(San Francisco: Berrett-Koehler, 2002).*

You may find the Process Observer form in Figure 2.9 effective in working with groups as they learn and practice the skills of dialogue. You can use it yourself to judge how others contribute to the practice of dialogue. And you can share it with the members of your group to help them understand their contributions.

F. What We Say and What We Believe

Barbara Omotani

Too often in schools, despite the admirable visions we create, we find ourselves doing things "the way we've always done them." Without careful examination of a school district's current reality, visioning, even combined with dialoguing, is pointless. In addition to taking a hard look at where the district wants to go, what will it look like when we get there? And how are we going to get from where we are now (current reality) to where we want to be (our goals)?

As Gary Wegenke pointed out earlier in this part, systemic structures and mental models help explain "the way we've always done things." Management guru Edwards Deming (one

Figure 2.9 Process Observer Form

Name	States Opinion	Shares Assumptions	Listens Deeply and/or Reflects	Encourages Others to Share Different Viewpoints	Actively Inquires Into Others' Opinions	Argues Judges Dominates Interrupts

Figure 2.10   What We Say and What We Do

Vision: All Kids Can Learn	Aligned With Vision (What we say)	Unaligned With Vision (What we do)
Staff's Efficacy Beliefs	All students can achieve to a high set of standards	Learning limited by expectations of what child brings to school
Student Groupings	Heterogeneous, flexible	Homogeneous, fixed
Grading	Assess what student knows against standards	Distribute grades across a "bell" curve
Retention Policies	All children will succeed because we are reflective about what we do	Grade level failure is common because we refuse to acknowledge that what we're doing belies the vision
Scheduling	All kids given time necessary to learn	All kids given equal time to learn
Attendance Policies	Absences = requirement to make up time	Absences = suspension
Achievement Results Analysis	Data disaggregated and studied	Data ignored

of the men responsible for the Japanese industrial miracle of the 1980s) reminds us that 80% of the barriers to organizational improvement lie in what's "taken for granted." In a lot of ways, what you need to figure out is the gap between what you and your district leaders say the district stands for and what your district is actually doing.

Figure 2.10 provides a template for beginning your examination of the discrepancies between what your district purports to believe and what is going on. It provides examples of common discrepancies. Completing this chart for your district gives you a way to begin a conversation—either within a building or districtwide. What is the vision that drives your school? Are educators' actions congruent with the vision? Where do the discrepancies occur?

I've found that most districts subscribe to the belief that "All Students Can Learn." Yet, in most cases daily behavior belies this lofty aim. In conversations, everyone agrees, "Yes, ABC is the ideal state." But the status quo rears its head: "We could never change XYZ." Mental models of the way things have always been done keep us from making progress toward our vision. They limit us to familiar ways of thinking and acting. In many instances, our mental models actually prevent us from acknowledging reality.

These and other constraints often get in the way of people creating their desired future. Your job as a leader becomes one of engaging others in a dialogue that enables them to examine why each person thinks the way he or she does. It should also assist people in reflecting on why they think the way they do while collectively breaking down the mental models blocking the organization from moving from today's reality to tomorrow's vision.

G. Tool: 10 Ways to Recognize a Learning Organization

James Ellsberry

If you want to gauge the extent to which your school system is a learning organization, consider these characteristics. Their absence may point the way to professional development needs.

You know you're in the presence of a learning organization if . . .

1. *People ask each other a lot of questions.* In an organization where people respect the work of others and value their own contributions to organizational goals, questions will be common. People are asked to clarify needs, results, and priorities for action. Questions lead to a deeper understanding about what makes the system successful.

2. *People listen to one another.* In a learning organization people engage in active listening. Listening is a sign of respect for another's point of view. It promotes mutual understanding (not always agreement) and helps to identify and clarify issues where agreement or disagreement exists. Active listening leads to more effective problem solving.

3. *People cue in one another.* People working in a system where learning is valued develop the habit of explaining their thinking as they share their ideas with others. This habit (practice) provides important information about the mental models that are driving one's thinking process. Cueing in one another enables others to ask questions or offer additional possibilities without putting anyone on the defensive.

4. *People have access to information.* Information is power. In the absence of relevant, timely, and accurate information, people can't make informed decisions. In systems where learning is honored, information is "transparent"; that is, information is

available to anyone who needs it. Access to information makes everyone in the system more effective.

5. *People are aware of what's going on.* Systems that "think" are characterized by employees who are well informed of, aware of, and sensitive to what other departments and individuals do in the context of the whole. Systems awareness leads to teamwork and increased learning.

6. *People are aware of the organization's ethos.* In a learning organization people embrace the rites, rituals, and traditions that define the culture. Telling stories about the organization and using shared metaphors and a common vocabulary are ways people celebrate and pass along the pride they feel in who they are and what they do.

7. *People take improvement seriously.* In systems where people learn together, real effort is dedicated to tracking progress. Performance is monitored, data recorded, and results assessed. The focus is on improvement, not change.

8. *People approach conflict in an open, straightforward manner.* In a healthy system, conflicts are not allowed to fester. Ways are provided to resolve conflicts quickly and fairly because conflict is perceived to be a normal part of relationships within the organization. (Dynamic tension—forces in opposition—is conflict.)

9. *People are self-motivated.* In a learning organization, control issues are minimal; external rewards and punishments are seldom a factor in driving performance. Motivation is driven by personal vision and individual pride in the performance of tasks related to the purpose and goals of the organization. Individual recognition comes with the success of the overall operation.

10. *People are open and honest in assessing current reality.* Ignorance is not bliss. When examining the results of individual and/or group performance, a healthy system demands accurate, truthful feedback. Corrective action or future goals cannot be established on the basis of misleading, inaccurate evaluations. Improvement efforts may be correlated with how much honesty a system can accept.

5. Reflective Practice

Obviously, we've given you a lot to bite off on leadership. Here, we give you an opportunity to chew on some of these issues.

We ask you to think about what you've read so far and apply it to the school situation in which you find yourself.

The exercise that follows can help you reflect on the concepts in this section. It should help you personalize the material and tailor it to your own use while deepening understanding of your leadership challenges. Working with partners from your administrative team provides an opportunity to practice the skills of dialogue.

A. Questions for Reflective Practice

Here are some key questions for reflection and for consideration.

What are the values that guide your district? As a leader, what do you think is important in the district and how do you try to symbolize and give voice to those values?

If you had to create an image of your district right now, what would it be? How about the board, staff, principals, and teachers? Similar images and metaphors or different ones?

What do I need to survive? Do individuals in my district understand the distinction between technical and adaptive challenges? If not, how do I create a common understanding of this framework?

What is needed to ensure that all children can succeed? What are the structural impediments to progress here? What mental models do educators and community members hold regarding children's chances for success? What is it about my thinking and behavior that gets in the way of children learning?

Can I map the iceberg? How about systemic structures impeding learning? Have we talked about the mental models that drive the systemic structures?

Where am I, and where is my staff, on the ladder of inference around specific issues? Do we engage in dialogue to surface these understandings? If you "suspended the elephant" over your staff table, what "blinking words" would emerge around the table?

Where is your balcony? How often do you get to it? Who are your confidantes and your critical friends? (Here's a hint: If there's no balcony, or you can't reach it, if you can't identify your confidantes and critical friends, you are in a lot of trouble.)

Where do you stand on the spectrum from "Lone Ranger" to "Lead Learner"? Can you figure out how to move yourself along the spectrum?

Map in your own mind the similarities and contrasts among Morgan's organizational images, Heifetz's adaptive challenges, and Senge's mental models? Do they track? Do they differ? If so, how, and what does that imply for your district?

Ask your board and your leadership team to go through the same exercise. How do their perceptions match yours? Are they comfortable with exercises such as this? If not, what does that imply for your relationship with them?

Part III
Coping With
Governance
Challenges

GOVERNANCE

Clearly we want you to adopt a new take on leadership, but we don't pretend that the traditional meat-and-potatoes view of organizational management doesn't make a difference. It does. Congratulations on your success in creating a new culture will turn to hisses the minute you get into a power struggle with the school board. Universal admiration for your skill in working with preschool providers can be transformed into pursed lips as soon as you cross local union leaders. And while everyone will applaud your efforts to lead learning, no one will tolerate your failure to balance the budget. You have to lead. But you have to manage, too. This part of *The Superintendent's Fieldbook* guides you through the minefield of union-board-management relations.

1. Orientation

James Harvey
Richard C. Wallace, Jr.

When it comes to difficult challenges in public administration, the task of overseeing a school system, particularly in urban communities, ranks right up there with the positions held down by police chiefs, city managers, and public transit directors.

Some school superintendents are responsible for a system that enrolls more students than the state university, while being the largest provider of food, transportation, and routine health screening in the community. Many districts—urban, rural, and suburban—are the largest employers in the area.

The very complexity of these organizations explains why toil, turmoil, and turnover are the lot in life of the superintendent, especially in big cities. The conventional wisdom that the position of superintendent changes every two years probably overstates the case, but newspapers around the country continually report on unpleasant terminations of superintendents' employment. Sometimes it's a budget crisis that precipitates the rupture. Often, it's a disagreement with the union that undoes the incumbent. Too frequently, it's a clash with a board member or a faction of the board over micromanagement of the district. In 2001, PBS broadcast a two-hour special describing life in the fast lane for an urban superintendent and concluded it was the "Toughest Job in America."

The American public was introduced to the complexities of the superintendent's assignment in 2001 when PBS broadcast The Toughest Job in America, *produced by the Merrow Report. Narrator John Merrow is the regular education reporter on PBS's* News Hour. *The Merrow Report can be located at* www.pbs.org/merrow /tv/tough/index .html.

School superintendents have long complained about the governance challenges of their work. Board members are supposed to provide democratic oversight of public schools. Yet too frequently their members are named in off-year elections with low voter turnout. It's often not at all clear that board members represent majority opinion in their communities. Indeed, turnout can be so low that as few as 5% of local citizens can elect board members, a situation rife for manipulation by special-interest groups. Groups bent on restoring creationism to the curriculum or intent on constructing classrooms criticizing American traditions, or teachers' unions determined to elect a board sympathetic to salary demands, can easily dominate local elections.

Although many boards are able to avoid these problems, the possibility of mischief around board elections is always present. So, too, is the human tendency of individuals on the board to mistake their oversight role for the opportunity to straighten out management. Board meddling and micromanagement is a near-universal complaint of school systems.

Another near-universal challenge is how to work with teachers' unions. Although adequacy of teachers' salaries and the perquisites of seniority receive some attention in public discussions, few people outside schools realize how central these issues are in school union-management relations.

The fact is that teachers' incomes don't stack up well with the salaries paid to other professionals. Their bargaining units never let management lose sight of that reality. While management may feel that computers, new textbooks, or revisions to the curriculum are the most important educational priority of the coming year, many union officials are inclined to look at every dollar spent elsewhere as money unavailable for salaries. And while reformers demand that the best teachers be put in the most challenging schools, unions insist that seniority (and the prerogative of choosing where to work that accompanies seniority) is a sacred cow.

Teachers' unions, of course, are simply one of the bargaining units that many superintendents work with. In large districts, it is not unheard of to have another half dozen or more unions representing different groups such as bus drivers, carpenters, electricians, maintenance personnel, and cafeteria employees. If you wind up in one of these districts, you'll find yourself bargaining with all of them.

In Homer's epic, Odysseus was required to pilot his boat through a narrow and treacherous strait. His vessel was threatened on one side by the flesh-eating Scylla and, on the other, by the whirlpool Charybdis. You're not likely to be devoured by the board or drowned by the union. But you're going to have to pilot your district through the very stormy waters raging between these two sides. This part of the fieldbook provides you with some useful charts and navigation aids.

2. It's Rough Out There

As superintendent, you're hired to lead learning. But no matter what you do, you'll frequently find yourself making peace between the board and the union. This section lays out what's involved.

A. Whipsawed: Boards, Unions, and the Central Office

Howard Fuller
James Harvey

Based on focus groups with superintendents in a variety of districts and a survey of those in the 100 largest districts, recent research indicates that superintendents, far from controlling their own agendas, are often whipsawed by the demands of competing power centers within the system.

The research described here was conducted by the Center on Reinventing Public Education at the University of Washington in September 2003. The full report, "An Impossible Job?" is available at the center's Web site: www.crpe.org/pubs/pdf/ImpossibleJob_reportweb.pdf.

Although people outside schools are likely to view the school superintendent as an imposing figure possessing impressive authority, the reality of the superintendent's position is more ambiguous. On paper, the managerial span of control is impressive, with central office staff, school principals, and teachers all reporting to the superintendent. But the fact is that superintendents report to school boards, elected or appointed, that frequently micromanage district affairs. In addition, central offices contain myriad personal and political relationships that are often used to sabotage, delay, or dilute a superintendent's initiatives.

Superintendents cite many impediments to effective districtwide leadership (see Figure 3.1). Overwhelming majorities of responding superintendents described local politics, conflicting public demands, mandates from

Figure 3.1   Challenges to District Leadership

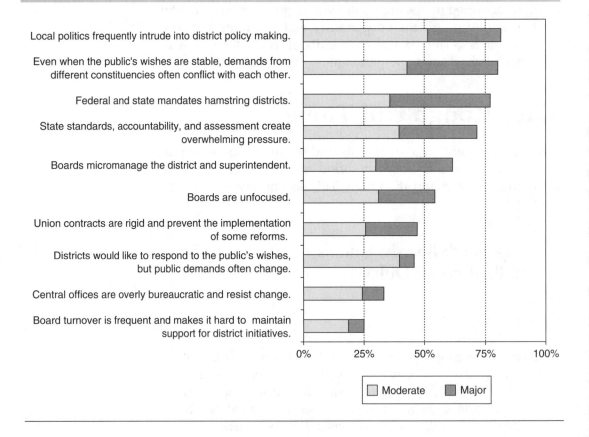

above, and pressures for accountability as either "moderate" or "major" problems (between 71 and 81% of respondents agreed).

The Board

One central challenge is board micromanagement, that is, straying from policy oversight and budget development into the nuts and bolts of day-to-day administration. A large majority of surveyed superintendents (61%) agreed that board micromanagement is a "moderate" or "major" problem. Fifty-four percent described lack of board focus as an impediment to district effectiveness. Although some interviewed superintendents spoke positively about their own school boards, the interviews conveyed a sense that boards in general are a problem, not the solution. A common theme wherever two or more superintendents are gathered together is a lengthy gripe session about dealing with this impossible board, or that troublesome board member, or how the board has started micromanaging the district.

Part of the concern centers on the perception commonly expressed during the interviews that, instead of protecting the school district from political pressures, boards have become a main conduit for such pressures. A reform-minded superintendent put it this way:

> I think the system wanted to reject us the way an organism would reject a foreign body. And we needed the board to be part of the vaccination. We needed them to be the protective shield but they weakened as time went on.

Another respondent identified changes in the quality of board members as a source of increased political pressure:

> In the old days, people who had stature would run for the board of education. We have a lot of situations now where people run for the board to gain stature. These tend to be the people that are most sensitive to political pressures and community groups.

Whatever the cause, many of the superintendents viewed one of their primary tasks as a struggle to get the board to focus on educational goals. Often this was a losing battle:

The biggest frustration was that we couldn't get the board to focus on one thing—student achievement.

I had lots of exposure to urban boards and in many cases it took you about 10 minutes to see that they were a large part of the problem.

Conflicts within the board itself appear to be endemic, according to the interviews. One superintendent described this problem as among the job's most challenging issues, one that made enormous demands on her energy:

The management of my board—the distrust they have for each other—[is a huge problem]. Obtaining board peace is a tremendous drain on my time.

Finally, board micromanagement is mentioned so frequently in these interviews that it has to be taken as a near-universal complaint about the job's structure.

I think what has happened in the last 10 years . . . is that boards have gone crazy and are really into micromanaging. I think that's the major problem.

Superintendents are at the beck and call of boards. There's just no question about it. You can be vocal and bullheaded, but eventually those who don't support student learning wear you down.

The city board has totally micromanaged the school district. I mean totally. Principals went to board members before they would go to the superintendent.

Another experienced and highly regarded superintendent reported that, shortly before he retired, his district elected a board that for the first time began to interfere in managerial decisions. "I'd get calls from staff saying they'd been ordered to do such and such, and I'd have to call the board members and tell them that's not their role."

Teachers' Unions

Although the superintendents were most concerned about boards, many (47% in the survey) also felt that relationships with teachers' unions were barriers to progress. While superintendents indicated clearly during interviews that they understood unions must protect their members' interests, many felt that the unions had focused so exclusively on economic issues that they had lost all sense of educational mission.

Superintendents' views about unions were not uniform. Much depended on whether superintendents presided over districts in states that sanctioned collective bargaining or prohibited it. For convenience, we refer to these as districts in "union" and "nonunion" states. More than two-thirds of superintendents in "union" states cited rigid union contracts that prevent the implementation of some reforms as either a "major" or "moderate" problem. By contrast, fewer than one in three superintendents from "nonunion" states considered union rigidity to be either a "major" or "moderate" challenge.

Our interviews and focus groups, primarily with superintendents from "rust belt" and West Coast districts in "union" states, reinforced this sense of a major problem with teachers' unions.

For more on contracts and negotiations, see Howard L. Fuller and colleagues, The Milwaukee Public Schools' Teacher Union Contract: Its History, Content, and Impact on Education, *(Milwaukee, WI: Institute for the Transformation of Learning, Marquette University, 1997). Fuller and his colleagues point to a voluminous written record of court cases, hearings, letters of understanding, and memoranda of agreement that create a separate "contract behind the contract."*

The big problem is that the teachers and the union don't take responsibility for education. The union's idea is that it has to protect the membership.

We cannot transfer teachers in most districts because of union contracts. You might be able to do it here and there, but it's not possible in most places.

When I was hired, the board recognized there was a problem with the union. The union was running the place.

One of the superintendents just quoted noted that, when he assumed his latest position, the union president was more powerful than the deputy superintendent. The union leader "had gone through many superintendents during his time in the district. He was by far the most powerful person in the district." What troubled this respondent most about the situation was his sense that a "culture of accommodation" had developed between the district and board on the one hand, and the union on the other. In accommodating that culture, the district, he thought, had "created a system that was based around the needs of adults as opposed to those of children."

Gulliver in Lilliput. Two different superintendents described a process of dealing with unions that was akin to Gulliver tied down by the tiny straps immobilizing him in the country of Lilliput. The image was graphic.

> *We had this 150-page union contract that contained more than a thousand rules. You could use it as a metaphor. You have Gulliver and the Lilliputians. You've got a thousand of these little ropes. None of them in and of itself can hold the system down, but you get enough of them in place . . . and the giant is immobilized.*

> *I've always supported the idea of unions. But I'm hamstrung. I feel like Gulliver in Lilliput.*

What comes through clearly in these interviews is the growing sense of frustration of urban superintendents forced to deal with external pressures to improve system performance and student learning in the face of union insistence that the first order of priority is pay and the second is working conditions. Adding to the frustration is the reality that, although boards and local politicians will support standards and student performance as system goals in public, in private their interests often align with the union's concern with pay and working conditions.

Becoming a Pickle. Nontraditional superintendents take a particular view of these issues. People who come into the superintendency from outside government or education are often struck by the sheer amount of resistance to change they encounter within the system.

One nontraditional superintendent found a graphic metaphor to describe the importance of swimming against the tide. He told his team (all imported from outside education) the following:

> *This is like a cucumber in a pickle jar: we're going to stay a cucumber for only so long—eventually we're going to become a pickle, and when we do, we're going to have to go because we won't be making a contribution. And I actually think that's what happened.*

The Iron Triangle: A Coalition of Boards, Unions, and the Central Staff

Many managers struggle with resistance from their organization's various stakeholders. This is not peculiar to the culture of school districts. In the automobile world, top management frequently finds itself at odds with designers, engineers, or marketing experts. High-tech leaders often report splits between the creative side of their empire and the financial side. However, respondents in this study point to a problem that in some ways seems unique to school leadership: not only do the constituencies individually resist a superintendent's authority, but they also join forces to block change. Some of the superintendents report a virtual "iron triangle" made up of boards, unions, and the central staff, a coalition that can work to block reforms deemed vital.

> *Boards are in bed with the unions. The boards say they don't agree with the unions, but their actions say they do. Often the union head is more in tune with what the board chair thinks than the superintendent. Plus, the unions were underwriting campaigns of board members to oppose us.*

> *There was this whole level of middle management that would curry favor with board members and board members would approach them for information, and you have lots of [middle managers] running to their patrons and their friends, and that was politically charged.*

Sometimes the groups successfully block change by forming alliances. At other times, different stakeholder groups frustrate initiatives because they cannot agree among themselves. One superintendent described the difficulties of dealing with both teachers and the teachers' union:

> *We shouldn't be in the position of using the grievance process to continually renegotiate the contract. School boards should authorize superintendents to resolve grievances and challenges.*
>
> "Mac" Bernd,
> Superintendent,
> Arlington
> Independent
> Schools, Texas

> *Teacher and union resistance is a big issue. Unions will not agree to anything that reallocates teachers or requires some to accept different hours or work rules. Even when unions cooperated, teachers in individual schools often blocked change. Many of us are whipsawed—we can get union cooperation or support from the grassroots, but rarely both.*

In practice, the forces against the superintendent can seem overwhelming. As one retired superintendent said,

"We underestimate the intelligence of our opponents and their capacity to organize themselves to oppose change."

Does the picture painted by this research accurately describe the district you lead? Or districts in which you have worked? If so, what can you do about these situations? Read on.

B. Tool: Working With Images of Organization

Luvern L. Cunningham

Remember what we had to say earlier about images of organization? Try to apply some of those images to the problems you're encountering with board members and union leaders. You may think you're leading a district that, like a finely tuned learning organization, assesses its own performance and works to improve it. But your board members may have a much different metaphor floating around in the dim recesses of their consciousness. They may think of the district as a finely tuned machine, disciplined in its pursuit of standards, with a curriculum and administration aligned around achievement of those standards. To them, you're not a leader but a mechanic. At their most unpleasant, they may see you as little more than a board flunkey, because the image that they could never describe in public (or perhaps even admit to themselves) is of a system based on politics and power.

Tables 3.1 and 3.2 will be more useful to you if you take their structure and add your descriptors of the behavior you see from school board and union members. Take it a step further: these tables have been effectively used in board development by superintendents who asked board members to describe their own behavior.

Meanwhile, your union may be working in concert with an entirely different image. You say you want to create a "learning organization," a district that functions like a brain. So does the union. But it puts a political twist on the metaphor, insisting that the components of the organization (specifically the union's members) have to conceptualize how this learning organization will be designed. Far from being a partnership involving all, the union may be intent on minimizing your role in reshaping the organization you're supposed to lead.

Knowing which metaphors drive your board members and unions may not entirely solve the challenges they pose for your working relationships. But they will help you understand why some of the games you see around you are being played, and they may give you some ideas about how to deal with them. Tables 3.1 and 3.2 provide templates that describe how each of the eight "images of organization"—four inherited images and four emerging

Table 3.1 Inherited Images of Organization (How the Board and Union Behave)

Image	The Board	The Union
Machine	No-nonsense bottom line; run a tight ship	Well prepared for struggle of negotiations
	Chair runs the show; short meetings; low-profile superintendent	Attracts support from other labor unions
	Limited citizen participation	Influences other bargaining units
	CEO/Board of Directors philosophy	Listens to national leadership about strategy
	Oriented around results	Skilled in building and maintaining membership
	Rigid reporting lines	Salaries and benefits outweigh learners' interests
	Power sought and respected	Labor specialists handle negotiations
	Diversity not a priority	Top leaders do not always reflect the rank and file
Political System	School board is first step on political ladder	Leaders well-known inside and outside jurisdiction
	Many candidates for board vacancies, often soliciting war chests	Skilled lobbying is a strong suit
	Board meetings broadcast on radio or TV	Always has best institutional memory around
	Polling often used; citizen participation championed	Secures favorable settlements, even in hard times
	Students are a means, not an end	Plays on constituencies' heartstrings
	Members seek personal media coverage	Monitors and nurtures special interests
	Committees and task forces are popular	Understands neighborhood and community media
	Will sacrifice superintendent for political advantage	Active in all elections, including those for school board
Psychic Prison	Salutes tradition	Contract provisions followed to the letter
	Supports phonics and opposes sex education	Focused on salaries and benefits
	Attracted to prayer in schools and creationism	Hidebound on educational issues
	Opposes innovation, outsiders, technology, and sex education	Building representatives are enforcers
	Board meetings are formal and by the book; turnover low	Building representatives often play hardball
	Seeks and supports conservative administrators	Expects loyalty from the rank and file
	Little participation in state associations	Leaders usually tougher than board or superintendent
	Fiscal conservatism is demanded and rewarded by reelection	Lukewarm on standards and assessment
Instrument of Domination	Relishes local control and fights to protect it	Prepared to take a strike; hang tough in negotiations
	Take-no-prisoners approach with management and union	Leadership dominated by former middle and high school teachers
	Oriented around fiscal conservatism and accountability	Uses rumor mill to inform membership
	Prefers weak superintendents and administrators	Threatens school officials from time to time
	Promotes loyalty through nepotism and sole-source contracts	Disinterested in achievement gap or issues of race and class
	Punishes those who challenge its power	Teachers' working conditions oppressive
	Disinterested in achievement gap or issues of race and class	Devoted to "I teach . . . you learn" pedagogy
	Board usually appointed and new members resemble old	Little interest in organizational development

Table 3.2   Emerging Images of Organization (How the Board and Union Behave)

Image	The Board	The Union
Culture	Improving academic achievement for all children is basic Diversity reflected in board membership Equity is a prominent and consistent value All sectors invited to speak to the board Policies in place to honor multiple views Members participate in state associations Members represent a broad range of constituencies	Consistently supports school improvement Respects diversity Committed to closing the achievement gap Local traditions are important Endorses minority recruitment and professional development Sensitive to community cultural change Supports policies for family leave and health benefits Acts on assumption that school cultures reflect community
Organism	Leading members understand systems thinking Joins professionals in support of academics Builds and sustains collaborations to meet needs Selects a superintendent with community-building skills Uses committees to do its work and worries about board growth Engages media in educating public Exploits technology for organizational growth	Joins in system's efforts at school improvement Comfortable working with the superintendent Supports reform and accountability Participates in local, state, and national educational movements Incorporates learning needs into contract Leaders are also learners Invests in union development
Brain	Focused on schools' educational mission Supports a "community of learners" philosophy Supports site-based management Champions excellence in student performance Works collaboratively with colleges and universities Creates partnerships with private research centers Sees union as ally in development	Leadership embraces organizational development Joins the board and administration in search for ways to improve learning Strong commitment to standards and reform Considers itself to be a learning community Bargained contracts reflect its commitments Engages in research Committed to technology and its application to learning
Flux and Transformation	Restless and impatient with the status quo Prizes innovation and change Challenges tradition Endorses alternative routes to licensure Frequent challenges to board leadership positions New-age administrative leadership sought and applauded Supports concept of multiple ways of learning Willing to take fiscal risks in pursuit of goals	Members aware of changing environment and possibly anxious Prospect of membership growth exists if change is threatening; possibility of backlash from anxious members National and local leaders struggle to understand change Opportunities exist for new rank-and-file leaders to emerge Partnerships with superintendent and board look more attractive Focus on children and their achievement

images (see page 23)—might play out from the perspective of your board and unions.

3. Working With Your Board

Nothing can make life better for a harried school superintendent than a board united behind her. And nothing can make her life more miserable than a badly divided board that routinely votes 5 to 4 or 4 to 3 on every significant issue before it.

Working with a representative board, whether elected or appointed, is like performing in front of a panel of Olympic judges every day. Few members of this panel hand out "10s." In this section we help you through the board thicket by describing typical challenges of board work and summarizing decades of experience from successful superintendents.

A. Getting It Right With the Board

Luvern L. Cunningham

Most people wind up reporting to an individual, a single superior. On occasion, a professional may have to make a report of some kind to a committee, but that's fairly infrequent, not a daily occurrence. The "line" relationship is with an individual.

As a school superintendent, you are placed in a unique employment system. It is hard to think of any other in the world that is similar. You will be hired by a collective known as a "school board" or a "school committee"; you will be expected to report to this group; and your work will be approved or challenged by it, sometimes on a daily basis.

Your tenure in office demands that you satisfy the expectations of this group. If it's a nine-member board, you must carry with you on every significant issue at least five votes. But that's a very uncomfortable working margin, because the board's makeup can change on short notice. Ideally, you should have the support of all nine board members. You should be so lucky to live in that administrative paradise. Many superintendents are happy with a working margin that provides them with six out of nine votes of support and consider themselves in Eden if they can count on seven votes consistently. Smaller seven- or five-member boards, of course, make your margin for mistakes with the board even narrower.

In my third year, when we could not reach an agreement with the union, the board lived through a long, bitter, divisive strike. It left scars in the community for years. Strikes aren't worth the damage they cause. When the teachers walk out, nobody wins.

Bertha Pendleton,
Superintendent,
San Diego Public
Schools, California

Now, here's the rub. Satisfying the expectations of the board (which is required if you are to survive in office) may or may not coincide with what is required if you are to succeed educationally in the district. To prosper in that sense, you have to raise standards, close the achievement gap, develop your principals, and work with issues of race and class. Sometimes this work can put you at cross-purposes with the board. There's a tricky balance here. You can be successful by one measure—surviving on the job. But can you survive and succeed educationally?

Getting it "right" with the board will be a key issue in your long-term success. Here are some ideas that promise to help.

Get Off to a Good Start

You should make sure that student learning is a central element in how the board will judge your success. The time to have this conversation is *not* after the board has decided it's unhappy with you because you've started moving principals around (in order to get the most effective administrators where they're most needed). The conversation has to begin during the recruitment phase. As one superintendent said, "We thought the board hired us to make change. It turns out it hired us to make the crisis go away. So here we are making change and it's not exactly what they wanted."

Misunderstandings that arise after you accept the job may be unavoidable. But during the recruitment process, you enjoy a very favorable opportunity to shape board expectations. You should not miss this chance, and you have only yourself to blame if, after taking the position, you discover the board has little respect for procedure or precedent and no interest in your long-term agenda for educational improvement. The time to nail down these issues is right up front.

Use Your Honeymoon Productively

No matter how troubled your school system is, you will enjoy a honeymoon in your new community. This is the period when the board members talk about what a great person they selected. The union leader insists that unless you succeed, the schools cannot succeed—and unless the schools succeed, teachers can't succeed. You'll get good copy and positive coverage in the local newspapers. You can do no wrong. You may even walk on water. It may last FDR's proverbial one hundred days. It may last a year or longer. However long it lasts, several things are apparent. First, life is wonderful. Next, the honeymoon will come to an end. And finally, you will want to use every opportunity during the honeymoon to strengthen the hand you've been dealt. Don't waste this time. Use it productively.

There's a lot to be done. In the crush of business and meeting new constituencies, you may lose sight of the essential first step. Reestablish the understandings reached during the selection process about district goals and objectives, particularly those related to learning. People have short memories. You don't want board members to forget why they hired you.

Now is also the time to make and cement relationships with internal and external constituencies. We know you won't make the following mistakes, but some superintendents do. One type of superintendent believes that change can be imposed on school systems from outside. This person is therefore likely to spend a lot of time with external constituencies—leaders from local churches and other houses of worship, community groups, and the business community—and essentially takes the support of internal constituents, such as teachers and principals, for granted. Another type believes these internal constituents need to be protected from external pressure. So he or she is likely to spend a lot of time assuaging the anxieties of teachers and principals, while fending off the criticism of business and community groups.

Neither strategy will succeed. You must pay attention to both your internal and external audiences during this honeymoon period. This is also the time to give the district the bad news about the problems you've diagnosed and the medicine that has to be prescribed. Ideally, the board has already agreed to an independent financial and educational audit to discover where the "bodies are buried" in the district. You may have to clean up some problems that you've inherited, but you shouldn't put yourself in a position of taking the blame for them.

If the ideal situation is out of the question, however, you need to do the next best thing. Surface big problems during the honeymoon period, when you still enjoy a presumption of innocence and the goodwill to deal with these problems. You will want to insist on a candid, independent, external review of the district and its potential problems. This should include a review not simply of educational and administrative issues, but also of the district's financial situation. You do not want to discover, a year into the job, that the district has been experiencing a slow-motion fiscal meltdown for the last five years. Sure, it began long before you arrived on the scene, but you're the only one around now to take the blame. And take it you will, unless you surface the issue so early in your tenure that most reasonable people in the community will not lay the blame at your feet.

The honeymoon period is also a good time to obtain an analysis of community opinion and resources. You need a very good sense of the community and its needs. A comprehensive needs analysis, including surveys and focus groups with key constituencies, can be conducted with the assistance of a local university. (Check Part VIII to see how you might launch a community engagement process.)

Finally, this is also the time to cement your relationship with the board while putting your administrative team in place. Who speaks for the board? What are the roles and responsibilities of the board officers? To whom does the legal counsel report? How will the board work through you to locate the information it requires from your central office? There's a concept of "relational distance" about the appropriate role of the board with respect to central office staff; you need to defend your staff from board intrusion.

There's a lot to be done during the honeymoon period. If you're too busy basking in the warm glow of the first hundred days to do the essential work required to stabilize your position, you may find yourself in the same position as a lot of newlyweds. When reality sets in, both sides begin exploring phone book entries under "lawyers—divorce."

Work on the Relationship to Sustain It Over Time

Like any relationship, the one between you and your board requires work. It requires a lot of work, over a long period of time. One experienced, and highly successful, superintendent found that quarterly meetings, which provided him with a "formative" evaluation, worked wonders for the relationship (see Section 3B). However you structure this relationship, building it should always start by recommitting to the goals and objectives you've already agreed on.

Of necessity, much of this work is oriented around policy and administration. You have to continually touch base with the board or its chair to make sure that management is on top of developing issues, that the budget is in good shape, that concerns about technology are addressed, and that everyone knows where the district stands with regard to union negotiations.

Much of this work also revolves around political issues, or at least around the "personalization" of policy. "Who gets credit" sounds silly among adults, but this is never a trivial matter. You may have a mature board that expects you to make most public announcements of small triumphs and steady progress, but don't count on it. It's as likely that the board expects you to stand in the background while it makes the announcements. Rumors that you are leaving, or are being shown the door, will crop up regularly. Get it straight with the board chair ahead of time how both of you will handle these questions—then make sure the rest of your board follows the script. What happens when the board chair (or the local business community) asks you to get involved in the next board election or to provide resources for community polling as part of the election? You don't want these questions to come up. Knock them down ahead of time with a crystal-clear policy that prohibits the central office meddling in elections.

Time to Go?

When it's time to go, you want to exit with dignity. Don't worry, you'll know when that time has arrived. Board members will forget the agreement to focus on learning and will begin second-guessing you about contracts or portable classrooms. Board turnover may become more frequent, creating unrest. What had been a relationship of mutual self-respect—with the board . . . between the board and superintendent . . . and between the board and community—begins to deteriorate. Those newspaper stories about your imminent demise? They appear more and more regularly. And the board chair seems less and less interested in dispelling them.

The endgame will begin with some variation of the following: The chair invites you to a lunch at which she reveals some grumbling among board members and influential community figures about whether or not to renew your contract. You find that board meetings have become less orderly and routine. Now, they seem to be taken up with complaints and criticism, along with demands that you respond to this charge or that. You notice board and public criticism if you leave town for professional meetings—the same meetings that had marked you as a "national figure" when the board hired you.

What to do? Sometimes it depends on where you are in the contract cycle. If the contract is about to expire, it will either be renewed or it will not. But if you have questions about the shape of the new contract and whether it is fair to you or not, it's probably time to think about updating your resumé.

The reality is that, unless the relationship has become irretrievably broken, the board will want to treat you with respect. And you should treat it with respect. The best solution here is often simply facing up to the obvious: Get together with the board chair to obtain agreement that your lawyer and the board's lawyer will work to plan a smooth exit that is fair to both parties. That's how you leave with your dignity—and that of the board and the community—intact.

B. Tips on Working With the Board

Richard C. Wallace, Jr.

Your relationship with your board will make or break you. Here's what experienced superintendents advise.

Pay attention to this relationship. Don't assume that lack of friction is good news. Problems can sneak up on you out of the blue. Below are some ideas for managing and nurturing a good relationship:

1. Regular workshops to address policy and to provide ongoing evaluation to the superintendent can be career savers.

2. When you are hired, establish in writing, from the word "go," the ground rules of your relationship with the board. These ground rules should include the formal terms of your evaluation.

3. Ideally, you should get the board to agree on its priorities early in your tenure. Use research, data, needs assessment, and focus groups to help the board agree on priorities. Then use those priorities as the touchstone against which you assess board requests for staff work.

4. Work with the chair if at all possible to minimize board micromanagement. When individual board members cross the line, you need to confront them immediately. Also, develop a conflict-of-interest policy to protect the board and your staff from themselves.

5. Insist that all staffing issues, including hiring and firing of principals, are your responsibility. You can't give this fundamental management role away to the board.

6. Empower the board to succeed by helping members make policy, address constituent concerns, and run a perpetual campaign in support of the schools.

SOURCE: Adapted from *The Urban Superintendent: Creating Great Schools While Surviving on the Job* (Report of a Colloquium for Former Urban Superintendents, Council of Great City Schools, September 2003).

C. School Finance 101:
No Surprises Around Money

Richard C. Wallace, Jr.

As superintendent, you can probably survive quite a bit of bad news. But there is one surprise where you will be held personally accountable. It is the shock of finding that the district has been spending more money than it has. It doesn't matter that there is a chief financial officer (CFO) in charge of the budget. All that will count is that both the board and you failed in your fiduciary responsibility to local taxpayers. Depending on how serious the shortfall is, a financial meltdown in your district is very likely to cost you your job.

If you don't understand school finance, learn about it. A dozen former superintendents at a meeting convened in Orlando, Florida, in February 2003, offered much useful advice, reprinted here. Get on top of your district's finances. If you don't, you may be buried by the rubble from a financial disaster.

Mishandling the budget is one of the surest ways to grease the skids for your exit. Here's how to get a handle on district finances.

1. Regular, annual, external audits are not an irritation but potential career savers.

2. In addition to audits, you need a financial analysis that explores how money is used, how much is received by formula and from "soft" sources, how much is committed (and to what), and how much is discretionary.

3. If you don't understand budgeting, get a tutor or go back to school. You can never be confident that you are on top of issues in your district unless you have a full grasp of the budget. Without it, you are not in command of your district; your budget director is.

4. Worry about increasing the financial literacy of your board members. For a high proportion of board members, the most complicated financial issue they have ever dealt with is their household budget.

5. Checks and balances are basic. One person should approve and another should write checks. And it's always a good idea to require two signatures on any check. Even in the nonprofit world, money has a remarkable habit of disappearing unless people keep their eyes on it.

6. The odds and ends of district finance create huge headaches. Establish procedures to monitor schools' "independent activity funds." And discourage board/staff use of district credit cards.

7. While you need to understand the budget, you should stay out of the details. It's typically hundreds of pages of minutiae. What you need to grasp is broad strategy and a sense of the budget options available to you to influence student achievement.

8. It's a good idea to allocate a minimum of 1% of the budget for professional development.

9. The budget needs to reflect district priorities, and it also needs to reflect yours.

10. If you are interested in a particular theme related to student achievement, fund this theme at the outset. It will be hard to finance it after everything else has been funded.

SOURCE: Adapted from *The Urban Superintendent: Creating Great Schools While Surviving on the Job* (Report of a Colloquium for Former Urban Superintendents, Council of Great City Schools, September 2003).

D. Tool: Are You and the Board Governing Learning Effectively?

Luvern L. Cunningham

How well are you and the board governing learning? Table 3.3 provides a checklist to help you assess and answer that question.

Table 3.3   Are You and the Board Governing Learning Effectively?

Issue	Yes	No	Other (explain)
Are policies focusing the board's work on student learning?			
Are learning goals reflected in teacher contracts?			
Is learning the responsibility of all employees?			
Is professional development directed to the improvement of learning?			
Is the budget intentionally designed to support student achievement?			
Do parents and citizens have easy access to student performance data?			
Do other local agencies contribute to your learning mission in clearly defined ways?			
Does the district have provisions in place for personnel and program oversight?			
Are planning initiatives directed toward the improvement of learning?			
Do you have the technology infrastructure required to support learning?			
Is training available to board members and candidates?			

Grading	
10 or 11 "yes" answers	Way to go!
7–9 "yes" answers	Keep up the good work.
4–6 "yes" answers	You have a lot of work to do.
0–3 "yes" answers	The community should have significant concerns about you and the board.

E. Tool: How Well Is Your Board Functioning?

Luvern L. Cunningham

Board effectiveness will determine your effectiveness. The checklist in Table 3.4 will help you to get started. It can be used for either discussion or assessment:

Table 3.4   How Well Is Your Board Functioning?

Circle the appropriate number below:
(1 = Very Poor; 2 = Below Average; 3 = Good; 4 = Excellent)

The School Board . . .

. . . spends most of its time and energy on education and student achievement.	1	2	3	4
. . . believes that advocacy for the educational interests of children is its primary responsibility.	1	2	3	4
. . . concentrates on goals and uses strategic planning to accomplish its purposes.	1	2	3	4
. . . works to ensure an adequate flow of resources and equity in their distribution.	1	2	3	4
. . . harnesses the strengths of diversity and integrates special needs and interests into the goals of the system.	1	2	3	4
. . . deals with controversy in an open and straightforward way.	1	2	3	4
. . . leads the community in matters of public education, seeking and using many forms of public participation.	1	2	3	4
. . . exercises continuing oversight of education programs and their management, draws information for this purpose from many sources, and knows enough to ask the right questions.	1	2	3	4
. . . works out, in consultation with the superintendent, separate areas of administrative and policy responsibilities and how these separations will be maintained.	1	2	3	4
. . . determines the mission and agenda of each committee, ensuring coherence and coordination of policy and oversight.	1	2	3	4
. . . establishes policy to govern its own policy making and policy oversight, including explicit budget lines to support those activities.	1	2	3	4
. . . invests in its own development, using diverse approaches that address the needs of individual board members and the board as a whole.	1	2	3	4
. . . uses policies and procedures for selecting and evaluating the superintendent.	1	2	3	4
. . . uses policies and procedures for evaluating itself.	1	2	3	4
. . . collaborates with other boards through statewide associations to influence state policy and how state leadership meets the needs of local schools.	1	2	3	4
. . . understands the role of the media and its influence on public perceptions and avoids manipulating the media for individual political gain.	1	2	3	4
. . . supports local control and is vigilant in safeguarding the rights of communities to determine what constitutes the educational well-being of children and their families.	1	2	3	4
. . . provides, in cooperation with the superintendent, for the orientation and preparation of new board members.	1	2	3	4

4. Dealing With Your Unions

Few things enrage critics of American public education more than the existence of teachers' unions. Many of these critics are convinced that collective bargaining is the major impediment standing between the United States and educational nirvana. And, in truth, union defense of seniority and protection of apparently incompetent teachers is difficult to square with a system committed to high standards for all.

Unions, of course, arose to protect individual teachers from the whims of central offices and boards. Jobs often depended on patronage. Elementary and secondary school teachers were on different salary schedules. Women received less money than men—and many faced the loss of their jobs if they married or became pregnant.

Critics are free to complain and make their case. You, on the other hand, have to work with teachers' unions (and unions representing other employees, also). This section provides you with some tools.

A. Working With Your Unions

James Harvey

Apart from teachers, it's hard to find anyone who has much that is positive to say about teachers' unions. In public discussions of school reform, unions, if mentioned at all, are likely to be demonized as reactionary bulwarks against change, staunch advocates of the status quo. On occasion, teachers join in the criticism, and, in recent years, thoughtful union leaders have tried to rethink how organized labor can improve its relationship with district management.

In many ways, union critics have a strong case to make. Union leaders imagining the school system as a political entity can easily convince themselves that they've waited out reform superintendents before and they can again. "Here comes another one!" is the cynical response. When superintendents who are trying to terminate incompetent teachers find themselves tied up in seemingly endless and costly hearings and procedural due-process snarls, they can easily decide that the potential benefits aren't worth the cost.

In some ways, however, the case isn't immediately self-evident. On a state-by-state and community-by-community basis, some of the worst schools in the United States are

Want to read the case against teachers' unions? You need The New York City Teachers' Union Contract: Shackling Principals' Leadership *(New York: The Manhattan Institute, 1999). It argues that school principals' hands are tied by contracts requiring seniority-based hiring and rigid work schedules, impeding the dismissal of poor teachers, and keeping principals from putting the right teachers in the right job.*

We have to end this process in which outbreaks of war between the union and district interrupt periods of chronic, long-term, festering resentment. In war, anything goes, with lots of casualties.

Adam Urbanski,
President, Rochester
Teachers' Association

found in states without unions. If unions are the problems their critics make them out to be, there's little evidence to support that in states with a political culture opposing collective bargaining.

Here's the issue: outside critics can afford to carp about unions and criticize teachers, but you have to work with the union. Teachers are your workforce. And here's a related reality: if organized labor and unions disappeared off the face of the earth tomorrow, you would still need a labor-relations strategy for dealing with your teachers. What would it be?

A Primer on Union Possibilities

Where did the teachers' unions come from? Is it possible to rethink their roles? The short answer is that they arose from a model of industrial unionism and that many of their best leaders are trying to rethink how they function.

A Legacy of Union-Management Strife. It's hard to recall now, but 40 years ago the National Education Association (NEA) counted administrators among its members, considered itself to be a "professional" association, and looked down its nose at an upstart American Federation of Teachers (AFT) that was busy organizing teachers. In those days, teacher salaries and benefits were low, and salaries for elementary and secondary teachers differed substantially. It was a profession dominated by women presumed to be supplementing their husbands' incomes. These women would be in the workforce for a short time, anyway, since they would undoubtedly return to the home as soon as their children arrived. In a world such as that, teacher strikes were inconceivable.

All of that started changing around the mid-1960s as the AFT succeeded in organizing more militant teachers and the NEA realized that a new era was at hand. Both organizations became quite militantly union minded, with an orientation that owed a great deal to the industrial union psychology of the 1930s and 40s. This was a militant unionism that saw workers as disenfranchised and management as an enemy; it defined the essential role of unions as defending employees from employer abuse.

Mind Workers. Another kind of unionism is possible. It's a type built on the realization that you, as superintendent, can't impose your vision on your teachers. It's grounded in the belief that some form of labor-relations strategy is needed if you are to work effectively with your major workforce. How are you going to do that? The old union model, according to experts such as Charles Taylor

Kerchner at Claremont Graduate School, was based on direct supervision of employees. Teachers' unions responded to direct supervision with the industrial union model with which we're familiar. Why not? Management wanted to behave like industrial employers; union leaders responded in kind.

But what if some of the newer images of organization we've been talking about came into being? What are the implications of the district as a brain or a learning environment for your unions? The new model, says Kerchner, should not make the mistake of thinking of school districts as akin to companies or plants. It should be based on what kind of employees teachers actually are. Teachers are not miners, hauling minerals out of the ground through brute force. They are not assembly-line employees placing the same nut on the same bolt as the line moves in front of them. They are classic examples of what Peter Drucker has called "knowledge workers," people who "think for a living." The organization representing them in labor relations should reflect what they do. It should also think for a living.

"Knowledge employees," according to Drucker, cannot be supervised. The very nature of what they do means that most of them know more than anybody else in the organization. If they don't, they are of little value to the organization. In this context, organizational performance (school district competence) will come to depend on attracting, holding, and motivating these knowledge workers.

Pipe Dream or Possibility? Is this new vision truly a possibility? Or is it a pipe dream? Some of the best thinkers in today's teachers' unions are already building on Kerchner's insights. It's not that they've given up on salaries, benefits, and working conditions, but they've added other considerations to the mix. Instructional quality is a major concern, with both major unions at the national level supporting improved standards. While acknowledging criticisms of teaching quality, support is also growing for peer review, professional development, mentoring, and national board certification. The Teacher Union Reform Network, or TURN, is also willing to consider salary and training incentives for teachers. Peer review as an alternative to conventional evaluation is also much favored for novice teachers and teachers at risk of disciplinary action. The challenge from the union perspective is to balance peer review and due-process rights for all teachers.

The new vision is moving forward in fits and starts. Alert union members might pay attention to emerging developments as they think about the future of collective bargaining in schools. Nationally, unionism is in decline as American jobs are shifted

Want to read the case for emerging models of unionism? You need Charles Kerchner's United Mind Workers *(San Francisco: Jossey-Bass, 1997).*

Interested in "knowledge workers"? The best source of information is Peter Drucker, Management Challenges for the 21st Century *(New York: HarperBusiness, 1999).*

Additional information on emerging models of teacher unionism can be found at the Web site for the Teacher Union Reform Network, www.turnexchange.net.

offshore to low-wage, nonunion sites. Little respect for union democracy in the private sector exists in the national conversation, and it is conceivable that even less respect exists for unions in public employment. Refusing to change, therefore, may not be a viable option for union leadership; change is likely coming one way or the other.

Trade Union or Professional Union? In a sense, what is at issue is whether teachers' unions will be trade unions or professional unions. If you are successful in working with your union to develop a more professional orientation around labor-relations issues, everyone will win. You will have an easier time bargaining with the union. Your community will see that unions are as concerned with learning, accountability, and teaching as a genuine profession, as they are with grievance procedures and protecting teachers' rights. Teachers will benefit the most. They will be paid like true professionals and will enjoy the authority and status that teachers elsewhere in the world enjoy.

B. Primer on Labor-Management Relations and Contracts

Luvern L. Cunningham

Few district employees, and even fewer citizens, know much about the details of local union contracts. Labor negotiations occur mostly behind closed doors, sheltered from public view. Some contracts are very brief; others, very lengthy. Here are some key issues around today's bargained contracts:

- Not all districts or states have them. In many states, collective bargaining for public employees is prohibited (as it is also for private employees).
- Bargaining processes and outcomes vary from district to district and state to state. There is no "one process that fits all."
- Collectively bargained agreements brought benefits to many school district employees throughout the twentieth century.
- The teacher contract is a "sacred text," exercising great influence over day-to-day school operations and efforts to improve schools and student achievement.
- Contracts with other employee groups have similar influences, often in terms of the length of the school day and the school year, access to school facilities, and standards of maintenance.

- Some longtime union heads are the most influential district leaders, often overshadowing superintendents and board members if considerable turnover exists.
- Despite the lack of detailed information available to the public, salaries and fringe benefits attract the greatest public interest.
- Contract sections governing professional development; selection of materials; and teacher qualifications, assignment, seniority, and evaluation profoundly influence student learning.
- In many districts, schisms between labor and management have existed for years, accompanied by a climate of acrimony that makes negotiations about learning difficult.
- The local "balance of power" is often swayed when state and national union leaders offer support to district labor leaders as the negotiating process gets under way.
- Evaluation of district employees, especially teachers and administrators, can be a source of great conflict and hostility, even in the case of professionals deemed incompetent by superintendents.
- An interest in professional unionism is emerging at national and local levels, suggesting that unions play a central role in issues such as teacher accountability, program quality, and implementation of standards-based reform.

C. A Conversation With Roger Erskine

James Harvey

Roger Erskine spent decades as an NEA organizer before settling down as the reform executive director of the Seattle Education Association in the 1990s. Displaced in a union coup as the decade drew to a close, he began a new career supporting school improvement from the outside; working with the nonprofit League of Education Voters, for example, he helped implement a successful ballot initiative to lower class sizes in Washington State. He shared his insights into emerging union thinking with us.

Tell us something about your background.

In 37 years with the union, I was involved with 324 strikes for union employees.

What needed to be done in Seattle?

When I arrived in Seattle, I found a city with 48,000 students, 4,800 teachers, substitutes, and aides, and 54% of the students on free and reduced lunches. We were serving at least 60% of the kids badly, principally the poor, minority, bilingual, or special education populations. Seattle schools were in trouble. School enrollment had dropped from 90,000 in the 1960s to 48,000 today due to demographic changes, suburban growth, and housing and desegregation issues. At the school level, the central administration was despised.

What about the union?

The union mirrored the dysfunction of the central office. No one was focused on kids. Everyone worried about adult issues. The contract was a set of minimum work rules.

What steps did you take?

We did several things. First, we sent a sign to every central administrator: "It's about the kids, stupid." Then I talked to the outgoing superintendent about creating a better legacy. We had a district statement of beliefs, value, and mission. I wanted to put that into the contract to help kids. Next, we started pushing the notion that "if it's good for the kids, it's good for us." We stopped defending teachers who were ineffective. The fourth-grade teacher doesn't want an incompetent teaching the third-grade class. Nobody wins. So we counseled 60 teachers out of the profession. The union began to be viewed as taking responsibility for the workforce as well as defending it.

Was that everything?

Oh, no. The superintendent and I started visiting schools together. That shocked people. It stopped the "blame game." I supported the superintendent when he took $8 million and 162 people out of central administration and sent the money to the schools.

What's this "system of schools" notion?

A new superintendent arrived, John Stanford, a former general. Very charismatic. He and I advanced the idea of a "system of schools" in place of a school system. That's what we have now in Seattle. You need a system—otherwise it changes every time someone waves a project at you. Each school is now site based, with a lot of data on the kids and their achievement, and 60% of the money has been decentralized to the schools.

How does the contract fit into that?

The contract now starts off as a trust agreement. This is what we stand for. It has the mission and so on in it. It's committed to kids. We moved 12 principals and 20 staff members from the schools because they just didn't get it.

Teacher evaluation is now tied to student performance. The contract is open all the time. If you have a problem, we reopen discussions and amend it, perhaps through a memorandum of understanding. If we don't trust each other, it's hard to know how to proceed. We started with more than 200 grievances annually, and by the time I left it was down to about 15.

What does the district have to do?

I think districts have to stop blaming unions for all their problems. You know, most elementary school principals see themselves as teachers. But that's not true at the middle- and high-school level. Principals at those levels see themselves as managers. That's a district problem, not a union problem. Districts are also hiring a lot of uncertified teachers to put in classrooms that otherwise would not have a teacher. Maybe 25% are uncertified in a lot of districts and another 25% have very little experience. Unions don't hire these teachers, school superintendents do.

> As is clear from this interview, union–management relations can be reconfigured, even in districts facing significant challenges. Still, it requires great courage from union leaders to take these risks.

D. Learn How to Bargain Like a Pro

Richard C. Wallace, Jr.

How do you bargain without giving away the store? Here's advice from a dozen experienced hands. Follow it to bargain like a pro.

Unions and Bargaining

Here are the fruits of decades of experience from the front lines:

1. Get legal advice in negotiating and administering contracts. The superintendent never sits at the negotiating table. That is a task for staff and attorneys.

2. Try to obtain a uniform negotiating calendar, unless you're prepared to have the district endlessly tied up in negotiations, union by union.

3. Encourage collaboration around the "main thing"—student achievement. Ideally, the contract becomes a living document that adjusts and changes continually as understanding of student achievement evolves.

It's not unknown for superintendents and boards to agree to contract provisions that will become unworkable in the future, long after superintendents and board members have moved on. Harvard's John F. Kennedy School of Government developed a case study of such a development in Buffalo, New York. There, the three main elements of the governance triangle bought labor peace by relying on unique provisions requiring the state to bail out Buffalo (and other big cities) if it ran out of money. As state finances tightened, of course, this house of cards collapsed. You can find the case study on the Web site of the Forum for the American School Superintendent at www.orgs.muohio .edu/forumscp/ BkgndPur.html.

4. Make the contract the instrument for advancing student learning. If it isn't in the contract, it's not really the "main thing."

5. Think of negotiating as a problem-solving mechanism, not a source of conflict. Ideally, it should be a perpetual tool for problem solving.

6. Keep language about the calendar out of the contract. It's likely to be too restrictive. Also make sure that you don't agree to "noneconomic" provisions with financial implications.

7. Find ways around problems. No union representative can give up the union's position on seniority. Insist that the superintendent has the right to assign personnel for the good of the district. Handle assignments on an "exception" basis if need be. Unions also want good schools.

8. Leaders and members are different constituencies. Often the leader is far ahead of members on key educational issues. In the same vein, you should inform all teachers of changes in the contract. That way, you define the change, not a bargaining or building representative.

9. Work with the board chair to have one spokesperson for the board's position during negotiations. You can't negotiate if the board is a Tower of Babel.

10. Don't agree to grievance procedures that create more trouble than they're worth. The grievance procedures should not become a source of grieving.

11. Keep up to speed on what's happening with union reform. Some of the most progressive ideas about how to advance learning are coming from union leaders themselves.

12. Watch out for union–board relationships. It's not a good sign if the union knows of the board's position before you do.

13. Remember that the contract is the union's "sacred text." If it isn't in the contract, it's not important.

SOURCE: Adapted from *The Urban Superintendent: Creating Great Schools While Surviving on the Job* (Report of a Colloquium for Former Urban Superintendents, Council of Great City Schools, September 2003).

E. Tool: What's Going On With the Union?

Luvern L. Cunningham

Have you established productive working relationships with your union? The checklist in Table 3.5 is a starting point. It gives you some ideas about strategies you might adopt.

Table 3.5   How Well Is Your Union Functioning?

Issue	Yes	No	Other (explain)
Is the union leadership open to the idea of incorporating learning goals into the contract?			
What about most members?			
Do you meet regularly with the head of the teachers' union?			
Are negotiations relatively relaxed and oriented around solving problems?			
Is there some union interest in exploring collaborative union-management relations more congenial to a learning organization?			
Have you ever convened a retreat involving top management, the board, and union representatives?			
If not, have you ever considered convening such a retreat?			
Is your current union leadership relatively secure (that is, does it feel threatened from within its own ranks)?			
If union leadership turns over suddenly, can you predict how that would change your relationship with teachers in the district?			
Is the union comfortable with the major elements of the reform strategy you are currently pursuing?			
Is the union leadership comfortable with professional development as a way to improve teaching competence?			
Would your union agree to differential pay, modifying seniority as a basis for assigning teachers, or streamlined procedures for counseling poor teachers out of the profession?			

5. General Rules of the Road

Recall from Part II that Ron Heifetz said that leaders can quite literally be killed. He was talking about national leaders and the risk of assassination many of them run. You may be threatened physically. Some superintendents are. Still, you are unlikely to run the risk of physical assault.

The bigger risk you run is of character assassination. That's never fun, and it can be painful. Don't think for a minute that your spouse will enjoy reading the caustic comments of parents or teachers in the local newspaper. You may have to worry about insults your children will hear at the local school. In the face of this kind of unpleasantness, how do you maintain your sanity and sense of self? You need to worry about protecting your own inner self, and your family's. This section offers some helpful guidance from people who've been through this fire and emerged whole.

A. Leading While Surviving Professionally and Emotionally

Richard C. Wallace, Jr.
James Harvey

This section is adapted from The Urban Superintendent: Creating Great Schools While Surviving on the Job *(Report of a Colloquium for Former Urban Superintendents, Council of Great City Schools, September 2003).*

You have a district to lead. Your district is full of families relying on you to educate their children. The board may be worried about proper deference at meetings. The union may be complaining about unreimbursed time from teachers. To the families in your community, however, these are sideshows. They want their children educated. How do you do that while surviving professionally and emotionally?

Experienced and successful superintendents offer two key pieces of advice. The first protects you professionally: make sure you have seven elements—elements that are necessary to lead any organization—in place. The next nurtures you personally: build shelters and create structures in which to protect yourself emotionally.

Organizational Leadership

Matt Prophet is a former military general who became superintendent in Portland, Oregon, in the early 1980s. He was one of the first of the "nontraditional" superintendents. He told us in 2003, "A long time ago in the military, I learned that seven elements define what is needed to lead any organization. The organization makes no difference—a military unit, a corporate division, a nonprofit or government entity, or a school system." The same seven elements must be in place if any leader is to be successful in shaping and directing the organization. As a school leader, you should be worrying about these seven organizational elements as well:

- You must have the right people. You can't do it all yourself, so you need good people in key leadership roles, at the district and school levels.
- You must have access to data about your system's performance. Otherwise you are probably operating in the dark and don't really understand your organization's own strengths and weaknesses.
- You need an effective delivery system. Having the right people or right ideas doesn't do you much good if you can't deliver what you set out to provide.
- Logistical systems are essential. Getting the bits and pieces of the organization moved around and where they need to be when they're required is often the difference between success and failure—in schools and corporations, as well in as military campaigns.
- You need a communications system. You need to be able to communicate effectively both within the organization and beyond it. Without such a system, you are unable to affect what goes on in your organization or communicate its needs and accomplishments outside the system.
- You absolutely have to have a methodology for evaluating the first five elements. This may well be the area of greatest organizational weakness, both in and out of schools. Everyone understands the importance of people and communications systems; fewer realize how important it is to evaluate every aspect of organizational operations.
- Finally, you need to understand that leadership success is a process, not a destination. You must endlessly recycle your understandings developed during the evaluation throughout the first five elements, engaging in what organizational theorists have lately come to call "continuous improvement" across every facet of organizational life.

This list might lack the complexity and detail of many educational theories, but it possesses the elegance and virtue of simplicity. You don't have to be charismatic to lead your district. If you are going to lead it effectively, however, you should be worrying relentlessly about this short list.

Emotional Survival

One of the things you will have to adjust to as superintendent is the realization that criticism comes with the territory. You'll need to develop a tough skin. Being on the receiving end of personal attacks, delivered either face-to-face or anonymously, is not easy on you or your family. Given the demands of this job, and the very high level of stress it imposes, superintendents have to be strong individuals. You will have to be, too. This is not a position for the faint of heart. It will not sit well with people still struggling to sort out their values. The first essential is that you know something about yourself.

Knowing yourself and your strengths and weaknesses is critical. Nobody is perfect. No superintendent is ideal. But at some gut level, superintendents must understand what they stand for and how they are likely to respond to stress. They should also understand their own personal biases. A superintendent inclined to blame students for failure is unlikely to be an ideal leader in a district with a lot of vulnerable children. A leader who likes to scapegoat teachers may find it hard to inspire their trust. Ideally, you will welcome challenge and respond well to it. But if you're inclined to head for the hills when unexpected surprises develop, you need to find people who can shore you up in that area. Make no mistake about it—stress, unexpected surprises, and downright unpleasantries are part of the job.

See Richard Wallace, From Vision to Practice: The Art of Educational Leadership (Thousand Oaks, CA: Corwin Press, 1995).

Ask yourself what you believe in. What are your values? What do you believe about learning? Asking these questions is critically important to maintaining your sense of self. Unless you know your core beliefs and values, you really can't be in a good position to defend them. You have to understand your core purpose in doing this work. Why are you doing this? Once you have a better fix on that, you'll be in a position to draw a line in the sand. You need to know what values and beliefs are so essential that the job isn't worth having if you have to compromise them. Actually, if you don't know that, then every developing problem potentially threatens your position.

Remember Ron Heifetz's advice from Part II: "It's not personal." Nothing will destroy you faster than assuming that attacks are directed at you personally. In politicized situations, opponents have a tendency to personalize their attacks, but what they're really opposed to are the positions you are taking. Understand that. If you weren't sitting in that chair, they'd be attacking someone else for attempting to lead the same changes. *It has nothing to do with you.*

Heifetz often speaks of the value of "critical friends" and of the need to leave the dance floor occasionally to get "up on the balcony." (See sections 3A, 3B, and 3C of Part II.) Both are solid pieces of advice. Following them may not save you, but you will never go wrong taking this advice. You must find ways to get trusted feedback from diverse sources. The world of school administration is littered with the wreckage of super-intendents who believed the sycophants who can be found in every organization.

Other Strategies for Dealing With Stress

There are some other tried-and-true methods of minimizing personal stress (see Section 5B). Get used to the idea that whatever you decide, you're wrong! "Should we close school this morning because it's beginning to snow and the forecast indicates a possibility it will get worse?" The answer is, "Yes," according to many parents worried about their children's safety. "Who are you kidding?" say others, already en route to work without child-care arrangements in place. "Should we offer extended-day services at cost to help parents in the workforce?" "Of course you should," say parents desperate for affordable and safe day care. "Over my dead body!" may be the response of defenders of "family values."

In a district enrolling several thousand students, whatever you decide will offend someone. Don't let the criticism slow you down. Do what you think is the right thing and move on. Otherwise you will be immobilized.

Next, it may take the patience of Job, but, while critics are busy personalizing their attacks on you, you must take care to focus on issues, not people. No matter how ugly things get, your responsibility is to stick to substance. The public needs to under-stand that your priorities are high-quality education, children's safety, and responsible administration of the public's business. The naysayers will say what they have to, regardless of what you do. Don't get down in the mud with them. Former Omaha, Nebraska, superintendent Norbert Schuermann offers succinct advice on this: "Remember, when you wrestle with a pig, the pig has fun and you get dirty!" Get used to the idea that conflict is the price you pay for leadership.

Put Yourself First

It's not selfish to say, "put yourself first." Unless you can preserve your sense of self, you cannot do what you went into education to do—help all children learn at high levels. To put your district's children at the top of policy priorities, you have to put yourself first. Otherwise you are no good to them. So, worry about maintaining your sense of self. Understand your strengths and weaknesses. Think about your values. Don't take any of it personally. And get up on the balcony every once in a while with people you trust to get your bearings and renew your commitment.

You'll find all of these efforts time well spent.

B. Ten Ground Rules for Survival

Richard C. Wallace, Jr.

How do you survive in the hothouse of the superintendent's office, both professionally and emotionally? Here are ten "rules of the road" from successful former superintendents.

Ten Rules of the Road for Survival

1. The "main thing" is to maintain student achievement as the primary objective; that is, never take your eyes off learning.

2. The most important element of the "main thing" is belief in students.

3. If what you are doing does not improve what happens in classrooms between teachers and students, it is probably not worth doing.

4. Accountability means making a year's worth of difference in the life of every student, every year.

5. It doesn't matter what you decide, you're wrong! Conflict is the price you pay for leadership.

6. Don't take it personally. Remember, if you wrestle with pigs, you get dirty and the pig has fun.

7. Listen to the people around you. They can keep you from falling flat on your face.

8. Leaders make their own good days. When leaders create real value for citizens, the public will respond enthusiastically.

9. Making permanent change means changing the things that are permanent.

10. All leaders are in transition, whether they succeed or fail.

SOURCE: Adapted from *The Urban Superintendent: Creating Great Schools While Surviving on the Job* (Report of a Colloquium for Former Urban Superintendents, Council of Great City Schools, September 2003).

6. Reflective Practice

The always formidable difficulties of school governance have become even more challenging in an era of high standards and greater accountability. The stakes have never been higher for you or for the students and families in your community.

This section provides an opportunity for you to reflect on how you can respond to these challenges.

A. Questions for Reflective Practice

Here are some key ideas you should be considering.

What's your experience with internal conflict in the district? Do you find yourself whipsawed by competing demands from boards, unions, and the central office? Or do these different power centers work reasonably well together?

Are you troubled by micromanagement by your board? Or is that not a significant issue in your experience?

Does the board (or individual board members) say one thing and do another? How do you account for shifting opinions about what to do on the board and among its members? Is there anything you can do to help stabilize the board around a central mission?

What about the union? Is your union more influential in the district than either you or the board? Or are you fairly comfortable with the role of the union and how it wields its influence in district affairs?

Are you able to put teachers where you most need them? Or do you find that seniority or other provisions in the agreement dictate teacher assignments?

Are there significant differences between your images and story line and those of your board and union? If so, what are the implications for district governance? Could these differences explain some of the disputes and tension in your district?

Are you confident that district finances are in good shape? What have you done to guarantee that the day never arrives when your CFO calls you to announce a major budget shortfall?

What have you done to encourage more openness about change in the union? Has it helped? Was it a waste of your time?

What have you done to preserve your sense of self? Where's your balcony? Who's your critical friend? What do you do to preserve a sense of your own value?

Part IV
Understanding Standards and Assessment

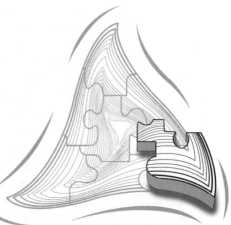

STANDARDS & ASSESSMENT

1. Orientation

It's a brave new world out there. Since *A Nation at Risk* in 1983 called attention to "a rising tide of mediocrity" undermining the educational foundations of the United States (pointedly including private schools in its critique), policymakers have relentlessly pursued a standards-based reform agenda. It's here to stay for the foreseeable future. This "commonplace" may be the most visible arena for your various publics, and you may be harshly judged if you do not demonstrate a thorough understanding of the issues and if you are not able to document progress.

In this section, you'll find a lot of what you need to cope with this new world, including descriptions of what's involved with the No Child Left Behind act (NCLB, or "Nickleby," as the bureaucrats call it), what it means, how it will influence your work, and the prospects for success in closing the achievement gap between now and 2014.

A. The Shape of the New Discussion

James Harvey

You may not remember what launched the standards-based reform movement, but most old-timers would

A Nation at Risk created a nationwide sensation when it was released by the White House in April 1983. Produced by the National Commission on Excellence in Education for Secretary of Education Terrell Bell, it argued that educational mediocrity was undermining American economic competitiveness. Whether they agree with that diagnosis or not, most observers date the intense public interest in school reform of the late twentieth century to that report. Twenty years later, similar analyses and recommendations continue to be made. See National Commission on Excellence in Education, A Nation at Risk: The Imperative for Educational Reform *(Washington, DC: U.S. Department of Education, April 1983).*

date it to April 26, 1983. That's the day the National Commission on Excellence in Education arrived at the White House with an alarming report for President Reagan asserting that the nation was literally at risk due to the poor quality of education in the United States. One of the remarkable things about the reform movement spawned by that report is that the energy behind it continues to this day.

First out of the box with reform suggestions were governors, eager to promise greater flexibility and independence at the local level in return for better results. Next, President George H. W. Bush partnered with Bill Clinton, then governor of Arkansas, to create six ambitious National Education Goals, beginning with the idea that all children should start school "ready to learn," that is, that they would have access to world-class preschool programs. Building on that theme, the first President Bush had his secretary of education (Lamar Alexander, now a U.S. senator from Tennessee) develop "America 2000." This was a program to encourage choice in schools, create model schools in every congressional district, develop new school designs through the New American Schools Development Corporation, and involve the community by worrying about "the other 93%" (the portion of time students spend out of school between birth and age 18).

President Bush's political opponents were not attracted to "America 2000," and most elements of the president's proposal (with the exception of New American Schools) disappeared when Governor Clinton defeated President Bush in 1992. Clinton's Department of Education developed a standards-based reform agenda based on a concept of alignment (see Section 2C). The idea of alignment was to improve system performance by conforming educational standards with assessments, classroom practice, and teacher education. Anxious about charges of federal interference in local education, and disrupted by his own political opponents, President Clinton's "Goals 2000" program made this a voluntary activity on the part of states.

No Child Left Behind

When President George W. Bush was inaugurated in 2001, he dramatically rewrote educational practice in terms of federal involvement. His program, No Child Left Behind, insists that states develop standards and assess them with mandatory statewide examinations, ultimately in every grade from third to tenth. The statewide examinations are to be benchmarked against the federal National Assessment of Educational Progress (NAEP), and it seems likely they will be required in every school, in every district in the United States.

For an overview of No Child Left Behind, see the next section, 1B: "No Child Left Behind and Adequate Yearly Progress" and Figure 1.1.

Passage of NCLB promises to transform your life. Now, every school and school district receiving funds under Title I of the Elementary and Secondary Education Act, including yours, will be expected to do more. You will be asked to demonstrate satisfactory performance on assessments administered in each grade, from three through ten. All of the schools in your district will also be required to demonstrate that no gap exists between performance of students from different racial, ethnic, or socioeconomic backgrounds. Moreover, your schools will be required to demonstrate satisfactory progress from year to year, and on the part of each disadvantaged group.

In all, there may be as many as 120 or more separate items on the pass-fail test that "Nickleby" puts before you and your district (tests in reading and writing in each of eight grades, with the 16 results cross-indexed against the racial, ethnic, and socioeconomic backgrounds of your students). Theoretically, unsatisfactory performance on any of these items could be cause for you, your schools, and your district to fail the test.

The penalties you face for institutional failure in this new accountability-driven system are substantial. They range from mildly remedial efforts, such as providing for tutoring, to coercive state takeovers and diverting funds to private schools. As the new law kicked into effect in the 2002–2003 school year, preliminary indications revealed that, depending on how things were defined, up to 85% of schools receiving federal funds in some states might be unable to meet the legislation's stringent new requirements. Indeed, by early 2004, resolutions denouncing various elements of NCLB were either pending or enacted in 12 states across the nation, including some legislatures in unshakable Republican strongholds where allegations about "unfunded mandates" and "federal intrusion" found ready ears.

Achievement Gap

Regardless of how NCLB develops, your schools will sooner or later be judged on their ability to close the achievement gap. The gap is often defined in racial terms, since so many minority students are from low-income families, but the gap is more likely to be a consequence of income and social class than of race or ethnicity. What is particularly troubling is that, after decades of success in closing the gap in the 1960s through the 1980s, it began to widen again during the 1990s.

With respect to the achievement gap, one very troubling reality is that most of the progress that has been made to date has been restricted to elementary-school students. Progress at the middle-school level is spotty at best and almost nonexistent in high schools.

Americans seem conflicted about standards and assessment, according to Gallup poll findings analyzed by R. J. Marzano, J. S. Kendall, and L. Cicchinelli in What Americans Believe Students Should Know: A Survey of U.S. Adults *(Aurora, CO: Mid-continent Research for Education and Learning, 1998). Of 248 standards in 15 subjects, only 102 are strongly endorsed by 50% or more of Americans, and just 33 garner the support of 66% or more.*

The challenge you will face here is dynamic and direct. To be effective, you must infuse your district with a passion for closing the gap. The first essential step is to put the issue on the table. District insiders have to understand that closing the gap is your priority. Next, you need to define the gap and use data to illuminate it.

Denial of course is routine, in schools as elsewhere. Too often, "successful" districts like to rely on "average" test-score results as evidence that the achievement gap is someone else's problem. Yet, even "successful" districts are finding themselves surprised when "averages" are pulled apart by school, income, and ethnicity. Invariably, they find that the "averages" conceal almost as much as they reveal.

The reality is that you do not enjoy many options in terms of data usage. Ignoring data is *not* an option under Nickleby. By requiring the nation's schools to describe their success in terms of what each student accomplishes, these provisions entirely modify the federal government's role in kindergarten through grade twelve. The legislation defines an accountable system as one involving several things:

• States create their own standards for what a child should know for all grades. Standards must be developed in math and reading immediately, and for science by the 2005–2006 school year.

• With standards in place, states must test every student's progress toward those standards by using tests aligned with them. Beginning in the 2002–2003 school year, schools were required to begin administering tests in at least one grade in all schools within each of three grade spans: grades 3–5, grades 6–8, and grades 9–10.

• Beginning in the 2005–2006 school year, tests in math and reading must be administered every year in every grade from three through eight. Beginning in the 2007–2008 school year, science achievement also must be tested in these grades.

• Each state, school district, and school will be expected to make adequate yearly progress toward meeting state standards. This progress will be measured for all students by sorting test results for those who are economically disadvantaged, are from racial or ethnic minority groups, have disabilities, or have limited English proficiency.

• School and district performance will be publicly reported in district and state report cards. Individual school results will be on the district report cards.

• If districts or schools continually fail to make adequate progress toward the standards, they will be held accountable. States will be required to implement corrective efforts ranging from financing tutoring for students, to paying for students to attend other schools, to taking over schools.

As the U.S. Department of Education Web site observed in 2003, failure will have no place to hide. And neither will you.

B. No Child Left Behind and Adequate Yearly Progress

James Harvey
Richard C. Wallace, Jr.

As a new superintendent, you have quite a challenge ahead as you grapple with the accountability provisions of No Child Left Behind. Here are some ideas about how to begin.

Coming to Grips With NCLB and "Adequate Yearly Progress"

Never before in the history of American education have school leaders been called on to follow student achievement as closely as they are now. Perhaps they should have been, but they were not, and you are unlikely to have been well prepared. Where to start?

You will be expected to speak authoritatively about the differences among performance tests, achievement tests, and aptitude tests. The language of "criterion-referenced" and "norm-referenced" test items should be second nature to you. And naturally, you will be familiar with the strengths and weaknesses of machine-scored versus hand-scored test items (and their financial implications). Does that all sound too much? Turn to Web sites such as those maintained by the Educational Testing Service (*www.ets.org*) and Achieve (*www.achieve.org*) to get a handle on the distinctions.

Next, you'll need to know which tests are most appropriate under which circumstances. (The reality is that your state education agency will define the assessments you use, but you need to know enough about these assessments to understand their effect within your community.) Try to avoid getting trapped in a situation in which one test(which might be perfectly appropriate for a specific purpose) is asked to do double or triple duty. Tests that are acceptable for program evaluation purposes may be entirely inappropriate for making judgments about individual students. You might want to turn to groups such as the National Center for Fair & Open Testing (*www.fairtest.org*) to learn more about these distinctions.

Finally, get accustomed to the idea that one of the most arcane and significant features of No Child Left Behind is the requirement for "adequate yearly progress." You will be expected to close the achievement gap among all groups in your district over 12 years. Your district must establish separate baselines for both reading and math, using 2001–2002 data, for each demographic group. The starting point will be the percentage of students in the state's lowest-achieving demographic group who are proficient—or in the school at the twentieth percentile of the state's schools, whichever is higher. Then you will be asked to raise the bar in equal increments over a 12-year period, with increases measured every two or three years. You'll have to raise the bar at least five times, and perhaps twelve. *And you will have to raise the bar, wherever it is set, for each demographic cluster.* You won't be able to hide behind the false security of districtwide averages. You can learn more about these requirements and how to implement them from your state education agency.

SOURCE: Adapted from *The Urban Superintendent: Creating Great Schools While Surviving on the Job* (Report of a Colloquium for Former Urban Superintendents, Council of Great City Schools, September 2003).

C. Here's the Deal on the Achievement Gap

James Harvey
Richard C. Wallace, Jr.

After 40 years of federal encouragement, the achievement gap has not been closed. It won't be closed with wishful thinking in the next 12 years, either. Here's the deal that you should insist on making with the public around the achievement gap.

1. We'll do our part, but the community needs to do its. We can do it, but the resources need to be put in place to get it done.

2. The resources include equalizing funds within districts, developing out-of-school community assets, and improving early education programming.

3. We will insist that the school board provide ample resources to students with the greatest need.

4. We will create a "no excuses" mentality by infusing a sense of urgency about this issue within the district. Specifically, we will improve the level of expectations for poor and minority children and we will use data to drive the discussion about the achievement gap.

5. We will communicate the sense of urgency by insisting that the district no longer ignore race and class, the 800-pound gorillas in our schools, and by putting the best principals and teachers in the schools that need them the most.

6. As part of the effort to close the achievement gap, we will also hold families and the community accountable. The best predictor of a student's performance is not race, income, or even parental education. It is whether the child comes to school. We cannot educate children who are not in class.

7. We will identify outstanding schools, teachers, and principals, and we will celebrate their accomplishments.

SOURCE: Adapted from *The Urban Superintendent: Creating Great Schools While Surviving on the Job* (Report of a Colloquium for Former Urban Superintendents, Council of Great City Schools, September 2003).

2. Where We Are on Standards and Assessment

The standards and assessment train left the station with dazzling speed. At the conclusion of the 2000 presidential election, standards and assessment were a state matter. Efforts by President Bill Clinton to encourage states and localities to voluntarily benchmark their programs against the fourth-grade reading and seventh-grade mathematics assessments used in the Third International Mathematics and Science Surveys (TIMSS) were never taken seriously in Congress. The Clinton administration (warding off allegations of federal interference) also struggled to encourage states to comply with voluntary efforts to set goals under its "Goals 2000" program. Surprisingly, given this background, bipartisan majorities in Congress enacted the Bush administration's No Child Left Behind statute in 2002, transforming the federal role in schools.

A. Emerging Demands

James Harvey

If the kids graduating from your schools are so stupid, how come things are so good? That seems like a reasonable question. If the nation was at risk in 1983, how come it stood bestride the world like a colossus in 2003?

Anthony P. Carnevale, former chair of the National Commission on Employment Policy, directs policy studies for the Educational Testing Service.

The answer that economist Tony Carnevale offers to this is fairly straightforward. The scale of the American economy, combined with massive investment in production facilities and flexibility, is what has carried the day so far. "Four good engineers can be better than one brilliant one," he told us a few years ago. We always seem to have enough people to get the job done. "Flexibility is a corporate term," he added, "when you're talking to people from labor, they use the term 'fired.' But the ability to add and subtract people in the workforce as demands change is a big economic benefit to the United States."

The Economic Demands

What does this have to do with American schools? A great deal, it turns out. Carnevale contends that the recipe for economic growth rests on four ingredients, mixed in roughly equal proportions. They are: human capital (the quality of your people), investment (the quality of your production equipment, processes, and transportation systems), scale (how big you are), and flexibility (how easily you change).

We need to worry about human capital, says Carnevale. The quality of a nation's human resources accounts for 25% of economic growth, according to Carnevale. In this area, we have little to brag about. "Whereas we look very strong on international comparisons of Gross National Product per capita, we don't look nearly as good on international comparisons of student achievement."

In an increasingly competitive world, therefore, it makes sense for policymakers to worry about the institutions that develop the nation's human capital. That's where your schools come in. And that's where the pressure on you is coming from.

For an extended discussion of these issues, see Anthony P. Carnevale, Help Wanted . . . College Required *(Princeton, NJ: ETS Leadership, 2000).*

The Moral Imperative

Apart from the larger macroeconomic issues, a moral imperative also stands out with great clarity. Education benefits in the United States are unevenly distributed. All of us know that. Few people understand it as well as you. You probably understand something else as well, if not with the energy and certainty Carnevale brings to the subject. In the United States, people who are well educated wield power and have access to the best jobs; people who are not lack power and take whatever work they can find. It's very simple. In the worst cases, the undereducated may create alternative cultures and economies, frequently finding themselves enmeshed with the criminal justice system. It's no coincidence that two-thirds of the nation's prisoners are functionally illiterate.

The Right Educational Stuff. The educational "right stuff" used to mean a lot of different things in the United States, says Carnevale. You once could be a "union guy" making a good living on an assembly line after dropping out of high school. In fact, 40% of union members were dropouts in the 1950s, he says. Forget that today. As the year 2000 faded into history, 40% of union members possessed some college education.

According to Carnevale, an educational and occupational hierarchy exists in the United States. There has been a substantial increase since 1979 in the proportion of workers with some college education or a college degree, accompanied by a marked decline in the proportion of workers with only a high school diploma or no diploma at all. High-technology jobs nearly doubled from 4% of employment to about 7.5% in the last 20 years. Positions in education and health care swelled from 10% of all jobs to 15%. White collar managerial and financial management jobs grew from 30% of the workforce to nearly 40%. All of these jobs require some college attendance; all of them pay reasonably well; and all of them have boomed in the last generation.

Look at Figure 4.1. It confirms what you already know. There is a hierarchy of occupations and earnings in the United States. The higher up the occupational food chain one advances, the

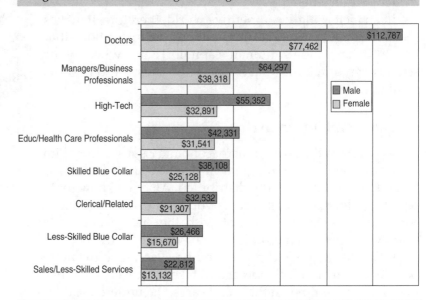

Figure 4.1   1998 Average Earnings of Workers

SOURCE: Carnevale et al., ETS, 1999

more attractive the rewards. The hierarchy moves from unskilled services and blue-collar work, through clerical and skilled blue-collar work. The hierarchy picks up when it gets to education and health care professionals, and salaries go through the roof for managers, business professionals, and doctors and other professionally trained employees (and entrepreneurs).

Schools as Sorting Machines

You have your work cut out for you. By the 1950s, American schools had already become well established as sorting machines, labeling teenagers as college-bound, run-of-the-mill, or low achievers. Those schools sent strong signals about who was on top, who was in the middle, and who belonged at the bottom of the pile.

Today, schools still operate as sorting machines. The signals are modestly more subtle but still effective. One of them lies in whether or not students enroll in "college prep," "vocational," or "general" programs. Another is the privilege of taking "honors" or "advanced placement" courses, an option never put before very many. Your challenge is to take this system and transform it into one with high expectations for all, a system in which no child is left behind.

Alfie Kohn, in The Schools Our Children Deserve: Moving Beyond Traditional Classrooms and "Tougher Standards" *(Boston: Mariner Books, 2000), cautions that increasing emphasis on tests and standards may be "squeezing the intellectual life out of classrooms."*

B. It's Not Good Enough: A Personal Perspective on Urban Student Achievement

Diana Lam

Inspiring comments from school administrator Diana Lam, an immigrant from Peru, remind us not to ignore children's dreams. In the words of the Nobel laureate William Butler Yeats: "In dreams begins responsibility."

If 50% of students in a poor urban high school enroll in college, it's hailed as a success story. But if only 75% of students in some suburban high schools go on to college, heads roll.

For too long, many Americans have expected too little of poor and minority children and the schools that teach them. The legacy of low expectations for poor and minority children has infected our schools, poisoning the futures of children who suffer the misfortune of growing up in America's cities. I am not interested in blaming socioeconomic factors or municipal budgets for the failure of children to reach high standards. These are excuses that paper over a harsh reality— every day in America, poor and minority students are deferring their dreams while we argue about what's going on.

Several school systems recognize that emotional intelligence plays a significant role in students' success, in and out of the classroom. Many turn to Daniel Golman's work: Emotional Intelligence: Why It Can Matter More Than IQ *(New York: Bantam Books, 1995).*

For me, the problem of low expectations is neither an abstract issue nor a debate about other children. It's deeply personal. Had I grown up with the yoke of low expectations around my neck, I would be someone else entirely. I grew up in Peru in a family of modest means, the daughter of a Chinese father and a Peruvian mother who had never finished elementary school. While their lack of formal education and their need to work endless hours to support the family limited their ability to help me in school, they instilled in me a respect for education. They also expected great effort from their daughter. My parents' influence was critical, yet exceptional teachers also shaped my life.

As a young girl, I dreamed of one day going to college in the United States. At the age of eight, I stood, my heart in my hand, and shared this dream with my third-grade teacher. How easily she might have squashed my hope and crushed my heart. A different teacher might have looked at an eight-year-old Peruvian child and thought to herself, "What are the chances of this girl studying in the United States?" Another teacher might have thought to help me by scaling back my dream to something more manageable, perhaps to learn a craft or go to secretarial school. But my teacher believed in me, breathing energy into my hope and mapping out the route to attain my ambition.

My third-grade teacher was gifted, for she knew that the power of children's dreams is the greatest inspiration in the world. She understood that the commitments children make in the deep recesses of their hearts explain incredible acts of courage and risk taking, the forces that truly shape societies. Her belief in me paid off. At the age of 16, I won a scholarship and moved to the United States to attend college. I carried with me the immigrant's dream of unbounded opportunity in a country where the air itself was filled with hope. A free and democratic society guarantees many rights to its citizens, but none is more precious than the legacy of hope that things will get better.

Many years later, I'm still not willing to let anyone scale down my dreams or steal my hope. Having worked as a senior administrator in several urban school districts where student achievement is unacceptably low, I have held another big dream. It is not to create a high-performing school; that has already been done. It is to bring the practices that we know work for poor and minority children to scale, creating a high-performing school district where every child in every classroom in every school is succeeding. This is the greatest challenge in public education.

For more information on Lauren Resnick's work, see Part VI.

Lauren Resnick's work guides my thinking. Resnick asserts that intelligence is not something that's inherited. She won't even sit still for the conventional view that you can work your way around limited intelligence. She insists that "intelligence," whatever it is, can be developed.

We can start to raise the bar for poor and minority children, challenging them to learn more and become more. And we need to approach this work with a sense of urgency, for the reality is that our children's futures depend on them.

The way schools are structured might matter a great deal to teaching practice, if we understood what kind of teaching practice we wanted, and if we understood the conditions necessary to give teachers access to the skill and knowledge they need to engage in that practice.

Richard Elmore, Penelope Peterson, and Sarah McCarthey, *Restructuring in the Classroom: Teaching, Learning, & School Organization* (San Francisco: Jossey-Bass, 1996)

As a child in Peru, I was challenged by my teachers. They supported me. The roots of my work as an educational reformer grew there, in the safety of a community where I was equipped with the intellectual faculties to pursue my sense of justice in the world. It's time to show the next generation that their dreams, too, have roots in reality and that their teachers, also, will give wings to their dreams.

C. Leaders Respond: Aligning the System

James Harvey

Much of the impetus for standards-based reform in the 1990s and for No Child Left Behind grew out of frustration with the pace and quality of reform efforts attempted in the 1980s, according to Marshall S. ("Mike") Smith, former dean of the

Stanford School of Education and undersecretary of education in the Clinton administration. The results for American students on cross-national studies of middle- and secondary-school students were disappointing, he told us. Too many schools, particularly in inner cities, were failing. And education reform efforts looked like fireflies—sparkles of promise school by school, but little that added up to systemic change.

See Section 3, "What the Data Tell You," for international comparisons of American student performance.

"States have the central constitutional authority for the conduct of education," said Smith, "under the Tenth Amendment to the United States Constitution." So that became a first principle of reform in the Clinton administration. Another was that all students can learn to far higher academic standards than they have in the past. And the third was what he terms a "clear moral responsibility to improve quality for the most needy."

Goals

With those principles in mind, Smith described the Clinton administration's strategy as developing school reforms that would, like reforms in other sectors of society, do the following:

- Establish clear, challenging goals
- Provide adequate quality resources to help reach the goals
- Align resources within the system to reach the goals
- Give people who are responsible for implementation the freedom and responsibility to reach the goals in the best ways they can
- Ensure mutual, reciprocal accountability—that is, up and down the line—that reinforces good practice and provides support and "know-how" to correct "bad" practice

This is a goal-oriented reform agenda, one in which the federal government sees itself as a mentor and encourager of state progress, not the arbiter of local school practice.

Within this structure, alignment then becomes the watchword. There is a sense of the machine metaphor about all this, a sense of bureaucratic compulsion at work. Yet, in reality, it's hard to take issue with much of the alignment logic.

Results

Robert Schwartz, founding president of Achieve, a coalition of governors and business leaders committed to standards-based reform, told us that practically every state, by the end of the 1990s, had a clear policy that set out the focus of standards-based reform. This was a far cry from the beginning of the decade, when perhaps only a dozen states had developed content standards or made any effort to align their systems.

Schwartz also pointed to other positive developments. Reading and math scores were up. Results for the SAT and ACT college entrance examinations were at their highest point in two decades. More students were taking and passing Advanced Placement examinations. And college attendance was higher than it had ever been.

Implementation Challenges

Both Smith and Schwartz pointed to significant policy issues that require attention. Schwartz, in particular, discerned "significant variation in how this is playing out across states." Standards in particular had become "wish lists," since they were developed by asking disciplinary leaders what they wanted to see in the standards. (That's only to be expected. No historian worth her salt would settle for anything less than 40% of the time available in the curriculum. History doubtless deserves that much time. The challenge is that the history demand is matched by teachers of English, mathematics, foreign language, and every other subject. The accumulated demands of disciplinary specialists, left to their own devices, would certainly create a 24/7 school.)

Most disciplinary leaders, according to Schwartz, have not "disciplined themselves to worry about issues of time or teacher preparation, or even whether these are things most teachers can do."

Tests are another central issue, he noted in his discussion with us. "If there's a gap between the standards and tests, the tests quickly take over and become *de facto* standards." In that regard, there was already, by 2000, a "real sense of testing overload in many places with too much testing of the wrong kind."

> *Am I worried about the emphasis on test results? I used to worry about things like that. But then I realized that there is nothing on these examinations that all of us wouldn't want our own kids to know.*
>
> Diana Lam,
> Superintendent,
> Providence Schools,
> Rhode Island

Schwartz, a staunch advocate of standards-based reform, also worried about two other aspects of accoun ability. First is the "opportunity to learn" challenge. This involves asking: "Has the child had the right curriculum? Are the teachers prepared? If my child was at risk, was I warned? Has the school tried to mobilize extra support for my child?" All of these things raise important legal, educational, and ethical concerns.

Next is the issue of how to think about accountability. Originally conceived as something revolving around schools and systems, it is now focused on high-stakes testing of students. "There's a need to balance accountability for kids with accountability for adults," he observed, suggesting that accountability can be thought of in three different ways. First is bureaucratic accountability, which worries about what each layer expects of the layer below. Next is lateral accountability, or how to build a professional culture across schools. The final method for thinking about accountability is a kind of consumer-oriented version, that is, situations in which institutions are accountable to clients and consumers. This third category opens up the possibility that standards-based and market-based reform might be in conflict, suggested Schwartz. The truth is that sometimes measures used to support bureaucratic account-ability are used to justify programs designed to encourage consumer-oriented accountability.

President Bush's enactment, of course, moves substantially beyond the modest encouragement developed in the 1990s by President Clinton and Achieve to encourage states to take standards-based reform more seriously. It takes align-ment to another level. It insists that standards be in place. It demands state compliance. It establishes very specific goals and timetables for closing the achievement gap.

And its success or failure will rise and fall on what you and your colleagues in your district do.

For more information about perspectives on accountability, see www.crpe.org (Center on Reinventing Public Education, Daniel J. Evans School of Public Affairs, University of Washington).

D. Effective State Accountability Systems

Luvern L. Cunningham

Researchers at the University of Washington developed the following description of an effective state accountability system. The seven elements described here level the playing field by encouraging reciprocal feedback between districts and the state and accounting for the needs of both.

An accountability system should have

- Fair, reliable, relevant, and understandable indicators of school performance
- Predictable and consistent incentives for performance
- Opportunities for schools to build their capacity, ensuring tools and resources for schools
- Flexibility for schools to adapt to help their students learn and meet state standards of performance
- A safety net, providing functional learning opportunities for students when school improvement is not possible
- A comprehensive public information campaign that helps schools and the public understand the process
- An independent body guiding the system and pro-viding a check and balance on the political oversight of the system

The American Evaluation Association issued a position statement on high-stakes testing in Pre-K–12 education. It went on record to oppose the use of tests as the sole or primary criterion for making decisions, arguing that such use creates serious negative consequences for students, educators, and schools. You can find this statement at www.aea@eval.org.

E. Tool: Assessing Your State's Accountability System

Luvern L. Cunningham

Accountability is a high-stakes part of life in the school trenches. Table 4.1 provides you with a checklist to help you review your state's assessments.

Table 4.1 Assessing Your State's Accountability System

Our State Accountability System:	Yes	No	Not Sure
1. Uses multiple measures of student performance to arrive at judgments of the success or failure of the state's educational system.			
2. Meets all the requirements of the No Child Left Behind legislation at the state and local levels.			
3. Ensures that the accountability system does not underserve (or do a disservice to) segments of the student population.			
4. Aligns state academic standards, curriculum, and assessments.			
5. Provides comprehensive information so that teachers, principals, central office administrators, parents, and community leaders can understand the accountability process.			
6. Provides regular, understandable reports to the public on the performance of the state's educational system, including plans for improving its performance.			
7. Reports annually and comprehensively on the costs of the accountability system to state taxpayers.			
8. Assures practitioners that standards guide test development and other instruments of measurement that are a part of the accountability system.			
9. Spells out clearly the placement of management and oversight responsibilities within the accountability system, including segments that may be delivered through outside contracts.			
10. Places school accountability in the context of public and community accountability for the well-being of children and youth outside schools, including mental health, substance abuse, juvenile justice, and correctional programs.			

NOTE: Scoring: Yes = +1; No = −1; Not Sure = 0.
Grades: 7–10 points—Congratulations; 4–6 points—Needs work; 1–3 points—You're not failing anyone on these results, are you?; 0 or below—Legislature flunks.

F. Tool: Single-Loop or Double-Loop Learning?

Nelda Cambron-McCabe

Decision making in our organizations moves between reflection and action. Ideally, we observe what has been happening; reflect on what we or others have done; compare this observation with our established norms; and then use the data to decide on our next course of action. Argyris and Schön described this process as *single-loop learning*, which may be effective in bringing about change in the short run.

> *Chris Argyris & Donald Schön*, Theory in Practice: Increasing Professional Effectiveness *(San Francisco: Jossey-Bass, 1974).*

As a system becomes more complex, however, this type of learning creates barriers to making necessary changes because single-loop learning fails to question the assumptions and norms of the organization.

Suppose, for example, that the behaviors and norms you're attempting to improve are ineffective or inappropriate for dealing with the changes you face. How do you know what's appropriate? Suppose the problem is not how well you do what you do but *what you choose to do* in the first place? The challenge isn't to do something properly; it's to figure out the proper thing to do.

Gareth Morgan, whom we met in Part II, highlights the limitations of single-loop thinking with the example of a household thermostat. The thermostat represents a simple system that moves through the single-loop cycle of monitoring the environment for deviation from the set temperature (or norm) and correcting it. The thermostat, using its single loop, cannot determine if the preset temperature is right for the number of the people in the room and thus adjust it accordingly. In other words, since the thermostat cannot question the established norm, it cannot change its behavior and learn to do its job more effectively. This act requires engaging in a second learning cycle (in communication with the first), often referred to as *double-loop learning*.

> *Bureaucracies not only impede the learning process, they also frequently behave as though individuals who question established procedures or the status quo are somehow disloyal to the organization's larger mission. This is a surefire recipe for guaranteeing single-loop thinking.*

Stretch out your time for reflection to include double-loop learning (thinking about the way you think). That way, you can challenge your own norms, attitudes, and assumptions. You can reconsider the tasks you've set for yourself and try to understand the ways your own choices may be affecting your organization.

According to Morgan and others in organization research, organizations rarely engage in double-loop learning. In fact, the bureaucracies of our organizations actually impede the learning process. Yet, it is this self-questioning ability that enables you and your organization to learn.

These questions engage reflection about standards and assessment. You can modify the list to reflect on any issue in your organization.

When you feel you are pushing against the system and your actions are not generating meaningful changes in your schools, slow down and take up the questions in the following exercise. They may be able to lead you into double-loop learning and meaningful transformation.

Questions for Double-Loop Reflection About Standards and Assessments

- What are we doing now to measure student progress? Why are we using this approach? What assumptions drive it?
- Do our current actions make sense educationally?
- Are we measuring what we think we are measuring?
- Are we measuring the appropriate things?
- Who benefits under this approach? Who loses?
- What beliefs, attitudes, and values prevent us from creating other alternatives?
- What are our aspirations for student learning?
- What aspect of my thinking must change to promote transformation of our present practices?

G. Tool: Are We "Shifting the Burden" in Schools?

Michael Goodman
Janis Dutton
Art Kleiner

In systems archetypes, a "shifting the burden" story usually begins with an urgent problem or symptom followed by demands to fix it. A "quick fix" is often obvious and immediate; it has the illusion of certainty and the reward of short-term efficiency. But it diverts attention away from the real or fundamental source of the problem and ultimately does not sustain itself. A better solution is more fundamental, but it takes longer and is much more uncertain. Building support for it is more difficult. Torn between these two approaches, we are naturally drawn to the quick fix. Mapping your story can help you determine if you are opting for short-term, quick fixes or long-term solutions. This tool demonstrates how to use the archetype with a particularly troubling school problem—student achievement.

Schools have felt increasing pressure from federal and state leaders and their communities to "prove" their competence by improving scores on standardized tests. But state standards have nothing to say about the fundamental reasons why performance in some schools might be worse than others, or about how to close the gap in any sustainable way. So the quick fix plays out: Typically from January through March, teachers convert their classrooms into preparatory courses for test-taking skills, and the initial results are indeed higher. The quick fix worked!

Once the test is over, however, most students forget the material acquired through the intensive drills. (Confess. Can you still remember how to solve a quadratic equation? Do you even remember what a quadratic equation is?) Students who have difficulty with tests, whatever the reason, see fewer opportunities to excel. They may see no reason to try. The result? Failure and dropout rates increase. In effect, the students who are not attuned to test taking are punished. This situation affects overall skill levels, which leads to lower overall performance. With the symptom reappearing, there is a renewed demand for another "quick fix"—raising the bar again, for even tougher standards and tests.

The causal-loop diagram in Figure 4.2 portrays this "shifting the burden" story. Faced with pressures to improve performance (in the center of the diagram), educators can either focus on improving test results (upper loop) or concentrate on the fundamental solution (bottom loop).

Everyone in the school system understands the dangers of the standardized test "quick fix." Yet everyone feels forced into the pattern. Why? Because the fundamental solutions require investment, time, and care. They require attentiveness to varied learning styles, in-depth staff development, curriculum revisions, nutrition, and much more, including perhaps many things in the community. Most of all, fundamental solutions are slower to produce results, and we cannot be certain of them. It is very difficult to endure the delay before results improve.

The loop on the right side maps the negative side effects of diverting attention and resources to quick fixes, such as eliminating learning activities or professional development not specific to the tests and short-circuiting teachable moments. When well-intentioned quick-fix efforts themselves become the problem, it is harder to seek and apply fundamental solutions. Often the availability of quick fixes reduces the perceived *need* for fundamental solutions.

This archetype can assist you as you reflect on other pressing issues. Follow these steps to gain insight into whether you are relying on quick fixes (or as Ron Heifetz would say, technical responses) or taking steps to develop fundamental solutions.

- What problem is creating a sense of urgency for you?
- What quick fixes are tempting you?

This section was adapted with permission from Peter Senge, Nelda Cambron-McCabe, Timothy Lucas, Bryan Smith, Janis Dutton, and Art Kleiner, Schools That Learn: A Fifth Discipline Fieldbook for Educators, Parents, and Everyone Who Cares About Education *(New York: Doubleday, 2000), pp. 359–364. This book can be consulted for an overview of archetypes and causal-loop diagrams.*

Figure 4.2   Causal-Loop Diagram

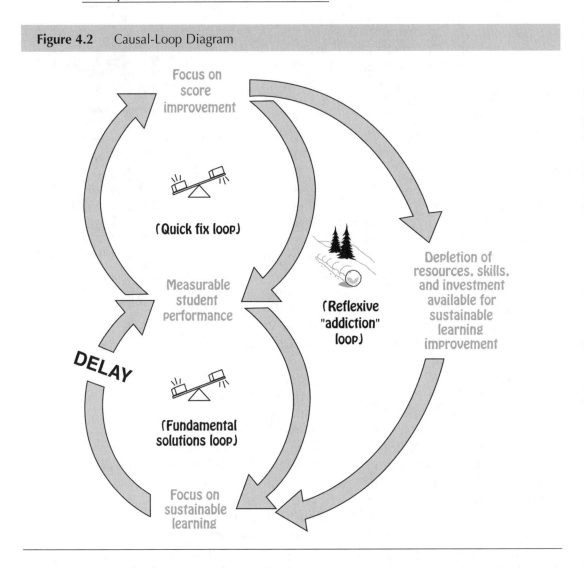

Remember several points as you use this archetype for reflection. First, various groups within the district may see different "fundamental solutions." This offers an opportunity to engage all constituencies in conversations to develop a shared understanding of the problem and options. Second, some problems must be addressed immediately with a quick fix. Using a quick fix buys time to pursue a fundamental solution as long as you do not lose sight of the fact that the quick fix is not the fundamental solution.

- What could be the unexpected results of these short-term fixes?
- What alternative approaches could you try if the quick-fix avenue were not available?
- Do any of these alternatives represent a more fundamental response to the problem?
- What kinds of investment would you need to really make them work?
- What time frame would be required?
- How can you sustain an approach involving substantial delays with your various publics?

3. What the Data Tell You

If the Promised Land is elimination of the achievement gap by 2014, you need to start thinking about how to part the Red Sea. Welcome aboard, Moses.

We hope you're good with data. If you're not, you need to find someone who is. You are going to be awash in numbers very soon; and if you can't interpret them, you'll need help. What are you going to do when presented with tables of reading and math results by grade level, by school, and by socioeconomic group, with additional breakdowns by stanine levels for each group and each school? Keeping it all straight will stretch the patience of Job.

What follows are graphs and tables providing some national and state-level data. They demonstrate several things. First, they help you understand the complex array of students showing up at your doorstep, in terms of ethnicity and socioeconomic background. Next, they indicate that policymakers are correct in worrying about student achievement. The performance of American students seems to decline, relative to the performance of their international peers, as they move through school. Finally, using data based on 800,000 test results in one state, we show you a snapshot of the achievement gap in seventh-grade mathematics. (It could just as easily be fourth-grade reading or tenth-grade social studies.) It gives you a better sense of what will be required to close the gap. Finally, we discuss data usage in your district and with your principals.

A. Tool: The Economic and Demographic Facts of Life

James Harvey

Here's an exercise for you. Table 4.2 contains national figures outlining the demographic and socioeconomic profile of American students. Get your hands on Bureau of the Census data for your district. Honest. It's available. In fact, the Census can give you data by ZIP code right down to the street and block level. Very handy stuff to have lying around. Fill in these categories for your district. Then have your principals fill them in for each of their schools. Check the Web site for the Bureau of the Census: *www.census.gov/main/www/cen2000.html.*

Table 4.2   The Economic and Demographic Facts of Life

The National Picture

Population	Number	In Poverty (0–17 years)	Language Isolated	Disabilities 1997 Data (0–15 years)
Children, 0–19	80,494	11,646	2,687	4,661
White, non-Hispanic	49,140	3,848	444	3,173
Black	12,061	3,570	235	800
Hispanic	13,677	3,653	1,887	533
Asian/Pacific Islander	2,924	353	105	63
Other Race	2,692	222	16	92

How Things Look in My District

Population	Number	In Poverty (0–17 years)	Language Isolated	Disabilities 1997 Data (0–15 years)
Children, 0–19				
White, non-Hispanic				
Black				
Hispanic				
Asian/Pacific Islander				
Other Race				

NOTES: All numbers in thousands; 2000 Census data unless otherwise noted. "Poverty": U.S. government definition. "Language isolated": Census definition of a household in which *all* family members 14 years or older have some difficulty with English; numbers by ethnicity in this column are the authors' estimates based on Census returns in which householders report speaking English "less than very well."

B. Data on Student Achievement

James Harvey

This is something you really need to understand. Findings from a number of international assessments reveal that academic achievement of American high school students is not up to international standards. Don't get too excited if you make progress, in elementary school; things will get harder in the middle and secondary years.

One analysis of the TIMSS data, shown in Figure 4.3, indicates that American students' performance relative to their foreign peers diminishes as they move through the elementary, middle, and secondary school years.

Figure 4.3   This figure reveals that fourth-grade students in 7 nations outperformed U.S. fourth graders in mathematics; U.S. fourth graders did just as well as peers in 6 other nations; and fourth graders from 12 nations performed below U.S. fourth graders. Grade 8 and 12 columns can be read in the same way

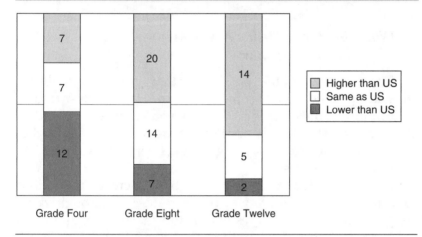

SOURCE: *Youth at the Crossroads: Facing High School and Beyond* (Washington, DC: The Education Trust, 2000). For additional reports and data on student achievement, visit this group's Web site at *www2.edtrust.org/edtrust*

C. The Achievement Gap: Whistling Past the Schoolyard

James Harvey
Mary Beth Celio

In the State of Washington, minority students are found in the bottom deciles of the achievement distribution at rates three to five times those of white students. Despite fairly impressive state progress in closing the achievement gap (averaging 2% a year), at current rates of progress, 80% of the gap will remain after 5 years and 50% after 10. States are (sensibly) levering minority students close to the standards bar over it. What is needed is a slingshot, not a lever.

The happy chatter from state leaders and educators about improved student performance on the Washington Assessment of Student Learning (WASL) is just so much whistling past the schoolyard. The dreams of the state's minority students and their parents are quietly being buried, and few officials are paying much attention. Despite apparently impressive improvement in minority achievement on the WASL exam, independent analyses indicate that the road ahead for minority students is much rockier than most of us want to believe.

The original version of this section appeared in the Seattle Post-Intelligencer, *Sunday, November 17, 2002.*

What the Public Hears: A Mixture of Good and Bad News

Even conceding the possibility that WASL isn't all it's cracked up to be, there's some good news in the latest results, according to public reports. The percentage of fourth graders meeting each standard is up. Results are also modestly higher across the board for seventh graders. Everyone is entitled to celebrate this progress.

But the bad news outweighs the good. There are indications some tenth graders are blowing off the test. And, although scores are going up, this year's results for fourth, seventh, and tenth grade are far short of where they need to be. Just 29% of fourth graders meet standards in all four areas tested (reading, writing, listening, and mathematics). In grade seven, the proportion drops to 22%. And just 30% of tenth graders meet all standards, a troubling figure because graduates of the Class of 2008 will have to master all four subjects to get a diploma.

Educational Disaster Unfolding Out of Sight

But public accounts of these results conceal an educational disaster unfolding among the state's minority students. Because reports based on averages and incremental improvement conceal almost as much as they reveal (even when reported by race, gender, and ethnicity), the scale of the problem is easy to overlook.

Our analyses of WASL results for nearly 800,000 students tested since 1998 indicate that focusing on year-to-year change obscures the central point: the racial achievement gap in Washington is more severe than most state officials appear to understand or have yet acknowledged publicly.

As in other states, WASL results show that African American, Native American, and Latino students stand about half the chance of meeting standards in reading and mathematics as students who are white or Asian American. Closer analysis reveals a harsher reality: It's not just that fewer of the minority students in trouble meet the standards, it's that they are not even close. Their performance abysmally misses the mark.

Seventh-grade math scores are typical of reading and math results in all three grades. Between 25 and 30% of Latino, African American, and Native American students score at rates comparable to the bottom 10% of white and Asian American students. About half of these minority students match scores produced by the bottom fifth of their white and Asian American peers.

There is no way to sugarcoat these results: on both sides of the Cascades, in cities and on farms and reservations, minority students in trouble are found at the bottom of the educational barrel at rates three to five times higher than they should be.

The North Central Regional Educational Laboratory has developed a range of resources related to student achievement. See, for example, Bridging the Great Divide: Broadening Perspectives on Closing the Achievement Gap *(Naperville, IL: Perspective Series, NCREL, 2002). See also the lab's "closing the achievement gap" Web site for additional materials:* www.ncrel.org/gap.

Will the Gap Be Closed?

Well, so what? We should be able to fix this.

In fact, some closing of the gap is evident in recent WASL results, particularly in fourth grade. Yet, despite improvement, there's not a lot of light at the end of this tunnel. All else being equal, a steady-as-we-go strategy won't work. If we stay the current course, we can't get far enough, fast enough.

Since 1998, in an encouraging and remarkable development, the scores of minorities at risk have been improving twice as fast as scores for white students. But to close the gap in the next five years, minority scores would have to improve three to four times as fast. Only Pollyanna could be optimistic about that possibility, since no district anywhere in the country has been able to pull it off. What progress has been made, here and elsewhere, has rested on nudging those minority students who are closest to the standards bar over it. But what's needed is not a nudge but a catapult.

At current rates of improvement, 80% of today's reading and math gap will remain after five years. Even after ten years, roughly half the gap will persist. We need to stop kidding ourselves about what it will take to fix this problem.

What to Do?

Familiar nostrums aren't going to change things. There needs to be direct, focused attention on the kids at the bottom of the pile, using every weapon in the state's arsenal.

Focus. In the most troubled schools, focused effort to improve instruction should be the primary order of business. Financial incentives to get the best teachers and principals into these schools are essential. And school leaders should be freed up to reconfigure staffs, add to and alter how time is used, and try out new technologies and teaching methods. If it takes more money, it takes more money. Business-as-usual in these schools is unconscionable.

Revitalize Communities. We also need to step up to the plate on out-of-school influences on learning. In Washington, as elsewhere, minority students are concentrated in schools with a lot of poverty. Over the years, one constant in educational research is the powerful relationship between income and achievement. As poverty goes up, test scores go down.

Poverty and its accomplices—unstable neighborhoods, single-parent homes, violence, and high rates of unemployment and substance abuse—explain as much as 60 to 70% of achievement differences in many studies.

In a technical sense, statisticians speak of poverty as "predicting" low achievement. As a practical matter, this doesn't mean poor kids can't learn, but it does mean the odds are stacked against them. Poverty doesn't explain everything, but it explains a lot.

A November 2003 analysis by the Northwest Evaluation Association reported startling differences in proficiency standards among states. In some states, standards are so low that 80% or more of the students in the nation could be expected to meet them; in others, standards are so high that 75% or more of students nationally could be expected to fail them. See G. Gage Kingsbury and colleagues, The State of Standards *(Portland, OR: Northwest Evaluation Association, 2003). The report can be found at* www.nwea.org.

For schools serving the most troubled neighborhoods, public officials need to think about complementing school-based efforts with community-revitalization strategies. Neighborhood investment programs to stabilize housing, build home ownership, generate economic development, and create jobs are all needed. And policy should encourage the efforts of faith- and community-based organizations to repair the shattered fabric of neighborhoods and families.

None of this will be easy, but, as Albert Einstein is said to have suggested, it's a form of insanity to repeat the same approaches over and over in the hope of getting a different result. And for decades, we've been pretending that schools alone can fix the achievement problem. Families and communities have a responsibility, too.

Review Standards. Finally, we should consider the possibility that the state's standards and assessment system is too ambitious for its own good. Everyone supports high standards. But if the standards are the wrong ones, or the assessments are inappropriate, or the system places imposing hurdles before minority students from the most troubled circumstances, standards may do the cause of quality more harm than good.

Are our standards too ambitious? They're apparently too broad. Research completed at the University of Washington's Center on Reinventing Public Education indicates that citizens, business leaders, and educators were talking past each other a decade ago when they came together to talk about standards. Basic skills interested corporate leaders, yet everything but the kitchen sink wound up in the standards after the state superintendent sought consensus among parents and curriculum specialists.

Regardless of what happens with WASL, we need to understand that, although schools need to do better, they also need help. If we don't act soon on that knowledge, we may as well continue whistling past the schoolyard. Because behind school walls the dreams of too many minority students are being deferred, drying up, in the memorable phrase of poet Langston Hughes, like raisins in the sun.

You're not in Washington State, you say? This is not your problem? Don't kid yourself. Wherever you are, this is precisely the problem you face.

D. The Achievement Gap: A Picture Is Worth a Thousand Words

James Harvey
Mary Beth Celio

Figure 4.4 shows the graph of the data that convinced University of Washington researchers that state policymakers were kidding themselves about the possibilities of closing the achievement gap with current strategies, approaches, and resources. Results for math and English skills in fourth and tenth grade were practically identical to the ones shown here for seventh grade.

E. What Do the Achievement Data Tell Us

James Harvey
Nelda Cambron-McCabe

Analyst Kati Haycock, director of The Education Trust, acknowledges that there is some legitimacy to the argument that schools

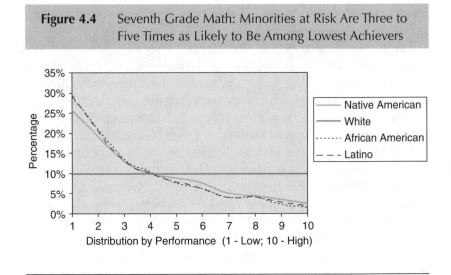

Figure 4.4   Seventh Grade Math: Minorities at Risk Are Three to Five Times as Likely to Be Among Lowest Achievers

are reasonably successful because they are holding their own in terms of achievement results, despite the near-collapse of other social institutions. Still, she pointed out to us, "holding our own" isn't good enough when we consider what kids actually know and what they need to know. "Rates of child abuse, poverty among children, and single-parent families have all increased," she says. "But when you look at data on minority children, only one in 50, sometimes one in 100, has mastered the skills they need."

The Flow

Glaring racial and ethnic disparities jump out of the data tracking the "flow" of students through the education system, says Haycock. For starters, one's chances of graduating from high school are heavily dependent on one's racial background. White students graduate from high school at a rate of 91%, compared with 87% for African American and 62% for Latino students.

The data on the educational life span of students, by race, are disturbing (see Table 4.3). At every stage of the process, white students have the advantage, followed by African American students, with Latino students bringing up the rear.

When analysts consider college graduation rates at age 24 by income level, very troubling disparities emerge, reports Haycock. By age 24, fully 48% of young men and women from high-income families have graduated from college; among

Table 4.3   Of Every 100 Kindergarten Students . . .

Who Are:	Graduate From High School	Complete Some College	Obtain Bachelor's Degree	Obtain Advanced Degree
White	93%	65%	33%	6%
African American	87%	50%	18%	2%
Latino	63%	32%	11%	Unknown
Native American	58%	Unknown	7%	Unknown

SOURCE: Developed from 2001 Census Population Surveys, The Education Trust, Washington, DC.

low-income young adults, the rate is only 7%. Haycock concludes, "This suggests that, unless you believe the children of the rich are seven times smarter than the children of the poor, there is something terribly wrong with the system."

"The point I want to make is simple," Haycock argues. "We have a myth in this country that we have a wonderful system of higher education, but a wretched public school system. The truth is that neither system is performing well. Both are producing poorly prepared graduates, and the sooner we get out of the blaming game, the better off we will be."

Why These Gaps Exist

These gaps exist, insists Haycock, because we take "kids who have less to begin with and then we give them less." Asked about school problems, she reports that adults of all kinds (business leaders, parents, and educators) invariably point to the same difficulties. The children are poor. The home doesn't have enough books. The parents don't care. Single-parent homes. And, of course, violence in the schools.

Young people point to a completely different set of problems. For students, the problem isn't poverty, Haycock says; it's teachers who don't know what they are doing. It's not lack of books at home; it's counselors underestimating their ability. It's not distracted parents, but disengaged principals. And it's not violence in the schools, but boring curriculum. Fewer than three in ten teenagers describe their schools as academically rigorous.

Haycock cites four main reasons for the gaps between the achievement of affluent or majority students on the one hand and low-income or minority students on the other.

• We teach different kids different things. Some kids are challenged, some are not. Poor kids are less likely than wealthy kids to be in the college preparatory track. African American and Latino students are less likely to have access to the "gateway" college-prep high school courses—algebra, calculus, physics, and chemistry. Kids are tracked, insists Haycock. Low-income students and minority students in the top quartile in high school are tracked into vocational education programs.

• Some schools have fewer instructional resources. Experienced teachers are more likely to be in schools in upper-income neighborhoods. School finance arrangements in many states continue to favor children of the well-to-do.

• We expect less of some kids than others. "Our staff was stunned at how little is expected of some students," said Haycock. "The assignments are miserable. There is more coloring in many urban middle schools than writing or math. Even at the high-school level, we found an extraordinary number of coloring assignments. We found an assignment paralleling an exercise from Maryland's fourth-grade assessment in a Philadelphia eleventh-grade class: Choose an historical figure. Do some research. Find a picture of that person; photocopy and decorate it; then develop one sentence on 3×5 cards about that person, completing four cards. Imagine that! Eleventh grade!"

• Many refuse to believe all students can learn. Such individuals are opposed to the idea that all low-income and minority students are capable of serious learning, says Haycock. Often the opposition comes from teachers, not just the community. "Poor kids can become the biggest beneficiaries of the standards movement," she concludes.

Driving home a main point, Haycock reports a distressing scene. The eleventh-grade teacher who assigned students fourth-grade assignments had the gall to wave the newly announced (and dreadful) test results of her class in front of Haycock and her colleagues while declaring triumphantly: "See. I told you these kids can't learn." Of course they couldn't; they'd never been taught.

Haycock succinctly identifies another four points you must take seriously if you're going to improve student results.

- You need clear goals. This is where you must articulate the standards and how you plan to assess them.

- You must ensure that all children receive a rigorous curriculum aligned with standards. Students who take a rigorous math curriculum score higher than those who do not. The data demonstrate the power of academically rigorous work.

- You must provide extra help for students who need it. Sometimes this means extra time; often it means more dollars.

- You must provide all students with effective, qualified teachers. Do your teachers have majors or minors in their teaching areas? Are classes in high-poverty schools taught more often by underqualified teachers?

The Education Trust's data have a sobering effect as we contemplate the overpowering impact of repeated years of poor teaching on low-income children. The statistical data indicating that tracking is alive and well disturbs most of us, particularly the revelation that even many of the best kids are tracked into vocational education—if they are poor or minority. "None of this is happening by chance," worries Peter Negroni, former Springfield (Massachusetts) superintendent. "Think about it. If we wanted to organize schools to systematically harm poor and minority youngsters, we couldn't do a better job of it."

> *Honest analysis of the data makes it clear that what schools do matters. What districts do matters. And, what states do matters.*
>
> Kati Haycock,
> July 2003

F. Tool: What Do You Do?

Nelda Cambron-McCabe

How you communicate will have a tremendous impact on the level of commitment and involvement of teachers, administrators, parents, and community members. Kati Haycock of the Education Trust provides pointed and important advice that can make a difference in your school district. These suggestions and others can be found on the Trust's Web site at *www2.edtrust.org/edtrust*

This checklist may help you avoid some of the most common pitfalls:

- Put your data out there—clear, honest, without spin.
- Explain to parents and the community why disaggregation is necessary—it is essential to understand the patterns; it allows you to give extra help where needed; and federal law now requires it.

- Own the numbers—which means no excuses (blaming demographics or the federal government), and the results are everybody's problem.
- Talk about opportunity gaps, not just achievement gaps—are all students receiving the same quality educational programs?
- Show evidence of success—celebrate schools that are making gains.
- Don't send out counterproductive messages—our kids are different than the wealthy suburban districts.

G. Tool: Communicating About Standards and Tests

Adam Kernan-Schloss

You'll need to bring the public along. Equally important, you'll need to reassure parents. You must be prepared to ask and answer the following eight questions. They provide a powerful point to begin conversations with community members in your district.

As the movement to raise academic standards continues—and as states and districts develop new high-stakes tests to see whether students meet standards—parents, students, and the public are asking more and more questions. At a minimum, school systems should be prepared to answer the following eight questions, in clear, jargon-free language.

Standards: Do You Have Clear Answers to These Four Questions?

- What are students expected to know and be able to do? Who made the decision and has it been discussed in the community?
- How is this achievement measured? (What mix of state proficiency and state and classroom tests, for example?) Do you give students a chance to show what they know?
- How good is good enough? And who determined that—educators, parents, experts, community, state? What level of performance is required to meet standards? Could you meet them?
- How can parents and community members help students achieve? (What specifically can parents and others do to help students improve performance?)

Tests: Do You Have Clear Answers to These Four Questions?

- What is the purpose of the tests the district is using? (To identify student weaknesses? Improve instruction? Identify failing schools? Graduate?) Be prepared to answer questions about whether students are tested too much.
- How is the district doing in terms of student performance? Improving? Holding steady? Moving backwards? How do results differ by racial/ethnic groups?
- How can the district improve? How can it learn from schools that are doing well, particularly those with the greatest challenges?
- How can parents and community members help students achieve? (Again, offer practical and specific advice for how members of your "village" can help improve performance.)

4. Questions for Reflective Practice

Here are some key ideas you should be considering.

Are you sure that the educators in your district understand the pressures on schools today? Do you understand these pressures? Do your teachers and principals?

What about the details of No Child Left Behind and its adequate yearly progress requirements? Are you confident that everyone understands what this entails?

When issues of race and class and the achievement gap come up in your district, do people fall silent? Or are they able to discuss these challenges openly? Is there a different answer to these questions in your community and in your schools?

Have you created, or are you creating, the infrastructure that will permit you to track progress in closing the achievement gap? Do your principals and teachers comprehend that this is your first priority?

Have you become a connoisseur of data? If not, where do you find the skills and confidence to understand what is happening in terms of closing the achievement gap?

Are you confident in discussing the economic and demographic facts of life with the business leaders in your community? With teachers and administrators? With community groups? Are you the only one talking about these things, or have you managed to transform this into a community conversation?

Have you completed the demographic mapping suggested in this part? Compared with national averages, how do things look in your district? What about individual schools? What do your principals and teachers make of these data? Do your principals and teachers understand where your students go (and what they do) after graduation?

Has your community agreed on standards for student performance? What level is expected? Has this information been broadly disseminated?

Have you closely examined students' assignments and the work they produce? Does this review reveal that all students are expected to achieve at high levels? Or do your schools expect less from certain groups of students?

Are students with the greatest needs receiving more resources (i.e., best teachers, enrichment opportunities, etc.)? Who speaks for these students?

Is your district speaking with one voice? Or are different parts of your district telling different people different things?

Part V
Addressing
Race and Class

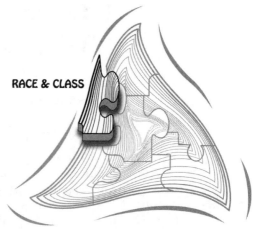

RACE & CLASS

It is as true today as it was two generations ago. Race remains what Swedish sociologist Gunnar Myrdal once described as the great "American dilemma." The legacy of centuries of oppression and prejudice remain with us, now made even more complex by burgeoning income inequality, clear class differences between and within groups, and growing diversity in the American population. How do you close the achievement gap? How can schools live out their historic promise of providing a second chance to all Americans in a society where inequality seems not to shrink but to grow? Discussions about race and class are among the most explosive and difficult you will ever hold as a superintendent. In this part of the fieldbook, you will learn some of the things to do and to avoid when trying to hold these difficult conversations. You'll learn also about what's going on inside schools—and what's going on outside them that might help you in your work.

1. Orientation: Why Race and Class?

Howard Fuller
James Harvey

Until No Child Left Behind came along, most of the discussion of school reform paid little attention to an unpleasant secret. Schools of all kinds, urban and rural, generally don't do a good job serving children of color and poverty. Race and class shape student achievement in ways both subtle and obvious.

> *When a community of people discovers that they share a concern, change begins. There is no power greater than a community discovering what it cares about.*
>
> Margaret Wheatley, *Turning to One Another: Simple Conversations to Restore Hope to the Future* (San Francisco: Berrett-Koehler Publishers, 2002)

The short answer to the question of why worry about race and class is that you probably cannot succeed as a school superintendent unless you worry about it. Nationally, more than one-third of all public school enrollment is made up of minority students—African American, Hispanic, Asian or Pacific Islander, or Native American. Nearly 20% of all children aged 5 to 17 live in poverty, with the proportion of poor minority children exceeding 40% and the number of African American children living in severe poverty doubling in recent years. While it is true that there are more white children who are poor than minority children, the proportion of minority children who are poor is much higher.

And these children are nearly as segregated today as they were in the days of legal Jim Crow. As the twenty-first century dawned, about one-half of white students attended public schools that enroll 10% or fewer minority students. About 2% of white students attended schools with enrollments of 75% or more minority students. Data for minority students were, of course, reversed: About 4% attended public schools with less than 10% minority enrollment. Nearly 50% of minority students attend public schools with enrollments that are 75% or more minority.

When these students arrive in your classrooms, what will their teachers look like? By that we mean, will the teaching force bear any resemblance to the students they are teaching? The answer, of course, is no. While the students are members of minority groups, young, and about evenly divided between boys and girls, the teaching force is primarily white, aging, and overwhelmingly female. More than four out of five teachers in the United States are white (about 86%); two-thirds of them are 40 years of age or older; and nearly three-quarters are women.

The challenge these demographics present to you as a practical matter is that, under the terms of the Bush administration's No Child Left Behind legislation (see Part IV), you are expected to preside over an educational revolution. In your school district, no distinctions on the basis of student achievement of the different groups in your district will be tolerated by the year 2013–2014. Equally to the point, between now and 2014, if your schools are not demonstrating "adequate yearly progress" in closing the achievement gap, the funds you are now spending may be redirected to pay for tutors, counseling, and extra assistance—or indeed to pay for education at private schools.

The issues in the long run are, if anything, more compelling. The dynamics of race and class are becoming ever more complex. In 2003, for example, the United States Bureau of the Census announced that, for the first time, Hispanic Americans were the nation's largest minority group. In the lifetime of superintendents launching their careers today, white Americans will become a statistical minority of the population.

This part begins to address these issues. Conversations about race and class are difficult to have, so we start out by providing some tools you can use to begin the conversation. Next, we explore what's happening both inside and outside schools. We explore the challenge of closing the achievement gap through the lens of disadvantaged students and students at the margin. Finally, we explore the assets students depend on in the effort to succeed in life before we turn to some questions and issues for reflection.

Why should you worry about race and class in the long run? Because our society cannot long function while it tolerates the class, income, and racial differences that are evident to anyone who takes the time to look. If it was true, as President Lincoln said nearly 150 years ago, that this nation cannot "endure half slave and half free," it is equally true that the nation cannot endure half wealthy and half

> *Race still matters in the United States. If you doubt that, examine Cornell West's* Race Matters *(New York: Vintage Books, 1994).*

> *Want a stunning insight into how class plays out in modern life? A picture is worth a thousand words. You'll probably have to find it on the Internet, but get your hands on a copy of 28-Up, a documentary by filmmaker Michael Apted, who also directed* Coal Miner's Daughter *and* Gorillas in the Mist. *Starting in England in 1964, he filmed 14 young people from different economic backgrounds at seven-year intervals beginning at age seven. The aspirations of wealthy young people were shaped by their parents, and most aspired to attend Oxford or Cambridge University. Generally, that's where they wound up. Children from low-income families were left to work out their own educational destinies, and most opted for less-demanding curricula and immediate work. That couldn't happen in the United States, you say? What about all those "legacy" admissions to Ivy League institutions?*

poor, with the differences defined more by race, privilege, and class than ability, merit, or effort. To say the same thing another way, unequal outcomes in a democracy might be defended on the grounds that everyone had an equal chance at the start. But if it turns out that significant numbers of students were not treated fairly at the outset, there can be no defense for unequal results.

2. Difficult Conversations

In the United States, conversations about race and class are nearly inevitably stilted, stylized, and difficult. Neither majority nor minority participants seem able to express honestly and openly what's on their minds, at least in formal public settings. Many people prefer to avoid the discussion, considering it to be the thinnest of ice on which to set foot. But it is a discussion that has to take place, a conversation that has to be held. Here are some examples of how to proceed and tools you might use as you begin this dialogue in your district. We don't pretend it will be easy, and you may make mistakes. With the help of the tools here, however, you can begin the engagement and experience some success.

A. Holding Difficult Conversations

Howard Fuller

The great silent dialogue in American education is about race and class. It's silent because so little is ever said publicly about the topic. The reality is that we didn't find this discussion any easier than you will. We found it difficult. You will too. But you're going to have to engage it.

Careful planning, honesty, determination, and sometimes just plain luck can help you broach these topics. Several factors appeared to be particularly valuable in framing the discussion:

- Structuring meetings around powerful individual stories
- Improving comfort levels by breaking large groups into smaller and smaller units
- Using skilled facilitators to help draw out the discussion

By the same token, several situations need to be avoided, lest they sabotage the conversation. These range from lack of adequate preparation to trying to deal with difficult issues in large groups. Section 2B gives some suggestions on how to work around these land mines.

Stories

Forget about the experts, at first. Try to find some people who are willing to share their lives with you. In the Danforth Forum, our success lay in finding four successful people, from very diverse backgrounds, all of whom started out life with huge obstacles in their path. If you can find people like that, just listen to what they have to say.

What you will hear is powerful. And it's often painful. Imagine sitting in a meeting in which four complete strangers share the following with you: being forced to listen to racist jokes in the classroom as a child . . . living a childhood of Appalachian poverty so severe that privies were unavailable . . . understanding, even as a child, that the deck was loaded against people who looked like you . . . trying to console your children scarred by racial slurs . . . waging a 70-year fight to obtain the honorable discharge and medals a father had earned but never received . . . confronting the prejudice and biases that divide even minority groups . . . examining the many ways in which class and caste blight dreams, divide society, and stunt American growth.

This is raw and tough stuff. But if you can set up the dynamics in which speakers can share material such as this—and you, your staff, your teachers, and your community can hear it—you will have made a tremendous start with the discussion. This conversation will leave you with new understandings of the dynamics of race and class in our life and schools. And it might leave you shaken.

Among the storytellers we listened to were the following: Beatriz, a national education leader who is Latino; Jacqueline, an African American woman who deferred her college plans to work as a parent activist; William, a professor emeritus at a Big 10 campus, who grew up poor and white in Appalachia; and Bernard, also an African American, now president of a foundation, who grew up in the North, during World War II, struggling with racism. Listen to their tales.

Beatriz. "I married an African American man," she began her story. "Now head of his own manufacturing firm, he was blacklisted by the chair of his Ph.D. program for objecting to

> *How do we frame a conversation about this so that our country's story has a happy ending? Because if it doesn't work for some of us, it can't work for any of us.*
>
> Peter Negroni,
> Superintendent,
> Springfield,
> Massachusetts,
> Schools

> *How you talk about this is critical. I remember saying to some of my African-American colleagues, "If you keep venting like that, nobody will say anything because you're blowing our white friends out of the room."*
>
> Lynn Beckwith, Jr.,
> Superintendent,
> University City,
> Missouri

Immigration trends profoundly influence schools and communities across the nation. For an intriguing look at the experience of immigrant children in four schools (Wisconsin, Colorado, Connecticut, and Iowa), see Portraits of Four Schools: Meeting the Needs of Immigrant Students and Their Families (New Haven, CT: Center in Child Development and Social Policy, Yale University, 2003). Also available at www.yale.edu/21C.

the chair's racist speeches. I have had to console my children after they heard racial slurs. And I've also had to encourage them when they were challenged for not being black enough."

She concluded her story by noting that the responsibility for addressing this state of affairs "rests with both blacks and whites. Both have prejudices to overcome; and both must recognize that unity is the only solution."

Jacqueline. Born in Chicago, Jacqueline moved to Milwaukee as a child. She recalls that at one point flyers were distributed in her neighborhood announcing a Ku Klux Klan rally near her house.

At Roosevelt Middle School in Milwaukee, she found herself attending what was thought to be "one of the worst schools in the city. Predominantly African American and Hispanic in enrollment, a majority of its teachers were from minority groups." At the end of eighth grade, said Jacqueline, she was transferred to another school with a majority enrollment of white students. "The idea was that we'd get a better education with white kids."

Unable to get Medicare, child care, or financial aid to go to college in her twenties, Jacqueline put off her college dreams in favor of consulting and civic activism. "I still have my own personal goal of going to college to become an engineer. But before I do that, I have to defer it to help eradicate racism, classism, and genderism."

William. This presentation was framed by class. He grew up, a poor Appalachian white boy in the 1930s, in a part of America little changed from the nineteenth century. So poor that the children literally evacuated outside the kitchen window (because there was no privy), he grew up in a largely dysfunctional family in which his alcoholic father ultimately deserted the family and "my mother went crazy trying to deal with that."

It's ironic that, after all these years, we're still struggling with the same issues around race and class.

Gerry House, Superintendent, Memphis Public Schools

William and his brothers and sisters used to run to the road to see a car go by; there were so few. They learned to "pole" coal off the top of passing freight cars with a stick, so that they'd have something to heat their shack. "A good poler could get a bushel of coal off a train easily. A bad one could easily get the pole driven through his body."

William's view of education's role in this is rich and textured. He noted, "My school could easily have destroyed me. It did not. Instead, it became my second home. It was the source of my sense of self-worth."

Bernard. "My generation, those of us over 65 years, was never confused about racism in the United States," said Bernard at the outset of his remarks. "We pursued full citizenship, accompanied by all its rights and responsibilities, as hard as we could. We knew what we had to do, and we had few illusions about how much help we would get. We loved America even when it had trouble loving us back."

The product of a strong family, whose father had a second-grade education and whose mother possessed a college degree, Bernard grew up in the steel-company town of Gary, Indiana.

One story tells it all: Bernard discovered that although his father was entitled to several medals for his service in the Army during World War I, he had never received them. "Seventy years after the armistice was signed, I finally obtained, from the Pentagon, the decorations and awards my father deserved. My mother and brothers and sisters never knew he'd earned them."

Small Groups

Large groups of people cannot process powerful information such as this. When the group is large, people may listen to presentations, but they won't talk about them. Increase people's comfort level around this difficult issue for discussion purposes by breaking down large groups into smaller ones. This rarely fails and almost always works. (See the tools for holding the conversation throughout this section.) In almost no small group will you encounter the dynamics that often develop in large groups: one or two individuals start to dominate the discussion so that the conversation turns into pro forma, sometimes angry, speeches and lectures.

These small sessions also provide an opportunity to use the dialogue and inquiry skills discussed in "Leading Your Schools," Part II.

Skilled Facilitators

Skilled and experienced facilitators are another key ingredient. They should include the broadest diversity possible: Latino scholars; African American activists; community leaders; and parents, teachers, and advocates for the disadvantaged are all good candidates. Working with a structured format helps. It should invite participants to explore their own understanding of issues related to race and class. In well-facilitated small-group discussions, we learned:

- Prejudice is not confined to any ethnic group but cuts across them all. Class is a common issue. Even people of color are divided along class lines.

- Board members and superintendents are frustrated by these issues; they want to change these dynamics; they have less power to do so than they thought.
- People in the small groups are often initially uncomfortable, afraid of saying the wrong thing. They get beyond that, but it is difficult.
- You can't get to a comfort level on these issues in one afternoon, and no amount of time is enough unless people are willing to struggle together.
- Adults are the problem, not children.

"The problem is changing," says one former superintendent, a Hispanic who was banned from hotels in the South under Jim Crow. "It used to be a black-white issue. Now we're talking about a more complex problem of diverse groups of white people and people of color competing with each other."

B. Kiva: A Tool for Talking

Luvern L. Cunningham

Think of the Kiva as a tool for talking, a technique for improving organizational learning and deepening social and political understanding. It has been used successfully for decades, in many contexts where difficult issues require intense reflection and analysis.

"Kiva" is a Native American term from the American Southwest. It defines a meeting place for the practice of tribal democracy. Its distinctive architectural features (circular, often around a fire pit) facilitate conversation, encourage all to speak, and designate levels of authority among tribal members. It incorporates several levels of seating and participation. The most influential tribal leaders occupy the seats closest to the fire. Leaders with less influence are seated in rows consistent with their power, behind the first row. All are encouraged to speak.

How to Make a Kiva Work for You

Modern American communities aren't tribes. Seating people by influence won't work. But you can define orders of seating based on roles, responsibilities, accountabilities—or anything that bonds people. Because Kivas are designed to clarify issues rather than confront opponents, they can be used to improve community understanding of even very controversial topics. For example, the objective of a Kiva might be to talk about the recent announcement that a local employer is leaving town, implementation of a new math curriculum, or racial tension in a local high school. Kiva participants could include students, parents, teachers, and administrators, all sharing their perspectives. At most normal school meetings, adults would dominate this discussion. Students would feel shut out. Even many parents would defer to teachers and administrators. In a Kiva setting, students and parents can both be explicitly invited into the conversation. In some cases, you might even want to mix and match the different groups; for example, do girls in the school experience racial tension differently from the boys? How do they handle it?

During the discussion, it is important to keep a detailed record of what is said (so that participants see that their point of view is being heard) either through newsprint or electronic feedback mechanisms or both. Then follow-up can be planned.

It Sounds Useful. What About the Nitty-Gritty of Organizing One?

Purpose. Clarity of purpose is essential. The Kiva concept will be novel to most participants. Particularly with difficult, complex, and emotion-laden problems, the purpose must be clearly stated. When race or class is on the table, a focus on "whose fault is this" will only encourage anger and acrimony. What the community needs to worry about is, "What's the situation and how can we improve it?"

Physical Arrangements. Attention to the arrangements of tables and chairs sounds trivial, but it is not. The basic configuration calls for chairs set in rows in either square or circular arrangements around a central open square (see Figure 5.1). The number of rows depends on the number of groups taking part. Usually, three or four groups (and hence rows) make up a Kiva. The members of the first group to respond to the facilitator's questions are seated in the front row. Seated directly behind group one are members of the other groups who will come to the front in a predetermined sequence.

Typical Kiva layout displaying moderator in center of square, surrounded by three different "circles" of participants. Observers can be seated on two opposite corners of the square, with note-takers at the two remaining corners.

Figure 5.1   Kiva Layout

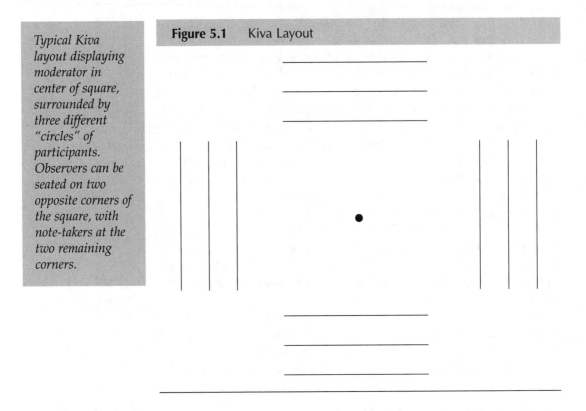

Read the description in Section 2C of the Kiva held in a jail. Do you think a similar process might be used in your district? Do you have staff who could be trained to facilitate? Should nondistrict facilitators be recruited to do this work?

Group and Kiva Size. If there is an ideal Kiva size, it is between 24 and 48 persons as primary participants. This means that the individual "ring" size around the open square ranges from 8 to 12. Participants are organized in rings, from inner to outer. The immediate audience is limited only by the size of the room.

Facilitation. A Kiva is managed by one or two trained facilitators who lead discussion, elicit observations and ideas, and maintain control of the dynamics while exhibiting flexibility. Facilitation is both an art and a science. Too much control is inhibiting; too little is unproductive. All comments must be honored and treated with respect. A bit of humor helps. Neutrality is essential; don't disparage anyone's contribution. And time limits must be observed.

Time. Kiva planners have to pay attention to time. The gravity of the problem and the number of participants (and their groupings) help determine time allocations. Fairness in time allocation is critical. If your Kiva about racial tension is divided into groups of Anglo, African American, and Latino parents and students, you must allocate time equally among the three groups. Facilitators will only create a disaster by providing significantly more time to one group than to the others.

Questions. Good questions from the facilitators are key. They must be clear and connect to the goals of the Kiva. Long, involved questions are often misleading and hard to follow, frequently introducing unnecessary discomfort. Some questions should be asked of each participant group to ensure under-standings of perspectives across groups. Questions can come from several sources, including the facilitators.

Physical Environment. Selecting the right place for the event contributes to effectiveness. Elbow room, good acoustics, comfortable seating and room temperature, microphones if necessary, and water all make a difference. Good lighting and easy access to restrooms help too.

Audiences. If there is an audience, and most often there is, members are seated behind the participants with care to ensure that audience members are able to see and hear. Should there be radio or television audiences, provision must be made for their technical needs.

Expert Observers. Two or three known and respected leaders, recognized for their ability to observe and comment, are invited to bear witness. Such commentary adds meaning, content, and value and it provides a basis to build on for succeeding meetings. Before the event ends, a facilitator invites commen-tary from the observers and expresses appreciation for their contributions.

The next section, on a Kiva held in a jail, gives you a sense of how the Kiva can be used.

C. The Kiva in Action

Luvern L. Cunningham

The scene is a tough jail in a major midwestern city, a "facility" for males aged 12 to 18 serving sentences of two years or more. Most are African American and some are guilty of appalling crimes, often drug related—armed robbery, rape, or murder. The jail is very old. Actually, it was once a school. On the former basketball court, people of all ages are seated on worn, squeaky folding chairs. The purpose: to begin to look at possible intergovernmental collaboration to improve the life chances of these young prisoners. An event unique in the jail is about to begin—a Kiva.

This Kiva is arranged to talk about the past, present, and future of 48 incarcerated young men. Three groups are seated in the Kiva's concentric rings, with observers behind them. The first group consists of 12 prisoners, all volunteers at this Kiva. The second is made up of prisoners' families—parents, grandparents, and guardians. The third row holds professionals from the jail, schools, and the city's juvenile justice system. Each ring has about 12 active participants. Each ring (row) comes to the front row in sequence. Security is tight. Observers represent city hall, district school administration, the state juvenile justice office, and some state and local politicians.

You will fail and feel uncomfortable many times. When a person begins this process and it fails the first time, you can't just say, "Well, I tried and it didn't work, so I'm out of here." If you'll continue trying, you'll see great strides forward. We have to insist that all children have the opportunity for a wonderful life.

Diana Lam,
Superintendent,
Providence, Rhode
Island

Two respected community members serve as facilitators: one a young African American male probation officer; the other an elderly African American woman. They enter the circle to begin the Kiva. They are skilled. Although they thought carefully in advance on the questions, their approach is flexible. While their demeanor is relaxed, the questions are penetrating. Some of the questions are addressed to all of the participants; others differ depending on the row.

The room is pin-drop quiet at the start. Answers from the prisoners are short, sometimes hostile. Some heads are down, avoiding the eyes of the facilitators. Those in the second group, the family representatives, are slow to respond, language halting at times, emotions on edge. Guilt, sorrow, anguish, and hopelessness are in the air. The participants in the professional row—candid, direct, and insightful—are given to speeches at times, but each member is sympathetic to the needs of the young men. Each group has 30 minutes. Then the observers comment. The observers are "all over the lot." Many are defensive, clearly protecting their part of the political and administrative infrastructure. Politicians, for the most part, talk in high-minded platitudes.

All the participants and observers talked about why the young men were in jail. They explored what life is like inside. They talked about their hopes for what would happen on release. Would the street take over? Would they go back to gangs? Would they be incarcerated again? Or was there some hope they would return to school or work? The programs of the professionals were described and critiqued, sometimes ridiculed.

From this Kiva, with its direct exposure and interaction among differing groups, new possibilities emerged. The schools, the probation department, and the juvenile justice authorities began exploring how to collaborate. Records began to move more quickly between agencies. Jail personnel began to attend professional development programs at the schools. School administrators and counselors visited the jail, where they saw firsthand what happens to school dropouts and how jail personnel work with angry, aggressive young males. Public officials acquired new insights into gang behavior and insisted that school officials and the mayor's staff meet together with male and female gang leaders.

What did the Kiva contribute? First, it offered an ordered environment for conversation. Second, it provided a neutral process to hear people out. Third, it guaranteed balanced participation from diverse groups in a compressed format. It hardly needs to be said that it encouraged communication among different groups, along with summarization and the opportunity to plan follow up.

Was it worth it? Perhaps not, if you define success as immediately solving every problem. But certainly so, by a more reasonable standard. That miasma of silence and hopelessness that pervaded the old gym at the outset? As the Kiva ended, it had been replaced with chatter and a sense of cautious optimism for the future.

D. Sabotaging the Conversation

Howard Fuller
James Harvey

Just as skillful preparation can make it possible to hold the conversation, sloppy or careless preparation can sabotage it. We don't always get it right. The reality is that, on occasion, the discussion of race and class is frustrating and incomplete. You can learn from the mistakes we made.

Three things consistently threatened to sabotage the conversation:

- Poor preparation
- Large groups, particularly those in which participants could not maintain eye contact with everyone
- Careless and insensitive use of language

Race and class are areas where you can't succeed by making it up as you go along.

Poor Preparation

Preparation may be the single most important factor in the success of any meeting about race and class. This cannot be overemphasized when convening a group around volatile matters that customarily are ignored in our society.

At various points in our planning, we turned to external experts when we felt we had reached roadblocks. In one instance, this was less than satisfactory for the group because of poor planning. The Forum planning group had outlined general expectations for a three-day meeting, but we turned over the detailed planning to someone who had been quite successful with our group previously. Unforeseen events in this individual's schedule resulted in lack of planning for the meeting and, consequently, in a meeting that was awkward and counterproductive. You must ensure that preparation receives your full attention when you embark on discussions of race and class in your district.

Large Groups

Don't create a situation in which you find large groups assembled for long periods over several days. You're inviting discomfort and disaster, particularly if you're unclear about the agenda. While we're at it, make sure that large-group circles, established so that everyone can see everyone else, are properly shaped. At one of our meetings, despite efforts to form a circle, some participants found themselves looking at the backs of the heads of several of their neighbors.

This experience reinforces an earlier learning experience. Small-group discussions to lay out the dimensions of the effort go well, but it is hard to maintain a sense of unity and purpose in the group as it expands. Some members dominate the discussion, sometimes expressing anger, while others withdraw. The lessons here are straightforward: understand that the problem will not be "solved" in one or two meetings. The conversation has to be relaunched every time it is brought up. Large groups should be avoided until the people involved have developed considerable experience holding the conversation in smaller and more intimate environments.

Careless and Insensitive Language

Language matters. Use of inappropriate terms can wreck the entire effort. Even people with the best of intentions can be struck by foot-in-the-mouth disease. When that happens, the best way to proceed is bring it up, challenge stereotypes, and move on.

An especially vivid example of this occurred at a meeting at the end of a lengthy day. The day began early and finished late. It ended, disastrously, with dinner and a major presentation followed by three respondents. The final respondent, a Native American woman, reported that, as an educator, she had always sought the "schools nobody else wants," schools in which student problems were the most difficult. "Most of my illegal students," she lamented, "were 'wetbacks' desperate for an education in an American school."

The use of this racially loaded term (not once, but several times) so offended several people that, the following morning, the group agreed to set aside the meeting agenda and discuss the incident. Three views emerged. First was the thought that the term is as offensive to Latinos as the worst racial epithet is to African Americans. Second was the view that, although the term is offensive, the word used to disparage African Americans is immeasurably more corrosive. Third, several people ascribed the incident to a slip of the tongue, brought on by a long day and the lateness of the hour. All agreed that holding this difficult conversation was essential to group learning.

Again, the lessons here were instructive. Don't overtire people when dealing with a difficult topic like this. Don't use language carelessly. When it happens, the group should not tolerate it. After raising the issue, accept an apology and move on.

E. Tools: Microlab, Peeling the Onion, and Active Listening

James Harvey

You will find yourself struggling with how to hold these conversations, sometimes successfully, sometimes less so. Here are some of the tools that worked for us:

Small-Group Discussions. The smaller, the better.

Skilled Facilitators. Sometimes involving a facilitator with a vested interest in the issue, but with no vested interest in the organization sponsoring the discussion, works well.

Randall Lindsey, Kikanza Robins, and Ray Terrell provide a wealth of individual and group activities to assist you in this difficult work. See their book, Cultural Proficiency: A Manual for School Leaders *(Thousand Oaks, CA: Corwin Press, 2003).*

Stand Up and Cross the Line. Launch meetings by inviting participants who are already seated to "stand up and cross" whatever line seems to divide the room. (Progress from easy through challenging questions. If you were born in August, cross the line. If you have children, cross the line. If you have ever been robbed, cross the line. If you have had a family member jailed, cross the line.) You'll be amazed at how fast racial and ethnic differences disappear as people start answering these questions.

The "Microlab." This is a structured, timed conversation (see "Microlab Guidelines and Sample Questions" by Emily White later in this section). It involves only four people who are not observed. Divide all participants *randomly* into groups of four who are required to sit closely together, facing each other. Friends and relatives should not be together. Using lots of "I" words, individuals are encouraged to take a minute each on each of the following questions (which are presented one at a time as each question is answered):

- How would you describe your background?
- What are your strengths and weaknesses?
- What is something you never want said again about the particular group you identify with?
- As a leader, what's your strength in dealing with diversity?

"Peeling the Onion." This is a protocol involving 4 to 12 people to develop an in-depth understanding of an issue, situation, or opportunity. It uses active listening to honor complexity and to avoid premature advice and solution finding (see "Tool: Peeling the Onion Protocol" by Emily White later in this section).

> *I have not failed. I've just found 10,000 ways that won't work.*
>
> Thomas A. Edison

You need to remember that sometimes these efforts will fail. But failure presents an opportunity to try again. Sometimes disappointment may develop because expectations about what is possible in the short run are poorly stated. As the "Stages of Collaboration" outlined in Table 5.1 emphasize, different goals require different strategies and diverse leadership approaches. It is likely that a purpose such as encouraging more congenial relationships may be easier to attain than equally worthwhile, but more challenging, goals such as working jointly together. At all stages, active listening from everyone is encouraged.

Tool: Stages of Collaboration

Table 5.1   Stages of Collaboration

Stage	Time Together/Meetings Look Like . . .	Leadership Looks Like . . .
Building Congeniality	• Anecdotes shared • Coaching/mentoring focus on helpful suggestions • Working to lessen competition and isolation • Appreciation and gratitude often expressed	• Meetings informative, free-flowing • Learning many things/not necessarily connected • Analytical/reactive • Centralized • Maintains tradition
Helping and Assisting	• Coaching and mentoring are top-down, follow-through is inconsistent • Feedback becomes more descriptive, less judgmental • Focus is less on complaints, more on conviction	• Problem-specific help given when requested • Encourages ongoing good-will and regard • Focus is on meeting needs of individuals • Beginning to look at needs of community as a whole
Sharing: Validating and Valuing Existing Practice	• Existing ideas are pooled • Mutual reinforcement of habits that are not always questioned deeply • Cooperation is stressed • Productive use of conflict begins	• Agendas are structured to allow time for sharing of practice, not just managing business • Language and habits of discourse are shaped • Critical thinking and appreciative listening are taught
Working Jointly: Building a Community of Leaders and Learners	• Critiquing of work, giving and getting feedback • Sharing of responsibility • Peer coaching/openness to critique become norms • Time together enhances understanding and imagination • Go from individual to collective practice • Problems seen as symptoms for community concern, not just individual intervention • Both veteran and new voices welcome	• Meetings transformative • Use of structures and protocols is a norm • Problem prevention, being proactive are norms • Openness and trust developed within and among groups • Norms are set with group • Teachers learn reflection • Obligation to school as community is taught • Assumptions are always questioned

SOURCE: Adapted by Emily White from Michael Fullan and Andy Hargreaves, *What's Worth Fighting for in Your School?* (New York: Teachers College Press, 1996).

Tool: Microlab Guidelines and Sample Questions

This was an exercise led by Emily White at one of the Forum meetings. It was designed to be taken back to superintendents' districts.

"Microlab" is a term for a small-group exercise that addresses a specific sequence of questions and promotes active listening. It uses a timed process. The microlab is useful for team building, "democratizing" participation, and strengthening diversity work because it is about equalizing communication and withholding judgment. It affirms people's ideas and helps build community.

Aim: To help participants learn more about themselves and others and to deepen the quality of collegial sharing.

Size: It works best with same-size groups of three to four people.

Time: Microlab takes 15 to 45 minutes; less time for groups of three addressing two to three questions, more time for groups of four addressing three to four questions. Allow time for the whole group to debrief at the end.

The time limit in this exercise provides safety. Crisp time boundaries help people take calculated risks and highlight aspects of listening. Sample questions might be: Describe your childhood. Can you remember something that hurt you emotionally as a child? What names have you been called that you never want to be called again?

Directions From the Leader

"I'll be directing what we're going to be sharing. It's not an open discussion. It's about listening and sharing nonjudgmentally. I will pose one question at a time. Each person gets approximately one minute to answer it in turn. The challenge is: no one is to talk or ask questions when it's someone else's turn [active listening practice]. I will time the activity and tell the groups when they should be halfway around their circle and when time is up, to go on to the next question. So, this is an opportunity for some openness and honesty, respecting confidentiality. When someone says something in your group, it is not to be repeated by anybody else. Can we all agree on that?"

Guideline for Participants

- Speak from your own experience. Say "I" when speaking about yourself.

- Speak from your own comfort level: not too risky, not too "blah."
- Respect shared confidences.
- Silence is OK. The person whose turn it is may need to think before starting.
- There is always the right to pass and go later.
- If someone doesn't get a full turn in one round, they should be the one to start in the next.

Tool: Peeling the Onion Protocol

This was an exercise led by Emily White at one of the Forum meetings. You will find this helpful as you try to probe a particular issue.

Goal: To develop an in-depth understanding of an issue, situation, or opportunity. The exercise uses active listening (see Table 5.2) to honor complexity and to avoid premature advice and solution finding.

Time: 25 to 40 minutes per group, set in advance.

Size: Groups of 4 to 12 people, with a facilitator.

Steps		
1.	Presenter describes an issue, opportunity, or incident	3–4 minutes
2.	Clarifying questions from group (Brief answers if beneficial)	3–4 minutes
3.	Go round 1. Presenter is silent, taking notes. Group members say: "A question or implication this raises for me is . . ." OR "A deeper issue I'd want to know more about is . . ."	7 minutes
4.	Check in (cross talk)—optional	2 minutes
5.	Go round 2. Presenter is silent. Group members ask: "What if . . . ?"	7 minutes
6.	Open conversation (Identify issues that have not been raised or probe a particular point that surfaced.)	5 minutes
7.	Debrief process	5 minutes

Tool: Active Listening Techniques

Table 5.2   Statements That Help the Other Person Talk

Statement	Purpose	To Do This	Examples
Encouraging	1. Convey interest	Don't agree or disagree	1. "Can you tell me . . . ?"
	2. Encourage other person	Use neutral words Use varying voice intonations	2. "What happened?"
Clarifying	1. To help you clarify what is said	Ask questions	1. "When did this happen?"
	2. To get more information	Restate wrong interpretation to force speaker to explain further	2. "You stated . . ."
Restating	1. To show you are listening and understanding what is being said	Restate basic ideas and facts	1. "So you would like your parents to trust you more, is that right?"
	2. To check your meaning and interpretation		
Reflecting	1. To show that you understand how the person feels	Reflect the speaker's basic feelings	1. "You seem very upset."
	2. To help the person evaluate his or her own feelings after hearing them expressed by someone else	Restate wrong interpretation to force speaker to explain further	2. "What does this mean to you?"
Summarizing	1. Review progress	Restate major ideas expressed	1. "These seem to be the key ideas you've expressed."
	2. Pull together important ideas and facts	Including feelings	
	3. Establish a basis for further discussion		
Validating	1. To acknowledge the worthiness of other people	Acknowledge the value of their issues and feelings	1. "I appreciate your willingness to resolve this matter."
		Show appreciation for their efforts and actions	

SOURCE: Adapted by Emily White from *Active Listening Techniques* (San Francisco: The Community Board Program, 1987).

3. What's Going On Inside Schools

The discussion about public education in the United States often proceeds like an argument. Critics contend that many people inside schools don't believe in children. In this view, teachers and administrators have little sympathy for the challenges and travails students will face when they graduate. The result? Educators have low expectations that minority students will succeed in class. School defenders, on the other hand, often claim that their critics have no real interest in learning. The critics' real motivation, in this view, lies in the destruction and privatization of public education. While each side is busy demonizing and caricaturing the other, neither has a monopoly on truth or virtue.

There's a lot going on inside schools. Some of it's good; some of it's appalling. You need to honestly assess what's happening in the schools for which you're responsible. This section can help you do that.

A. The Achievement Gap: Where Do We Find Hope?

James Harvey

All of us understand that racial and ethnic achievement gaps in American classrooms have deep roots reaching out far beyond the schoolhouse walls. Not content with using that as an excuse, however, several ambitious reform groups have worked hard to define schools and districts in which school performance is improving and the achievement gap is closing. Although none can point to a district that has closed the achievement gap, most of these efforts offer important clues about how to proceed. The best data and lessons can be found in analyses completed by the Council of Great City Schools, Manpower Demonstration Research Corporation, and The Education Trust.

Richard Rothstein draws on extensive research to analyze the causes of the achievement gap. See Class and Schools: Using Social, Economic, and Educational Reform to Close the Black-White Achievement Gap *(New York: Economic Policy Institute, Teachers College, Columbia University, 2004).*

Beating the Odds

The nature of the challenge is well defined by the title of a series of reports in recent years from the Council of Great City Schools (CGCS), "Beating the Odds." The Council never declares victory and always offers its conclusions

Beating the Odds III:
A City-by-City Analysis
of Student Performance
and Achievement Gaps
on State Assessments
*(March 2003) can be
found on the Web site of
the Council of Great City
Schools at* www.cgcs.
org/reports/beat_
the_oddsIII.html.

with great caution, but in general it finds that its member school districts (all large urban areas) are making gains in math scores on state assessments.

This analysis provides accountability data from 59 big-city school districts in 36 states, city by city, year by year, and grade by grade in both mathematics and reading. It concludes that

- Mathematics achievement is improving in urban schools and reading achievement is beginning to improve.
- Gaps in both math and reading achievement may be narrowing.
- More urban districts showed improvements in math and reading in 2002 than in 2000.
- Urban-school performance in both math and reading remains below national averages.

The Council's report is impressive for the care with which it reports its findings and the authors' refusal to go beyond their data.

Case Studies

The MDRC Study,
Foundations for
Success: Case Studies
of How Urban School
Systems Improve
Student Achievement
*(2002) can be located at
the MDRC Web site at*
www.mdrc.org
/publications/47
/execsum.html.

In an effort to go beyond data analysis, CGCS worked with a nationally known research organization, the Manpower Development Research Center (MDRC), to explore several promising urban districts more closely. The hope was that a case-study approach would produce more robust findings.

The resulting report was quite encouraging. After examining promising efforts in Charlotte-Mecklenburg (North Carolina), Houston Independent Schools (Texas), Sacramento City Unified (California), and the "Chancellor's district" in New York City, MDRC researchers concluded that districts willing to take a comprehensive, systemwide approach to reform "may be more effective" than districts that undertake reform solely on a school-by-school basis. The research also found several overarching similarities in districts improving student achievement. Among these factors were the following:

- Stable leadership that focused relentlessly on improving achievement
- Accountability systems that included measurable district-wide and school goals, along with performance timetables
- Districtwide instructional coherence and sometimes prescriptive curriculum, along with districtwide professional development

- Systems for monitoring reform implementation (see Part VI, Section 3) and regular testing and detailed data assessment
- Initiation of reforms in elementary grades, working up through middle and secondary schools
- Focus on the district's lowest-performing schools and groups

Since the report was released, questions have been raised about the accuracy of the data reported for the Houston Independent Schools (particularly the dropout data), but on balance these factors are widely agreed to be essential elements in a comprehensive reform effort.

Dispelling the Myth

A series of reports from The Education Trust is by far the most upbeat assessment of school performance. The Trust analysis sets out to answer the question first posed by educational researcher Ron Edmonds 20 years ago ("How many effective schools would you have to see to be persuaded of the educability of poor children?"). It identifies several thousand "high-flying" schools that score in the top one-third of the schools in their states, despite high rates of poverty and minority enrollment.

The report identifies 1,320 schools that enroll large proportions of students who are both minority and poor; 3,592 schools that enroll large proportions of low-income students; and 2,305 schools that enroll large proportions of minority students. All of them are high performing by the Trust's definition. Two important caveats need to be made: the performance standard is "at least one year of high performance on one or more state assessments." So it is possible that a year's data on one test would justify a place on this list. Also, although these schools are "high-flying," no claim is made that they have closed the achievement gap. They rank, on at least one measure, in the top one-third of the schools in their state. This report also includes a list of promising reform variables, several of them parallel to the findings of the Council of Great City Schools and MDRC:

The 2002 version of Dispelling the Myth can be located at the Web site of The Education Trust, www2.edtrust.org.

- Standards as a framework for assessing curriculum and instruction, student work, and teaching
- More instructional time for reading and mathematics
- Substantial investments in professional development
- Comprehensive systems for monitoring student performance

- Parental support of efforts to help students meet standards
- State and local accountability systems with real consequences for adults in the school
- Use of assessments to help guide instruction and use of resources

In short, what each of these three sources of information demonstrates is that the standards-based reform movement has achieved several things. It has begun to generate the data required to understand the dimensions of the achievement gap. It is beginning to develop a database of successful practices. And all of us, in and out of schools, are beginning to understand that, although we may be halfway home, we still have a long way to go.

B. Can We Close the Gap?

Howard Fuller
James Harvey

> *Interviews and surveys with superintendents from large districts reveal significant differences of opinion about whether or not current efforts can close the achievement gap in the next five years, according to a 2003 report for the Wallace Foundation.*

Many large school districts around the nation are making progress in improving the achievement of minority students, but none has been able to close the achievement gap. When superintendents talk about student learning, they often refer to an "achievement gap" between middle-class children and those from a lower socioeconomic status (who often are members of minority groups as well). For urban superintendents, one of the most important tasks in assisting student learning is to concentrate on those who are most at risk educationally to try to close this gap. During the interviews conducted as part of this study, all superintendents—majority and minority, men and women—universally agreed on the nature and severity of the challenge. Nobody said, in effect, this is not a problem or the problem is overstated. Here are typical comments:

No question about it. There are huge problems in terms of minority dropout rates and the achievement gap.

The achievement gap is a very big problem. In my former district, Hispanics and African Americans range from the bottom quartile to the lower end of the third quartile; low-income Caucasians range from the middle of the second quartile to the middle of third; and middle-class whites range from the middle of the top quartile to the 90th percentile.

The survey results, as well, show that most superintendents are deeply troubled by the achievement gap. Nearly nine out of ten (89%) "agree" or "strongly agree" with the statement "The racial achievement gap between students is a critical and chronic challenge." Across the board, therefore, widespread agreement exists that the achievement gap is perhaps the compelling educational issue of our time.

See The Black-White Test Score Gap, *edited by Christopher Jencks and Meredith Phillips (Washington, DC: Brookings Institution, 1998), for a thorough and scholarly examination of the achievement gap in the United States.*

Can We Close the Gap?

With regard to whether current efforts to eliminate the gap are adequate, the study received different answers from survey respondents, who were asked to put their answers on paper, and from interviewees, who were interviewed personally and in depth.

Of the superintendents surveyed who see the achievement gap as a critical and chronic challenge, a majority (67%) believe that the programs the district has in place are capable of closing the gap within five years. In contrast, interviewed superintendents felt that what they were currently able to do was not enough.

Race and District Complexity as Factors in Superintendents' Reponses

Both the race of the superintendent and the complexity of the district affect the response to the survey question about the possibility of closing the gap. Figure 5.2 demonstrates these contrasts between superintendents from highly complex districts (defined as districts in bigger cities, with larger enrollments, more schools, and both more minority students and more students living in poverty).

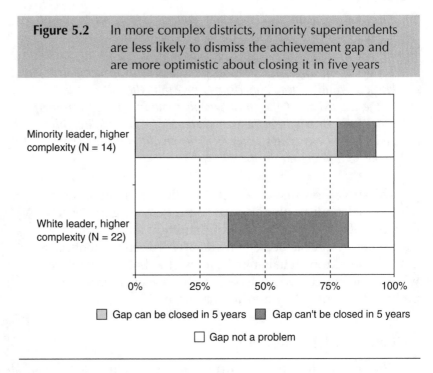

Figure 5.2   In more complex districts, minority superintendents are less likely to dismiss the achievement gap and are more optimistic about closing it in five years

The complete report from which this research is abstracted is entitled An Impossible Job? The View From the Urban Superintendent's Chair, *a report to the Wallace Foundation from the Center on Reinventing Public Education at the University of Washington. It can be found at* www.crpe.org /pubs/pdf/Impossible Job_reportweb.pdf.

Some survey superintendents, both majority and minority, deny the existence of an achievement gap. Nearly one in eight white superintendents (13%) reported that the gap is not a problem. Only one in 16 minority superintendents (6%) shared that view.

Interestingly, for both white and minority superintendents, those in highly complex districts are more likely to report that the gap is not a problem than are those in less-complex districts. Nearly twice as many white superintendents in highly complex districts agreed the gap is not a problem, compared with those in less-complex districts: 18% compared with 10%. Although 7% of minority leaders of highly complex districts reported the gap is not a problem, no minority superintendent in a less-complex district did so.

It is difficult to interpret these results. Some superintendents may have felt uncomfortable making racial achievement comparisons. Others may have believed that an achievement gap is not a problem "in my district." It is also conceivable that racial minorities are so highly concentrated in some highly complex districts that the achievement gap as traditionally understood is meaningless because few white students are enrolled.

Beyond that, we find a paradox. Although, in general, minority superintendents are much less likely than white superintendents to dismiss the existence of an achievement gap, they are also much more likely to believe the gap can be closed in the next five years.

Once again, it is difficult to interpret these findings. Perceptions, attitudes, and value systems may lie at the root of these differences. It is possible that minority superintendents view the achievement gap as their primary personal and professional challenge and believe they have the will and the tools to meet it. Meanwhile, white superintendents in the most highly complex districts may view financial issues or pressures of state accountability systems as the major issues, while finding little reason to be optimistic that the gap can be closed in five years.

Despite the misgivings of a fairly sizable group of surveyed superintendents, the reality is that most superintendents, whether minority or white, agree that they will have the problem of the achievement gap under control in half a decade.

The confidence of most superintendents in the survey stands in stark contrast to the opinions of interviewed superintendents. The superintendents who were interviewed reported that they were unable to do the minimal things necessary to make a start in closing the gap. They were up-front about the frustration they experience due to their inability to put the best teachers where they are most needed. They have trouble focusing resources on schools, classrooms, and children needing the most help. Even these elementary, small, first efforts—so clearly essential to any effort to close the gap—are beyond their authority.

The following are typical of the comments received during the interviews:

> *To close the achievement gap, you need to be able to change how every dollar is spent. This means reallocating funds away from existing programs and maybe even schools in middle-class neighborhoods.*

> *Middle-class parents are often the biggest challenge. They want their children's schools unchanged. It matters a lot to them that their schools have lots of languages and lots of science options; they also know that major investments in schools serving the disadvantaged would threaten what they now enjoy.*

An excellent book recommended for discussions of race and class is Beverly Daniel Tatum's Why Are All the Black Kids Sitting Together in the Cafeteria? *(New York: Basic Books, 1999).*

The upshot, according to the interviews, is that superintendents find themselves talking a good game of reform, but many believe that what they are doing will not be enough.

C. Tool: Thinking About Learners at the Fringes

Luvern L. Cunningham

To see how one community studied mobility, look at Columbus Public Schools Student Mobility Research Project Report *(Columbus, OH: Community Research Partners, John Glenn Institute, Ohio State University, 2003).*

The accountability movement marching through American schools is designed to salvage forgotten children and youth. But it might leave some strewn by the wayside. It's not clear that policymakers have thought through carefully what accountability really means for students in foster care, youth in jail, or children who are homeless, are recent immigrants, or do not speak English. Millions of children with special needs run the risk of being overlooked in a general effort to improve achievement. For example, recent research documents that students who move twice in an academic year have far lower grades and perform much more poorly on standardized tests. Data disaggregation, useful as it is, may not go far enough to sort out all these populations and their experience as learners.

As superintendent, you have to be the voice for these learners at the margins. Use the following list of questions to get the discussion started in your community:

- What do you know about kids in your district who are immigrants, homeless, under foster care, under the jurisdiction of other authorities, and are moving between schools in your system?
- How many of each of them are there?
- Have you visited students, for example, in jail? What about those under the jurisdiction of other community authorities?
- What provisions are there for prompt transfer of student records, and other information, to other schools, school districts, or jurisdictions?
- Do you have functioning partnerships with the police, courts, the juvenile justice system, children's services, hospitals and clinics, and other jurisdictions serving your students?
- Would the category of "African American boys" be recognized in your district as meriting special attention?
- Are exchanges of professional development programs taking place between and among your schools and the other community institutions serving learners at the margins?
- Are there up-to-date policies and practices within your district, and among other jurisdictions, covering privacy and confidentiality?

- Does the performance of learners in these categories appear in the district's accountability system?
- Are special efforts in place to communicate with parents of immigrant children, foster parents, and parents of those under incarceration or under other jurisdictions?

4. . . . And What's Going On Outside Them

A generation or two ago, it wasn't unusual for policymakers and the public to believe that school achievement problems in low-income neighborhoods needed to be approached in a pincerlike campaign. One pincer would operate inside the schools, which were thought to be pretty good and simply needed to be improved and beefed up. The other would operate outside the schools and would work to eliminate the disadvantages in health care, housing, jobs, and community infrastructure in many neighborhoods. Reforms of recent years have swept both pincers away and replaced them with an accountability-based demand that schools improve student performance and close the achievement gap.

This section attempts to restore some of the balance of that earlier conversation.

A. Schools Can't Do It Alone

Neal Schmidt

Concerns about student learning and the achievement gap are well founded, but these problems cannot be addressed in schools alone. Here's the deal we must strike with public officials: we need help from you, our public officials, in two vital areas that support our work. The first is in early childhood education; the second in out-of-school opportunities to advance learning. In a sense, we have to meld the curriculum of the home, the school, and the community.

Early Learning. The commonsense instinct to worry about experience early in life has received a powerful impetus in recent decades from medical science. We now know much more about how the human brain develops than we did even 20 years ago. But we have yet to fashion policy to take advantage of this exciting new knowledge. Research on early development reveals the enormous plasticity of the human brain in the first years of life.

This is the period when brain tissue grows, the cerebral cortex is "wired," cognition develops, and speech and the capacity to manipulate language grow and mature.

Think about it. The research clearly demonstrates that every single child, no matter where they are born, possesses the capacity to speak any of some 200 languages. But our brains are "wired" by age seven to speak the language we hear around us. That's the reason the Japanese have trouble saying "Chevrolet" and we have trouble speaking Chinese or mastering a French accent at the age of 14. We've missed not just the "teachable moment" for second-language acquisition but the "teachable years." Many of the major tools children employ in learning, in short, are well along in their development before they step through the school door.

In addition, many children enter school already far in advance of their classmates. Research indicates, for example, that a child of college-educated parents begins kindergarten with a working vocabulary of perhaps 20,000 words, compared with just 5,000 for the children of high-school dropouts.

The old adage has it that "an ounce of prevention is worth a pound of cure." If schools are to succeed, they need to start worrying about early childhood learning and development. At a minimum, they should be advocates for programs like Head Start that serve infants, toddlers, and preschoolers. More than that, they should be actively aligning their own kindergarten activities with local preschool efforts so that schools are "ready" when the children arrive. The potential benefit is easy to define. Most children start life equally equipped to learn and grow. Preventing an achievement gap from developing is likely to be easier than fixing it after the fact.

The Other 93%. In the 1980s, researcher Joan Bergstrom at Wheelock College in Boston reported a finding that people had trouble accepting. From birth through age 18, Bergstrom said, nearly 80% of a student's waking time is spent outside school. Schools were never intended to do it all, and they can't do it all by themselves, she concluded. By 1991, Secretary of Education Lamar Alexander pointed to the fact that a child spends 93% of his or her time from birth through age 18 outside of school, and this time is an important asset in the school-reform agenda. He and former President Bush advocated a community-reinforcement element to school reform as part of their "America 2000" strategy. Like the national goal of school readiness, America 2000 has disappeared from the public radar screen. You cannot afford to let it disappear from yours.

See also Part VII of this fieldbook for examples of districts that entered collaboration activities around early childhood education.

In a sense, what will be required here is a commitment to building a bridge between the curriculum of the school and the curriculum of the home and neighborhood. Finding ways to help school personnel access the richness of students' experience out-side school . . . providing incentives to encourage staff to live in the community . . . empowering parents to become more knowl-edgeable about the system . . . and developing reciprocal relation-ships so that community centers, voluntary organizations, libraries, and churches become part of the community's educa-tional fabric—all of these activities are important. They can help make sure no child is left behind outside of school. The goal is no small order. It should be to weave together the neighborhood's fabric so that good schools are able to work with caring families in strong and healthy communities.

B. An Asset-Based Approach

James Harvey

Here's an exercise for you. At your next staff meeting, ask your teachers and administrators to think through, in private, what and who accounted for their success. After they've had a few minutes to think about that, ask for a show of hands. How many people thought of a parent? How many thought of another adult who acted as a mentor and sounding board? How many thought of a teacher? How many thought of a particular school? You will almost certainly capture everyone in the room with those four categories, but, just to be sure, ask if anyone came up with other possibilities.

Most public discussions about young people focus on what's wrong with them. The subtext of much of what we hear about race and class is that things would be better if only these young people were white and middle class. Yet, according to research developed by the Search Institute in Minnesota, a much more productive approach would be to concentrate on the assets of young people, not their deficits.

This research defines as important some 40 family and community assets related to the development of children, teenagers, and young adults. Some constellation of these assets, not all of them, is important. Most young people can draw on about 20 of them as they grow up, which turns out to be a kind of critical mass for adult success. Kids with fewer then 10 of these assets in their lives are likely to wind up in trouble; those with 30 or more normally hit the ground running when they reach adulthood.

Lisa Delpit's book Other People's Children: Cultural Conflict in the Classroom *(New York: The New Press, 1995) is a treasure trove for teachers, especially those teaching in culturally diverse classrooms; it is equally important for superintendents and other school administrators. It is a marvelous book, filled with the wisdom of practice.*

There's something terribly wrong with the way we talk about young people in our society, argues Clay Roberts from the Search Institute. On one level, we devote pages of newsprint and hours of media time to catastrophes such as the shootings at Columbine High School, as though the teenagers who wreaked havoc on their school were typical. But this ignores the fact that a tiny fraction of young people are capable of terrible things and that 95% of youth do wonderful things with their time.

On another level, according to Roberts, professionals talk about young people in ways that have nothing to do with the reality of teenage lives. "As a junior high school history teacher, I used to listen to the kids outside the school on Friday as they waited for a ride home," he says. "The conversation was always the same: What are you doing this weekend? Any good parties? Who got drunk last weekend? Who might get wasted tonight? Who's getting some? And, who isn't?"

These are the things typical middle-class teenagers think about, argues Roberts. Yet we behave as though kids need programs. "They don't need programs, what they need are people." Roberts calls for a new emphasis on "asset building."

These 40 assets are based on research involving almost 100,000 sixth through twelfth graders in 213 towns and cities across the United States. (See Sections 4C and 4D for details.) Externally, the assets involve

- Support from family and neighborhood
- A sense of empowerment
- Clear boundaries and expectations
- Constructive use of free time

The internal assets involve

- Commitment to learning
- Positive values
- Social competencies
- Positive sense of self

Schools are important in young people's development, but they are not the only thing, according to Roberts. A lot of the assets come from the home and the community, not the school. "The best predictor of a child's success is whether that child came from a healthy, strong, supportive family," asserts Roberts. "The second best predictor is bonding with school." However, it is clear that combinations of assets are much more important than any single asset. The more assets young people have, the better their chances of avoiding destructive behaviors later, says Roberts (see Table 5.3).

Table 5.3   The Power of Assets

Behaviors	Youth With 0–10 Assets	Youth With 11–20 Assets	Youth With 21–30 Assets	Youth With 31–40 Assets
Negative				
Problem Alcohol Use	53%	30%	11%	3%
Illicit Drug Use	42%	19%	6%	1%
Sexual Activity	33%	21%	10%	3%
Violence	61%	35%	16%	6%
Positive				
Succeed in School	7%	19%	35%	53%
Value Diversity	34%	53%	69%	87%
Maintain Good Health	25%	46%	69%	88%
Delay Gratification	27%	42%	56%	72%

The data on 100,000 middle- and high-school students indicate that youth with the most assets are far less likely to engage in high-risk behavior involving alcohol, drugs, violence, and sexual activity than those with fewer assets. Fully 53% of students with 10 or fewer assets experience problems with alcohol abuse, for example. By contrast, only 3% of those with 31 or more assets to draw on encounter the same problem. The patterns involving illicit drug usage, sexual activity, and violence are very similar.

Conversely, the more assets young people can draw on, the more positive their attitudes and behaviors. More than 50% of young people with 31 or more assets succeed in school, compared with just 7% of those with 10 or fewer. Similar positive patterns prevail on such attitudes and behaviors as valuing diversity, maintaining good health, and delaying gratification.

Roberts offers a self-evident truth when he says, "Those of us who came from difficult circumstances know that some of the most important people in our young lives had a vision for us that we didn't have for ourselves. They believed in us when we couldn't believe in our own future."

One of the challenges you will face in dealing with race and class is how to create situations in which more and more assets can be provided to young people who need them.

Assumptions about poverty in this country have developed over the past half century, influenced by the 1962 Michael Harrington book, The Other America, and the subsequent War on Poverty social policy. Now comes a refreshing revisit to matters of poverty and their presence in classrooms and schools. Superintendents who know this volume like it and, what's more, use it with teachers and their communities. Pick it up. Ruby K. Payne, A Framework for Understanding Poverty (Highlands, TX: RFT Publishing Company, 1998).

C. 20 External Developmental Assets

Support

- *Family Support.* Family life provides high levels of love and support.
- *Positive Family Communication.* Young person and parent(s) communicate.
- *Other Adult Relationships.* Young person receives support from three or more nonparent adults.
- *Caring Neighborhood.* Young person experiences caring neighbors.
- *Caring School Climate.* School provides caring, encouraging environment.
- *Parent Involvement in Schooling.* Parent(s) actively involved in helping young person succeed.

Empowerment

- *Community Values Youth.* Young people perceive that adults value youth.
- *Youth as Resources.* Young people are given useful roles in the community.
- *Service to Others.* Young people serve in the community one hour or more a week.
- *Safety.* Young person feels safe at home, at school, and in the neighborhood.

Boundaries and Expectations

- *Family Boundaries.* Family has clear rules and consequences and monitors young person's whereabouts.
- *School Boundaries.* School provides clear rules and consequences.
- *Neighborhood Boundaries.* Neighbors take responsibility for monitoring young people's behavior.
- *Adult Role Models.* Parent(s) and other adults model positive, responsible behavior.
- *Positive Peer Influence.* Young person's best friends model responsible behavior.
- *High Expectations.* Both parent(s) and teachers encourage the young person to do well.

Constructive Use of Time

- *Creative Activities.* Young person spends three or more hours per week in lessons or practice in music, theater, or other arts.
- *Youth Programs.* Young person spends three or more hours per week in sports, clubs, or organizations at school or in the community.
- *Religious Community.* Young person spends one or more hours per week in activities in a religious institution.
- *Time at Home.* Young person is out with friends "with nothing special to do" two or fewer nights per week.

SOURCE: *Research on the 40 Developmental Assets,* The Search Institute, Minneapolis, MN. The report can be found at *www.search-institute.org*

D. 20 Internal Developmental Assets

Commitment to Learning

- *Achievement Motivation.* Young person is motivated to do well in school.
- *School Engagement.* Young person is actively engaged in learning.
- *Homework.* Young person reports doing at least one hour of homework every school day.
- *Bonding to School.* Young person cares about his or her school.
- *Reading for Pleasure.* Young person reads for pleasure three or more hours per week.

Positive Values

- *Caring.* Young person places high value on helping other people.
- *Equality and Social Justice.* Young person places high value on promoting equality and reducing hunger and poverty.
- *Integrity.* Young person acts on convictions and stands up for her or his beliefs.

- *Honesty.* Young person "tells the truth even when it is not easy."
- *Responsibility.* Young person accepts and takes personal responsibility.
- *Restraint.* Young person believes it is important not to be sexually active or to use alcohol or other drugs.

Social Competencies

- *Planning and Decision Making.* Young person knows how to plan ahead and make choices.
- *Interpersonal Competence.* Young person has empathy, sensitivity, and friendship skills.
- *Cultural Competence.* Young person has knowledge of and comfort with people of different cultural/racial/ethnic backgrounds.
- *Resistance Skills.* Young person can resist negative peer pressure and dangerous situations.
- *Peaceful Conflict Resolution.* Young person seeks to resolve conflict nonviolently.

Positive Identity

- *Person Power.* Young person feels he or she has control over "things that happen to me."
- *Self-Esteem.* Young person reports having high self-esteem.
- *Sense of Purpose.* Young person reports that "my life has a purpose."
- *Positive View of Personal Future.* Young person is optimistic about her or his personal future.

SOURCE: *Research on the 40 Developmental Assets,* The Search Institute, Minneapolis, MN. The report can be found at *www.search-institute.org*

5. Reflective Practice

At least twice before, American society has tried to resolve the ambiguities of its racial and economic past through the schools. The first was shortly after the Civil War ended when segregated schools were encouraged to reinforce the indignities of Jim Crow. That worked in a society in which power and control were powerful images of organization and schools were used as instruments of domination. But the effects on American life were profound, long lasting, and pernicious. The second attempt, in the 1950s, was a nobler effort. It was the hope of building an integrated America by desegregating schools (while largely ignoring segregation in housing, employment, and access to economic opportunity). As noted at the outset of this section, the second attempt ended with about half of minority students in schools that are 75% or more minority.

Will the effort to close the achievement gap be any more successful than these two prior efforts. Who knows? Here, we take a look at some of the unanswered questions.

A. The Superintendents' Take on Race and Class

Linda Powell Pruitt

Want to know what your peers in the superintendency consider when thinking about race and class? Here are some results from one of the few studies that asked the men and women who sit behind the superintendent's desk how they view these challenges. The short answer is that they see the issue as complex and underdeveloped with a lot of work still to be done.

Has race, class, and the achievement gap been an issue in your district? Has there been a critical incident in your district related to these issues?

In answer to this question, almost all respondents started on safe ground. They first described their districts in terms of student demographics, generally including percentages of ethnic groups, issues of language and bilingual instruction, and some sense of the dynamics of recent immigration. Some went beyond that description to talk about teacher, administrator, and board race/class percentages and how those interacted in the climate of the district. Several mentioned race and class dynamics in hiring decisions at the district level and in board composition, election, and negotiation.

Those who saw the achievement gap as important painted a similar picture. Student population is changing dramatically; teacher and administrator ranks are changing far more slowly; and political processes are not changing at all. This creates a climate where teachers no longer know the students or their communities. Often, politicians understand neither. Structures of power and privilege remain intact and do not "look like" the students they serve. Teacher preparation programs were criticized because they do not provide new teachers the skills necessary to work with young people today.

This study examines perceptions around race and class from 17 members of the Forum for the American School Superintendent. Each participant responded to a set of open-ended questions around race, class, and the achievement gap. A comparison group of 6 California superintendents (bringing the total respondents to 23) is also included in the analysis because no significant differences were found between this group and the Forum participants. The superintendents responded to questions about critical incidents, problems, resources, and remaining challenges.

When you look at the results society achieves for poor and minority children, you begin to suspect at some point that these results are intentional.

Peter Negroni,
Superintendent,
Springfield,
Massachusetts,
Schools

Respondents characterized and described the issues of race, class, and the achievement gap in a broad range of ways. These descriptions ranged from "not an issue" to "there is nothing in the district that race doesn't influence." This seemed related to a basic underlying factor. If the issue was framed as being narrowly about test scores, then race (and maybe class) were not "issues," especially if the district was all white. Many were very poor districts, for whom poverty was the major issue. Others saw the achievement gap as a symbol or measure of the district's racial climate. One stated, "what this is really about is not just high test scores, this is about breaking down stereotypes [about low-income students]."

However, there seemed to be an unexamined agreement that it was the *presence of students of color* in a mostly white system that made race an issue. Adult behaviors or district policies were less often framed as an immediate issue. Three respondents said that it was *their* professional/political/ethical issue even though their district could "live with" a gap between white middle-class children and poor children of color. One superintendent stated that, while it was not a particular issue in the district, "nationwide we have a tremendous race and class issue to be worked on." Several mentioned including a commitment to this question in their preliminary contract negotiations with a district.

In districts with multicultural student populations, disaggregated data was universally seen as important in starting a conversation about the gap. Being able to demonstrate and quantify the existence of a gap was important in harnessing community energy as well as in measuring progress toward closing it. However, one respondent pointed out that the related challenge was fighting the "causality" explanation for achievement scores: that the color/class of these students "causes" their low scores.

In some communities, "closing the gap" is associated with lowering standards. Several superintendents noted that it was critical to communicate with the community in a reassuring way. The goal had to be stated as raising achievement for all students while raising achievement for poor children more quickly. Several stated that they routinely faced the following questions: "Why are you spending money on this [efforts to close the gap]?" and "Why are you [just] interested in 'these' kids?"

Critical incidents named included publication of disaggregated data, controversy over programs to support minority hiring and retention, hiring and placement of principals, and an employee's use of a racial epithet. Several superintendents went out of their way to mention the heated nature of debates about bilingual education; it is very hard to build common ground and support while defusing "English-only" rhetoric.

All in all, a picture emerges of superintendents interested in exploring issues of race and class who are either not quite sure how to proceed or who make the effort swimming upstream in their districts.

What problems/obstacles have you experienced in other conversations about these issues?

Almost all respondents used this question as an opportunity to talk about varied and specific problems and obstacles in their own districts. One superintendent described a basic tension in how the achievement gap is framed: "I think we still operate from the premise that we have 'broke' kids and it's a matter of fixing the kids rather than it is our responsibility, as professionals, to create the outcomes we want."

Several superintendents reported a general feeling of hopelessness in communities of color; community members are accustomed to doing badly on standardized tests and having overall low performing schools. One superintendent was concerned that the community had given in to a "dynamic of resignation." Another stated that the public tended to "judge school quality on the basis of their perception of the students who attend."

One superintendent was surprised by the initial response that raising issues of diversity was seen as divisive; one board member held a strong belief that the conversation itself would be damaging.

Trust that meaningful conversations can change your world.

Margaret Wheatley, *Turning to One Another* (2002)

One respondent expressed a strong sentiment held by many: "The obstacle is the mindset of generations of bad habits on race and class issues." Denial by the mainstream community that America is a "class oriented" society leads to a blindness to the differing and powerful constraints on poor rural children. Several focused this mindset on teachers. Persuading them to change their attitudes about whether students can and will achieve at higher levels is a huge challenge. One respondent stated flatly that teachers are a problem because they live outside the community and have no connection to the culture of the students. Too many of them are "just there to get a check."

Dwindling resources and union tensions are a major issue. In some districts, resources have been cut every year in recent memory, while needs have continued to grow. Failed bond issues, past deficits, salary freezes, and contentious challenges like school closings demand much of the superintendent's attention. Tensions with the union were mentioned by most superintendents in unionized districts. Conflicts often occur over improving or changing classroom practices for underperforming students. Perceived as "anti-teacher," these measures are sometimes resisted by union leadership although welcomed by the rank and file.

Some superintendents mentioned external but related issues in the community that influence the school system's ability to deal with race and the achievement gap. One example was an "underground Christian and Jewish tension" functioning between African American churches and local synagogues. This tension was described as both "hidden and prevalent." Another observed that demographic shifts often place stress on old wounds *within* and *across* communities of color (e.g., African American and Latino).

What resources, actions, or attitudes have you found helpful in addressing race and class issues in your district?

In keeping with their assumption that the children were the primary "site" of the problem, some superintendents initiated direct programs to improve the academic achievement of students of color. These superintendents were inclined to promote more diversity among extracurricular activities and encourage afterschool, tutoring, and mentoring programs for minority students.

Others, however, reported working on interventions to improve school culture. They might invite a theater group to work with students using "stop-action" and discussion techniques. Some encouraged racially mixed groups of older students to conduct middle-school groups that are student facilitated. "Changing the testing environment," defined as communicating clearly the meaning and importance of statewide testing to students and to parents, was also heavily favored by these superintendents.

Some superintendents focused on instruction as the intervention with the greatest and quickest impact. These respondents were attracted to direct instruction at the high-school level and to promoting literacy and improvement in all subjects. Generally, providing greater access to better instruction was heavily favored. "Providing the basic kids with some of what we give the gifted kids," was one respondent's comment. Also mentioned were the efforts to eliminate barriers for students underrepresented in advanced courses, to provide open access to all Advanced Placement courses, and to have the district pay for the Preliminary Scholastic Assessment Test for every student.

Others took a larger view that included parents and families. These respondents wanted to encourage greater parental involvement, and some of them were inclined to full-service schools that would help provide low-income students and children of color with more social services. Favorite solutions also included intensive professional development for teachers, administrators, and board members; diversity training for all employee groups on an ongoing basis; and staff development oriented around communications, curriculum, meeting the needs of all learners, and social cooperation.

One respondent described focusing "very precisely on the skills that students need to do well" on the state achievement tests, and requiring "very high quality professionalism as opposed to programs with a lot of catchy names." This means that teachers understand "the variables of motivation, how to approach students who come from non-middle-class backgrounds and have an excellent knowledge of curriculum."

"Just identifying the issue" of the achievement gap was noted as a critical act. Taking the leadership to say that the gap exists and is unacceptable has been important. The superintendent must be proactive, positive, and persistent. Being able to "keep the system from being distracted," maintaining a relentless focus on the issue, was described by one respondent as the superintendent's most difficult assignment.

What do you think remains unaddressed about these issues in your district?

Superintendents were clear that the agenda is both difficult and underdeveloped; it is far from settled and much remains to be done. Their comments were as varied as their districts:

• There is a real challenge to creating the belief that all children can learn and that most parents support the success of their children. One respondent noted that the community as a whole hasn't grasped the difficulty of dealing with race and class.

• One superintendent asked if districts are "afraid to be successful," and several others raised variations on this theme. This fear leads to a sense of resignation on the parts of school staff and communities. "While education used to be seen as the way out of poverty, now poverty seems to be used as a reason for children not getting an education."

- What are the unexpected outcomes of some of our efforts? In one district, successful African American students graduate from a racially integrated high school and go to colleges where they become part of "Black Only" groups. Is that a success? Another noted that their success-oriented philosophy had inadvertently hurt the community, by promoting the idea that once you go to college, you "don't come back *here.*"

- The recruitment of teachers—especially teachers of color— who have the knowledge, skills, and attitudes to be successful with all students is a perennial problem.

- The role of the media in communicating and interpreting issues of race and class was mentioned as a problem by many. One superintendent noted that during his tenure the media had moved from being positive and supportive of initiatives to covering events in a manner "designed to create an adversarial environment" in the district.

Key Themes

Several themes emerged from these conversations, issues cutting across individual views and district realities.

1. *Each superintendent's situation was highly idiosyncratic.* Each told a detailed and specific story that included the history of his or her district, the economic climate, the roles and fates of previous superintendents, and the like. Overall, several variables seemed to make the most dramatic difference: size of district, general district achievement, the size of the achievement gap, the history of desegregation and busing, media relations, and union climate. Several suburban interviewees compared themselves to the "big city" superintendents who describe having more to contend with regarding visibility, generating common ground, raised stakes, and the like. One suburban superintendent said candidly, "I have it much easier than some of my colleagues."

2. *The respondent's race and class identity was also a key factor.* A complex form of achievement gap exists among school leaders. Superintendents demonstrated dramatically differing levels of proficiency in their ability to talk about race and class as personal, professional, and political issues in education. There seemed to be widely differing abilities to use themselves and their own experience. Superintendents of color all indicated that

they brought a "different perspective" on these issues than their white colleagues. Superintendents of color were also more likely to report personal attacks as relatively routine (although painful) parts of their job than were white superintendents.

3. *The issue of authority or "who is in charge" was woven throughout many of the stories.* Some superintendents described particular difficulties in change initiatives in their districts. All innovation raises the question of authority and power: teachers, parents, and external stakeholders question, challenge, and even undermine change efforts. Resistance seemed most likely to any intervention that focused attention on systemic rather than student issues and that threatened a shift in adult power. One respondent noted that significant improvements were likely to be team efforts; superintendents were likely to have to "allow for some shared ownership in these outcomes. In their eyes, they are losing some of their authority by doing that."

4. *There was wide variation in complexity of professional understanding of the role of superintendent.* Many images emerged from these interviews, including manager, moral leader, orchestra conductor, and politician. An individual conforming to each image has advantages and blind spots when leading change interventions around issues of race and class. The complexity in these differing images seemed directly related to a sense of what one respondent labeled as "efficacy" or the belief that leadership actions could help close the achievement gap.

5. *Superintendents often understand the dynamics of race and class along the lines of Heifetz's continuum of adaptive–technical change.* (See Part II, "Leading Your Schools.") Most see issues of race and class as classical "adaptive work" for leaders. That is, they see their task as being to focus the issue, raise the question, and encourage dialogue about the issue as an opportunity to learn. Others gravitate toward the issue as a technical problem. These respondents are more inclined to focus on answers instead of raising questions, and to encourage the dissemination of information and workable solutions. Both groups are interested in what they can do themselves, and with their communities, to make progress.

6. *Examining race and class is a continuing struggle.* Several respondents expressed the sentiment that "these issues had been circled" for a long time and now might be the time to "meet them head-on." Participants acknowledged concern about the willingness and capacity to engage in a deep conversation about these issues. One noted, "We've addressed these issues, but I

don't think we've been honest with each other . . . You notice when we start talking about race and class, a high degree of tension comes into the room, and it's the same thing [back in my district]." Another said, "There are significant issues that we have to get out [on the table]. This whole issue of race and class weaves its magic by the fact that it's usually avoided rather than confronted."

It's undoubtedly true that these issues continue to challenge educators. Why wouldn't they? They continue to challenge the nation.

B. Questions for Reflective Practice

Here are some key questions you should be considering. Encourage your staff to think about them, too.

What's the breakdown by race and class in your community? How many gated communities? How many trailer parks, units of subsidized housing, and homeless shelters? Line up your teaching staff against these categories. How many of your teachers live in your district?

If you asked your teachers and staff about an achievement gap in the district, what would they say? How about parents? Community leaders?

Is closing the achievement gap a personal and professional priority for you? How about your administrative staff and teachers?

Can you be sure that financial resources allocated to individual schools don't contribute to the gap? Are some facilities newer or better equipped and maintained? Do the most senior and highest-paid teachers cluster in some schools and avoid others?

Are you able to break down the data in your district by race and class? If so, what does it tell you? If not, why not?

In an effort to close the gap, what has been tried so far? Have you tried to reassign teachers? Beef up remediation? Increase enrollment of some groups of students in AP and honors courses? What has succeeded? What has failed?

Have you tried to hold a conversation about race and class in your district? If so, what happened and how did you build on it? If not, why not?

Do your teachers find all the African American kids sitting together in the cafeteria? Undoubtedly they do. Has any thought been given to what that means? Is it a good thing or not?

What about your board? Where are board members on issues of race and class? Do they bring up these challenges or do they wish you'd stop talking about them?

Have you tried to listen to the voices of students on this issue? If so, what have you learned?

What's the status of your relationship with preschool programs? Do you wonder who these preschool providers are and wish they'd go away? Or have you entered active partnerships with them?

How about your relationship with community-based programs and churches? Are they arrows in your quiver as you seek to close the achievement gap or simply another group out there with which you have little contact?

Have you explored an assets-based approach to help challenged young people? How effective was it?

Part VI
Developing
Your Principals

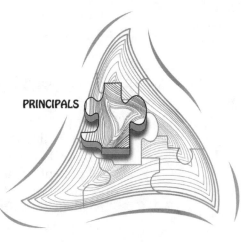

PRINCIPALS

By far, your most significant, substantive challenge as superintendent will be how to focus the intellectual resources of the school district on better teaching and learning. Developing your principals, our next commonplace, provides your single greatest leverage point. Research and common sense support the importance of strong building-level leadership for improving student learning. In this part, we share a framework that superintendents can use to develop principals as leaders of learning. We begin by acknowledging the complexity of the principal's job. Then, the primary emphasis is placed on (1) leading student learning and (2) facilitating the change process.

A number of teaching and learning models exist to guide educators as they take up these challenges. Lauren Resnick's work at the Institute for Learning, at the University of Pittsburgh, can inform your professional development. Her nine principles of learning are directed at how educators organize the instructional environment and the kinds of curriculum and pedagogy that are needed for students to meet high academic expectations.

Bringing about change is difficult. Frequently, a lot of time and effort goes into designing programs that don't change very much. To avoid this trap, you need to understand the nature of change and how it can be advanced in your institution. Gene Hall from the University of Nevada, Las Vegas, is our guide here. He examines the personal side of change, the anxieties and worries your people bring to the process, and how they can be addressed.

1. Leading Student Learning

Few people describe schools as learning communities or learning organizations. As elaborated in Gareth Morgan's metaphors, schools take on mechanical characteristics focused on efficiency, alignment of tasks, and adherence to rules and regulations to ensure uniform outcomes. Superintendents face tremendous challenges in attempting to move schools from this traditional, entrenched stance to one that nurtures collaborative working relationships and learning among teachers, students, and principals. Our work with school districts, however, shows clearly that this is a necessary step for transforming existing schools and must begin with the development of principals. You can't build learning communities without concentrating on student learning.

A. What Does It Take to Lead a School?

This section is drawn from a useful paper on school leadership developed with Wallace Foundation funding at the University of Washington. The paper, entitled Making Sense of Leading Schools: A Study of the School Principalship *(September 2003), by Brad Portin and colleagues, is available at the Center on Reinventing Public Education's Web site (www.crpe.org).*

Brad Portin

"In the great scheme of things, schools may be relatively small organizations, but their leadership challenges are far from small or simple." That's a central conclusion of a two-year study of the school principalship that I completed with my colleagues at the University of Washington in 2003.

As we went about our work, we realized that a lot of the current attention to school leadership looks at all the things principals "might" do and treats them as if they are the things all principals "should" do—and that principals should do them all.

Based on in-depth interviews with educators (principals, vice principals, and teachers) in 21 schools, public and private, in four different cities, we drew five major conclusions about the nature of the principal's work:

1. The core of the principal's job is diagnosing his or her particular school's needs and, given the resources and talents available, deciding how to meet them.

2. Regardless of school type—elementary or secondary, public or private—schools need leadership in seven critical

areas: instructional, cultural, managerial, human resources, strategic, external development, and micropolitical.

3. Principals are responsible for ensuring that leadership happens in all seven critical areas, but they don't have to provide it. Principals can be "one-man" bands, leaders of jazz combos, or orchestra conductors (see Figure 6.1).

4. Governance matters, and a school's governance structure affects the ways key leadership functions are performed.

5. Principals learn by doing. However trained, most principals think they learned the skills they need "on the job."

From an extensive list of tasks, functions, roles, and duties, the team identified seven common functions of leadership evident in all types of schools and performed by someone in each of them. Table 6.1 lists these seven areas and describes generic actions associated with each.

Table 6.1   School Critical Functions and Associated Actions

Critical Function	Actions
Instructional Leadership	Assuring quality of instruction, modeling teaching practice, supervising curriculum, and assuring quality of teaching resources.
Cultural Leadership	Tending to the symbolic resources of the school (e.g., its traditions, climate, and history).
Managerial Leadership	Overseeing the operations of the school (e.g., its budget, schedule, facilities, safety and security, and transportation).
Human Resource Leadership	Recruiting, hiring, firing, inducting, and mentoring teachers and administrators; developing leadership capacity and professional-development opportunities.
Strategic Leadership	Promoting vision, mission, and goals—and developing a means to reach them.
External Development Leadership	Representing the school in the community, developing capital, tending to public relations, recruiting students, buffering and mediating external interests, and advocating for the school's interests.
Micropolitical Leadership	Buffering and mediating internal interests, while maximizing resources (financial and human).

These functions were performed in various ways in different schools, as Figure 6.1 illustrates.

Figure 6.1   Leaders, Responsibilities, and the Seven Core Functions

Consolidating seven functions within the principal: The Principal as One-Man Band

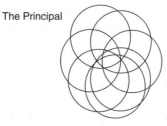

The Principal

Shared leadership between principal and other designated leaders in the school: The Principal as Jazz Band Leader

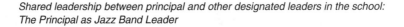

The Principal

Assistant Principal

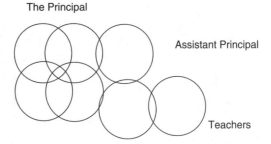

Teachers

Distinct leadership roles between independent school principals and level heads: The Principal as Orchestra Conductor

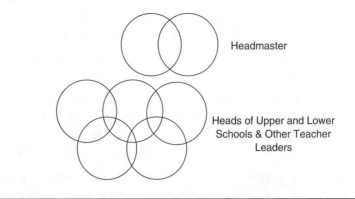

Headmaster

Heads of Upper and Lower Schools & Other Teacher Leaders

In some schools, the seven critical leadership areas (represented by the seven circles) are tightly coupled around the principal. The principal remains centrally involved, if not entirely responsible, for each of the core functions. The top diagram displays what is almost a formula for a beleaguered principal—a one-man band responsible for just about everything in the school, from the lyrics and melody to the bass line and harmonics.

The middle diagram displays a more distributed leadership model. This principal encourages "leadership" throughout the organization, very much the way the leader of a jazz combo expects her musicians to solo. Here the principal lays down the basic melody line and encourages individual band members to improvise around the theme. This is more of a shared leadership model, sometimes contingent on available talent, sometimes on the disposition of the principal.

The bottom diagram illustrates how, in other schools, the seven critical leadership areas are even more broadly distributed among various people. Here the principal is more akin to an orchestra conductor—playing nothing himself, but making sure the many individual parts are expertly performed and harmonize and work together smoothly. This particular model accurately describes what is apparent in many private schools. In these schools, the school leader is seen as the "headmaster," not the principal. It seems apparent that there are many different ways to lead.

Given today's emphasis on instructional accountability, these distinctions are important. In no case was a principal walled off from the instructional work of the school. But neither did all principals present themselves as the "instructional exemplar" of the school—capable of teaching any class at any time. Yet, even these principals could identify good instruction when they saw it and would incorporate visits to the classroom into their regular practice. But their comments suggest that identifying good teaching is not the same thing as helping others teach well. Clearly, instructional leadership merits the attention it receives in the press and research.

B. Effort-Based Education: Principles for Teaching and Learning

Richard C. Wallace, Jr.

Superintendents find Lauren Resnick's model—with its challenge to the traditional thinking that inherited ability determines what a student can learn—extremely effective. Resnick notes that schools are built on the assumption that aptitude governs achievement. She counters with the argument that a student's effort creates ability. That is, students can "become smart by working at the right kinds of learning tasks." This section introduces you to how the Principles of Learning can be used to shift the day-to-day work of educators toward an effort-based focus.

Resnick, a distinguished psychologist at the Learning Research Development Center (LRDC) at the University of Pittsburgh, insists that the "brain's capacity to learn and adapt continues throughout life, right into the assisted-living facility." Superintendents and principals will find especially useful one article challenging traditional mindsets about learning and abilities: Lauren Resnick, "From Aptitude to Effort: A New Foundation for Our Schools," Daedalus, vol. 124, no. 4 (Fall 1995).

See Lauren Resnick, "Making America Smarter," Education Week, vol. 18 (June 16, 1999), for further elaboration on learnable intelligence. New findings from emerging neuroscience research support Resnick's claims. These are discussed in Part VII.

Aptitude primarily determines what students learn in school? Lauren Resnick denounces this deeply rooted conception of learning in numerous settings with superintendents and principals. Her decades of research on how students learn have led to the development of nine Principles of Learning grounded in the belief that educators can harness student effort to create ability (see Table 6.2).

Resnick has adopted an "incremental view of intelligence." That is, intelligence is something that expands and grows. "It's not true," says Resnick, "that the brain is fixed at the end of the first year; the brain's capacity to learn and adapt continues throughout life." She argues, "People can *get smart.*" If students believe this, they invest more energy when confronted with something new. However, it's not simply brute effort that leads to greater mastery. Resnick clarifies: "Incremental thinkers are particularly likely to apply self-regulatory, meta-cognitive skills when they encounter task difficulties, to focus on analyzing the task and generating alternative strategies. Most important, they seek out opportunities to hone their skills and knowledge, treating task difficulty (and thus occasional setbacks) as part of the learning challenge rather than as evidence that they lack intelligence. They get on an upward spiral in which their intelligence is actually increasing. Meanwhile, their peers who think of intelligence as fixed try to avoid difficult tasks for fear of displaying their lack of intelligence. They enter a downward spiral by avoiding the very occasions in which they could learn smarter ways of behaving."

Resnick argues that "targeted effort" is what you and your administrative and teaching peers should be pursuing. It's counterintuitive, given the conceptions we've inherited, Resnick acknowledges, "but the view emerging today is that *effort creates ability.* That is to say, smart isn't something you are, it's something you become."

Schools can consciously set out to "socialize intelligence," believes Resnick. That is, they can routinely challenge students

Table 6.2   Principles of Learning

1. *Organize for Effort.* Replace the assumption that aptitude determines how much students can learn with the belief that sustained, directed effort yields high achievement. Support means setting high minimum standards, matching the curriculum to the standards, providing expert instruction, and giving students extra time if needed.

2. *Establish Clear Expectations.* Define explicitly what we expect students to learn so that school professionals, parents, community members, and students can understand it. When expectations are clear, students can take responsibility for their own learning. All children are given a chance to work toward demanding expectations.

3. *Insist on Fair and Credible Evaluations.* Assessment processes must be aligned with the standards and curriculum. Students and parents must find assessments fair, and community members and employers must see them as credible.

4. *Recognize Accomplishments.* Everyone likes recognition. If we expect hard work from students, we should celebrate their authentic accomplishments.

5. *Create Academic Rigor in a Thinking Curriculum.* Thinking and problem solving are the "new basics" of the twenty-first century. Thinking requires a solid foundation of knowledge. Curriculum must include commitment to a knowledge core, high thinking demand, and active use of knowledge.

6. *Accountable Talk.* Teachers should encourage "accountable talk" in their classrooms—talk that is accurate, uses appropriate knowledge, encourages rigorous thinking, and responds to and develops what others in the classroom have said.

7. *Socialize Intelligence.* By calling on students to use the skills of intelligent thinking—and by holding them responsible for doing so—educators can "teach" intelligence. Interactions with others are critical in constructing understanding and meaning.

8. *Encourage the Self-Management of Learning.* If students are to develop as learners, they must be encouraged to develop and use an array of self-monitoring and self-management strategies.

9. *Understand Learning as Apprenticeship.* The historic value of apprenticeship to learning can be brought into schools by encouraging learning environments in which complex thinking is modeled and analyzed, and by providing mentoring and coaching as students undertake extended projects.

SOURCE: Adapted from materials provided by LRDC, University of Pittsburgh.

Forum superintendents and their principals worked with the Institute for Learning at the University of Pittsburgh to create effort-based schools built on rigorous academic standards. Resnick began with intensive training sessions with principals and then expanded to direct, ongoing work in a number of the districts with teachers. The core set of nine principles in Table 6.2 guided this work.

For in-depth information about the Principles of Learning and their application, see www .instituteforlearning .org/. A CD-ROM also is available to introduce the principles.

to engage in strategic problem solving and self-monitoring of what they know. These two attributes—strategic problem solving and self-monitoring—are really what metacognition is all about, she says.

"We can't teach intelligence but we can socialize it," argues Resnick. "Kids will get smarter. In fact, that's what we do with gifted and talented programs and it's time we took those techniques to all children." It's also what first-rate private and parochial schools do, too.

Schools that set out to socialize intelligence will challenge students, expect them to "act smart," provide them time to "act smart," and hold them accountable for their work. "Educators have to be very demanding for this to work," Resnick says. But if it does work, it develops students with a set of beliefs, skills, and dispositions that are powerful tools for learning. These students will be convinced that difficult problems can yield to analysis, and they will be able to monitor their own development well enough to know when they need to ask for help.

She concludes: "What we need to be about is ensuring that children are using their minds all day, every day, and in every subject." We need to set students on the "upward getting-smarter spiral."

Think about that. You have the children in your schools for only perhaps 10% of their time. You can't afford to waste it. If you don't use 100% of school time for socializing intelligence, we won't make it.

C. White Plains Applies the Principles of Learning

Saul Yanofsky
Constance W. Iervolino

Perhaps the central challenge of the standards-based reform movement is the need to reconcile the polarization between the views of those who insist that all children can learn to very high standards and those who believe that many cannot. In White Plains, New York, we found that Resnick's Principles of Learning offered a promising way to confront this dilemma.

Like many other states, New York has been in the throes of the standards movement for some time. Although most people are in agreement with the concept of higher standards, all of this intimidated parents and educators. In particular, the new requirement that all students pass five Regents examinations (challenging optional tests for college-bound students originally developed by the State Board of Regents) brought a measure of contention into the statewide debate. Public opinion became focused on comparative school achievement data. In competitive Westchester County, stress among staff, students, and parents escalated.

Meanwhile, many staff members had minimal expectations for a sizable number of students. They felt it was unrealistic and unreasonable to expect these students to pass the new assessments. Predictably, these staff members wasted time and energy blaming the state for the assessments and were quick to offer excuses for student failure. Particularly in a diverse district like White Plains, where more than half of the student population is classified as minority or English Language Learners, there was a definite gap in achievement between these students and the more advantaged middle-class student population. Ironically, most teachers still saw themselves as "good teachers," even though many students were not achieving. They rationalized that students were either not ready, not working, or not supported at home.

Two books by Jo Blase and Joseph Blase helped superintendents in their focus on instructional leadership—Handbook of Instructional Leadership: How Really Good Principals Promote Teaching and Learning *(Thousand Oaks, CA: Corwin Press, 1998) and* The Fire Is Back: Principals Sharing School Governance *(Thousand Oaks, CA: Corwin Press, 1997).*

Instruction was largely teacher centered; even in some classrooms that purported to be "doing" writers' workshops, often it was the teacher who still collected student papers to do the proofreading and correcting. The study of science that was supposedly more constructivist because it was "hands-on" often was not connected to any core concepts, scaffolding content, or essential questions; rather, it consisted of a series of unrelated activities.

Clearly, a framework was needed to serve as an umbrella under which teaching and learning could be defined and understood. We adopted Lauren Resnick's Principles of Learning as that framework. These principles became the lens through which we viewed curriculum and instruction and the mechanism for communicating our mission and for aligning curriculum to standards. Inevitably, the principles became the yardstick by which we measured our progress.

"Scaffolded" curriculum was articulated from grade to grade, and report cards were revised to reflect new specific performance indicators of achievement. Grade-level and department teams met to clarify curricular objectives, and the shift from teacher-dominated to student-centered classrooms slowly began. Measuring what students were learning by looking at student work brought a new dimension to formal post-observation conferences and teachers' conversations. The principles and the intrinsic core belief that "effort creates ability" became the foundation of our work.

Classroom visits escalated into "learning walks." These structured classroom visits provided a common form and language with which both administrators and teachers could look at instructional practices. The principles helped staff to set consistent expectations for what classroom learning environments should look like. In White Plains, we were delighted to see some elementary and middle-school teachers begin to visit colleagues' classrooms and talk about what they saw.

Our administrators also became more skilled in both observation and discussion. The practice of learning walks became embedded in our principal and later assistant principal meetings. Teachers at first were quite vocally opposed to what they termed "drive-bys"; in an attempt to kill the practice, they asked the union to raise objections. Gradually, however, teachers became more comfortable (or at least tolerant), realizing that the order of business had changed. Every attempt was made to include teachers in the process by regularly asking them what feedback they would like to receive during the learning walks. We also found it useful to have teachers participate in the walks.

We didn't try to do it all at once in White Plains. We began by concentrating on two of the Principles of Learning: *Establish Clear Expectations* and *Organize for Effort;* we added two more principles the following year—*Insist on Fair and Credible Evaluations* and *Create Academic Rigor in a Thinking Curriculum. Accountable Talk* came on line in year four.

The principles were essential. Staging their implementation carefully was important. But the key to our success in White Plains was being forced to reflect on whether instructional practice in the classroom matched our aspirations for student learning. It wasn't always easy. It would be misleading to suggest that every classroom reflected the Principles of Learning. But we were clear in our goals, progress was made, and the Principles of Learning defined where we were heading.

D. Reflection Exercise: A Teaching or a Learning System?

Nelda Cambron-McCabe

How do you differentiate between a teaching system and a learning system?

Reflective practice was an integral part of our Forum leadership development work. Often this was personal reflection, but at other points it included engaging each other in dialogue around a particular issue or concern. In one session with superintendents and their school board members, we posed the following question: How do you differentiate between a teaching system and a learning system?

These questions can help a group of teachers, administrators, and others reflect on their understandings about teaching and learning and the implications for students' learning.

- How do you differentiate between a teaching system and a learning system?
- What does a teaching system look like in a classroom?
- What does a learning system look like in a classroom?
- Is there a difference in expected outcomes?
- What is the student's role/responsibility in a teaching system? In a learning system?
- How does change occur in a teaching system? In a learning system?
- What constitutes success in a teaching system? In a learning system?

2. The Instructional Leader's Toolkit

Theory is helpful. But how do you put this complex new way of understanding learning into practice? Here's a way of understanding your job as an instructional leader along with several tools for your toolkit.

A. The Instructional Leader's Tools

Otto Graf

> *Forum superintendents found Otto Graf's on-site work with their principals to be invaluable, as the principals took up the challenge of instructional leadership. Graf raises provocative questions that force a reconsideration of the "business as usual" stance prevalent in schools and provides tools for principals to shift their orientation to teaching and learning issues.*

Ask any principal to list the top priorities of his or her job, and most will include instructional leadership. Next, ask the principal to review his or her work calendar to see how the use of time corresponds to this priority. In most cases, the time devoted to the role of instructional leader does not begin to match the priority given that role.

Taking up instructional leadership involves a shift in perspective. This begins by making questions about student learning central to each day's work.

- How can I have an impact on what happens, in every classroom, for every student?
- How can I ensure that every child is held to and enabled to meet high standards?
- How will I talk to teachers and students about what is being learned and how performance is evaluated?

Nine Tools for the Instructional Leader

All instructional leaders should be able to put their hands on the following tools easily:

1. *Data.* Collecting and analyzing data about student performance, classroom by classroom and subject by subject, is imperative.

2. *Clinical Supervision.* Principals need to be comfortable assessing and guiding teachers based on actual observation of their classroom performance.

3. *Self-Evaluation.* Encouraging teachers to collect and analyze their own data about what's going on in their classroom is powerful.

4. *Videotaping.* The videotape offers vivid accounts of the lesson and what teachers and students are doing.

5. *The Portfolio.* Ideally, portfolios should capture the work of both students and teachers.

6. *Peer Observation and Collegial Discussions.* Nothing convinces a teacher about the merits of a new approach more than counsel from colleagues and peers.

7. *Professional Learning Communities.* Encourage every adult in the building to understand that they're all in this together.

8. *The Walkthrough.* This tool provides a fresh ritual for collecting data and sharing perceptions.

9. *The Debriefing.* An essential corollary to the Walkthrough permits verbal and written feedback to individual teachers and the whole faculty about learning in the school.

B. The Walkthrough

Otto Graf

The Walkthrough observation technique creates a fresh ritual for collecting data and, afterward in a debriefing, sharing perceptions and ideas. In a sense, it brings the teacher and the principal into the cultural center of instruction. The Walkthrough provides a very real indicator that instruction and learning are the priority in the school. It also signifies that the teacher and principal play major roles in the instruction and learning process. Over a period of time, Walkthroughs can forge a relationship between the principal and teacher as colleagues who work closely together in the area of instruction. Principals and teachers begin focusing on those things that make the difference in improving academic achievement. The process of coaching each other becomes a significant factor in shaping what happens in the school.

How often do you as principal conduct a Walkthrough? To be part of the culture of the school, a Walkthrough should be conducted on a regular basis. Most principals set a goal to see every teacher a minimum of two times per month. Over the course of a school year, a principal can take 20 "snapshots" of a teacher's classroom. Using multiple "snapshots," principals can collect important data about the implementation of the curriculum, the differentiation of instruction, the performance of students, and the ability of students to evaluate what constitutes good work. Here's the 14-step process.

1. *Conduct a preliminary Walkthrough* to learn important information about the staff, students, curriculum, and school. The goal of this Walkthrough is to see the school in operation and to begin collecting baseline data around a wide spectrum of instructional practices.

2. *Conduct a Walkthrough meeting* with the staff. This meeting sets the stage for the Walkthrough and helps to establish clear expectations for the staff's participation. Specific school goals, special programs, or areas of focus for the school should also be reviewed at this meeting.

3. *Establish guidelines* for all participants in the Walkthrough. Clear expectations need to be established concerning professional behavior for individuals involved in this process. Participants must maintain the highest degree of confidentiality regarding what is observed in the classrooms. While feedback is important, negative or judgmental comments to others regarding teachers or students are not appropriate.

4. *Establish the focus* for subsequent Walkthroughs. The principal and teachers work together to identify the specific elements of effective instruction that they wish to target for implementation. This step includes the identification of "look-fors"—a precise descriptor of teaching strategies that tell the observer what the strategy looks like when applied in the classroom.

5. *Connect the "look-fors"* to established standards. "Look-fors" in the classroom should reflect the district's standards for curriculum and instruction. This is an important step in developing a common language and a matching set of indicators for instruction and learning.

6. *Create an agenda for the Walkthrough.* The principal should establish an agenda specifying "look-fors" for the Walkthrough and communicate it to everyone involved. The exact number of classroom visits may vary, but a typical Walkthrough includes five to ten classrooms.

7. *Identify data* to be collected (e.g., student-learning behaviors, student work, teacher behaviors, materials used, physical arrangement of the classroom, and class activities).

8. *Collect data.* The person conducting the Walkthrough should collect data. Note specific examples of effective practice and exact details about the implementation/use of "look-fors."

9. *Observe student behaviors* that influence learning. The Walkthrough should focus primarily on student work. Walkthrough participants may observe students' behaviors, level of engagement, and quality of work. Talking to students about what they are doing and how they evaluate their work presents a wonderful opportunity for assessing teaching and learning.

10. *Validate effective practice.* The Walkthrough begins as a process for validating powerful teaching practice, effective use

of guiding principles of learning, and effective learning strategies demonstrated by students.

11. *Debrief with teachers.* Debriefing with teachers and, in some instances, with students is a critical step in the Walkthrough process. (See Table 6.3 for debriefing options.) Feedback based on observation is a powerful tool.

Table 6.3   Debriefing Options Following a Walkthrough

Oral Feedback. Provide verbal feedback to teachers about something observed during the Walkthrough. Be specific and connect the feedback to "look-fors" or elements of effective instruction.

Written Feedback. Write a general narrative about what was observed during the Walkthrough and distribute the information to the entire staff. The narrative includes specific examples (without identifying a particular teacher or classroom) and evidence of how "look-fors" are present in the school. Short e-mail notes to individual teachers can be effective, also.

Debriefing the Faculty. Conduct a short meeting to debrief the faculty immediately after completing the Walkthrough. The meeting is generally held after school, and attendance is most often voluntary. This meeting begins with a general overview of effective practices observed during the Walkthrough and specific evidence of "look-fors" employed in classrooms. Feedback is focused on what is present in the school and not on individual teachers.

Group Conference. Conduct a group conference with teachers to highlight and validate the teachers' use of effective practices and/or implementation of "look-fors." The conference begins with a general overview about what was observed during the Walkthrough. This is followed by giving each teacher one or two specific examples of effective teaching strategies or "look-fors" that he or she demonstrated during the Walkthrough.

Growth Conference. Conduct a group conference focused on improvement. To create a specific growth objective for the conference, use framing questions, identify areas of consideration, encourage teachers to complete a self-reflection sheet, examine student work, or share instructional artifacts from students and the classroom.

Clinical Supervision Conference. Conduct a one-on-one conference with a teacher to reflect on the teacher's performance or the performance of his or her students.

Study Groups. Form small learning communities. Provide the time and resources for teachers to meet and discuss instruction and learning. Study groups can explore new strategies/research, share best practices, and engage in action research projects in classrooms.

Other Tools. Videotape lessons; prepare professional portfolios; examine student work; share teaching artifacts; review teachers' lesson plans; devise projects.

12. *Debrief staff.* Providing feedback to the staff as a whole is critical. This process begins by validating effective teaching and learning practices and encouraging their continued use. As the process develops, ample opportunities exist to engage teachers in sharing ideas and strategies with each other to create a strong learning community.

13. *Coach each other.* The Walkthrough provides an excellent opportunity for participants to talk about instruction and learning and to coach each other. While this process begins with the principal and other administrators walking through classrooms and the school, engaging teachers in the process improves everyone's learning.

14. *Create a new school culture* emphasizing improved teaching and learning. The Walkthrough should be seen as part of the culture and not as an event. To make this process a part of the culture, principals must establish a visible and continuing presence in classrooms.

C. Your Task as a Superintendent

Nelda Cambron-McCabe

What must a superintendent do to support principals taking up the challenge of leading student learning? We've laid out an ambitious responsibility for principals that fundamentally changes the very nature of their work. From our experiences, we identified some common behaviors across superintendents that made it possible for principals to lead student learning. Forum superintendents elaborate on these points here.

Harvard's Richard Elmore has developed powerful insights into the challenges of improving school leadership. See Building a New Structure for School Leadership *(New York: Albert Shanker Institute, 2000).*

1. Student Learning Begins at the Top, With the Superintendent

Superintendents set the tone by what they do, what they say, and what they value. When student learning is constantly part of your rhetoric and actions, you create a space for principals to engage their staffs and communities. The real question from my learning is "How do we help superintendents understand that their role is to create safe practice fields for principals taking up the student learning challenge?"

—Les Omotani, Superintendent, West Des Moines, Iowa

If you believe the principalship is the key for student learning, you must be prepared to adopt an instructional framework or philosophy to set the stage for the work. It's a paradigm shift in how you think about learning. Resnick's Principles represent a way of thinking and looking at learning that shifts the whole energy of the organization as to how instruction takes place. It left no doubt about where we stood on student learning.

—William Symons, Superintendent,
Charlottesville, Virginia

Do you engage in regular conversations about student learning? Are you familiar with student work? Your responses to these questions send clear messages about what you value.

—Carol Choye, Superintendent, Scotch
Plains–Fanwood, New Jersey

We turned our attention to focusing the schools' core beliefs and mission on the needs of students. The work of teaching and learning needed to become the central shared value. Everyone, including me, needed to acknowledge and demonstrate in their work that the core business of the entire district was raising student achievement.

—Saul Yanofsky, Superintendent,
White Plains, New York

2. Principals Need Time to Reflect and Learn

Real support for principals is giving them time for reflection and learning during the workday. It may be the only way to shift their mindset about the nature of the work.

—Les Omotani, Superintendent,
West Des Moines, Iowa

Sometimes a good dose of inspiration is all it takes. So, learn about Lorraine Monroe, founder of Frederick Douglass Academy in Harlem. The success of the children in this legendary school are credited to Monroe and her "Monroe Doctrine." See Nothing's Impossible: Leadership Lessons From Inside and Outside the Classroom *(New York: Time Books, 1997).*

"What is it that we can do to create space for you to lead student learning?" That's the question we regularly posed to our principals and assistant principals. This helped us sort out the mundane burdens that were being inflicted on the building-level administration.

—Ben Canada, Superintendent,
Portland, Oregon

I'm always looking for tools to help principals reflect on their own practice and learning, to construct what they need to reach the next level of development. It's not about giving them a formula to apply or a program to implement but rather the tools that allow them to reflect and grow.

—Dan Colgan, Superintendent,
St. Joseph, Missouri

3. Principals Need Specific Skills and Knowledge in Creating Learning Communities to Engage Teachers and Others

Learning communities run counter to the individualistic culture that is found in most schools. As such, we found that our monthly administrative meetings needed to be focused on developing skills to shift this culture. We took a deliberate and systematic approach to prepare school principals.

—Steve Norton, Cache County
School District, Utah

You need to have a focus for the professional development of principals. Initially, our leadership academy attempted to do too many things. When we focused on student learning, we were able to narrow our approach and provide very targeted skill development for principals to work collaboratively with their staffs.

—James Hager, Superintendent, Washoe
County School District, Reno, Nevada

4. Principals Must Quit Doing Some Things They're Doing Now

Superintendents have a unique role in helping principals structure their time. Principals are under incredible pressure from many areas—union, parents, discipline, building issues. If we expect them to be leaders of student learning, then we must help them carve out that time and give them permission to let certain things go. We have to say these things are not important in your role as principal.

—Pendery Clark, Superintendent, Douglas
County School District, Minden, Nevada

5. Principals Must Be Protected From Internal and External Pressures That Divert Their Time and Energy From Student Learning

As superintendent, I must control the demands that the central office makes on principals. Quite frankly, that's where a lot of the pressure originates, whether from finance, personnel, or facilities. The difficult part of this task is getting the central office staff to see their role as supportive of principals and buildings as opposed to having their own agenda that often conflicts with the needs of schools and principals.

—George Russell, Superintendent, Eugene, Oregon

As superintendent, my role is running interference for principals so they can stay focused on student learning. "Leaders of learning" is not just a phrase in my district; it has real meaning, and my actions reinforce it continuously with principals, parents, board members, and the community.

—Carol Choye, Superintendent, Scotch
Plains–Fanwood, New Jersey

6. Principals Must Model Leading Student Learning as a Fundamental Way to Change What Happens in Schools

Principals need very practical modeling. The "Walkthrough" has been extremely powerful for us because it's modeling. I'm not just telling principals to walk through the classrooms. I'm doing it with them. We're collaboratively identifying the "look-fors" to guide our inquiry and then debriefing what we learned.

—Dan Colgan, Superintendent,
St. Joseph, Missouri

7. Superintendents and School Boards Must Create New Policies, Structures, and Practices to Frame the Student Learning Agenda

We reexamined many long-accepted practices. If something did not connect with student learning, then we had to raise hard questions about why we were doing it.

—James Hager, Superintendent, Washoe
County School District, Nevada

We needed to change our teaching and assessment practices, our student support programs, our interaction with parents and the community. The school system seriously needed to build anew, but we were aware that without reexamining our beliefs, the programs of a "new" school system would woefully resemble those of the past quarter century.

—Alan Beitman, Superintendent, Manchester
Public Schools, Connecticut

8. The New Expectations for Principals Must Be Clearly Understood by All

For me, committing this new leadership understanding to writing was pivotal. If it's a living document, board members and others (including me) don't run to principals demanding that they take care of brush fires when those inevitable calls come through from parents and other groups. Involving board members and principals in joint retreats for conversation about what all this means makes it more than another piece of paper.

—Neil Schmidt, Superintendent,
Santa Monica, California

9. Superintendents Ultimately Must Raise the Tough Questions

With our students, three quartiles are doing exceptionally well, and therein lies the problem. Admirable test scores statewide and nationally conceal an entire group of kids. The fact is, we're doing a fabulous job getting most students through the system. What we had not examined was the bottom quartile and how really low some of the kids' scores were. Making that data public was important even though it was met with disbelief and almost open rebellion in some of the upper-income schools.

—Steve Norton, Superintendent,
Cache County School District, Logan, Utah

10. Distribute Leadership in Your District

As part of our reform plan in Newport News, we set out to distribute leadership among principals in our district. We created new learning communities. In them, students take responsibility for their learning; the community is effectively engaged in leadership roles; high standards for all are the norm; all courses, including Advanced Placement, are open to all students; leadership means the community, not the principal; children succeed; the gap has been closed; and these schools are driven by a broader moral purpose.

Interested in the broad moral purpose of schools? See Michael Fullan's Leading a Culture of Change *(San Francisco: Jossey-Bass, 2001).*

—Wayne D. Lett, Superintendent,
Newport News, Virginia

D. Where Do We Find Principals?
Growing Our Own in Cache County, Utah

Steven C. Norton
Stephen W. Zsiray, Jr.

Recognizing that effective school leadership is the cornerstone for increasing student success requires school districts to identify, select, and develop quality principals. Cache County School District in Utah has constructed a comprehensive process to attract and retain building-level leaders who lead student learning. Our six-step process may inform your efforts.

1. Leadership Identification

Finding and encouraging individuals to consider the school principalship is a formidable task all too familiar to superintendents. We look inside to our own teachers, using an ongoing, systematic process. Our administrative team identifies outstanding classroom teachers; teachers participating on school and district committees; teachers who hold leadership positions in local, state, and national organizations; and teachers who are involved in community leadership.

2. Professional Preparation

Interest in administrative leadership isn't sufficient. The Cache County School District works in partnership with two administrative leadership preparation programs—Utah State University and Idaho State University. The district administrative leadership team members interact regularly with the faculty members in the two programs as well as teach courses and serve on graduate students' committees. This partnership gives us confidence that a match exists between the preparation programs and our goals for instructional improvement.

3. Administrative Leadership Screening Process

A screening process gives us insight into the leadership ability of aspiring principals. Key components of the process include

- Selection and briefing of the screening team
- Candidate response to written problems
- Candidate response to oral questions
- Performance in handling a case in a simulated board meeting

The screening team includes teachers, parents, administrators, classified staff, and university personnel. The team is briefed on how to analyze candidate answers and the need to be consistent in their evaluations of each candidate. The candidates write responses to questions that are relevant to district goals and aspirations. These questions include topics such as philosophy of education, situational issues relevant to school instruction, organizational issues that affect the school district, and state and national issues. A rubric is used to score the responses. The following is a sample written problem:

Your school's most recent standardized test scores indicate poor performance in mathematics. In fact, student math scores fell well below the predicted scoring range for your school. This is the third consecutive year test scores have been below the scoring range. Local newspapers have reported the disappointing scores, and you, the principal, have received complaints from parents blaming the test results on inadequate school leadership and instruction. What steps, if any, do you plan to take to address the situation?

Additionally, candidates respond to a series of oral questions in a roundtable format. Each member of the screening committee poses a question. For example, a parent might ask, "What is parent involvement supposed to look like in my school?" Both written and oral questions are designed to give the committee an opportunity to compare candidates' responses and analyze their understanding of key issues, particularly concerning student learning.

The final aspect of the screening process is the *school board simulation*. Candidates prepare a written response to a problem and then make a formal presentation to the school board, composed of screening committee members. In this simulation exercise, candidates are judged on their ability to define a problem, understand its various dimensions, develop a solution, and then convince the school board that their approach is viable. A sample problem could involve the approval of a school improvement plan, a student disciplinary action, or a personnel issue such as teacher dismissal. At the completion of the screening process, a candidate's performance is scored for all elements of the process. A final cumulative score of 80% ensures inclusion in the interview process. Presently, 71 individuals are in the district pool, and 20 have scores 80% or better (range 91.8 to 52.6).

4. Interview Process

A two-tiered interview process is used. The first interview involves the site-based committee of the school where the vacancy occurs. If the opening were for an assistant principal of a school, the committee would include the principal, one or two teachers and parents from the site-based committee, a classified staff member from the site-based committee, and a district office administrator. A standard set of questions relative to the district goals is provided, as well as questions developed by the interview team that are relevant to the unique issues of the school. At the end of the process, a list of three unranked final candidates is submitted to the superintendent. The superintendent, a member of his or her leadership team, and the school principal interview the three finalists. After discussion with the district interview committee, the superintendent makes the selection.

5. Instructional Development

Instructional development for both new and aspiring administrative leaders is provided to the candidates in the leadership pool. Aspiring leaders are encouraged to take leadership roles in the school district. Some serve as trainers for reading, literacy, or technology programs. Others chair key operational committees in the school district, including efforts to examine career ladders and character education. In addition, an annual leadership workshop is provided for new and aspiring school administrators. This workshop has now expanded to include individuals from 12 school districts in the area.

In White Plains, we worked to create "leadership density." This meant developing new opportunities for teachers to aspire to and assume leadership responsibilities. New roles emerged. These included instructional specialists, who were districtwide staff developers in math and English. Two lead teacher positions were funded for each elementary school, which permitted classroom teachers to work with the principal while keeping their instructional role in the classroom.

Saul Yanofsky,
Superintendent,
White Plains,
New York

Saul Yanofsky, superintendent in White Plains, New York, notes, "Reflection in both instructional and administrative practices was modeled and encouraged in our district. The work of Judith Warren Little and Milbrey McLaughlin on collective practice, work culture, and commitment to shared practice of teaching guided us." You should also explore J. W. Little and M. McLaughlin, Teachers Work: Individualism, Colleagues, and Contexts (New York: Teachers College Press, 1993).

6. Building a Learning Community Among Principals

District-level meetings have been geared toward the building of a learning community around instructional leadership. Monthly meetings range from book discussions on instructional practice to a discussion on how effort-based learning principles are implemented in the classroom. Meetings are not limited to these formally scheduled sessions. School principals are encouraged to meet as groups and discuss instructional issues. The Internet is a catalyst to generate discussions through e-mail, net-meetings online, and videoconferencing, all of which have been used to facilitate the sharing of ideas. We attempt to engage in practices to establish learning communities that reflect the unique nature of the individual schools, as well as maintain a sense of the big picture.

The bottom line of our learning community effort is student learning. Perhaps Richard Slavin says it best when he notes that educational reforms have limits unless the reforms can improve the methods and materials every teacher uses with every student, in every subject, every day.

E. Leadership Academies: Making Learning a Priority

Portland, Oregon

Dr. Benjamin Canada designed Portland's monthly Administrator Academy meetings around three themes:

- Administrator as instructional leader
- Administrator as effective building/program manager
- Administrator as effective human resources manager

A committee of Portland building and program administrators guides the Academy agendas. Proposals for academy sessions must demonstrate that the session content will build knowledge and skills and strengthen administrators' leadership and management practice. Over the past three years, major sessions included ESL/bilingual practices; supervision and evaluation; effective math, science, and language instructional practices; school-improvement planning; communicating with parents and communities; crisis management; employment law; and student assessment.

Washoe County School District, Nevada

James Hager, Superintendent of Washoe County School District, Nevada, says that "Pass It On" is pivotal to principals' survival. Both former and current administrators participate in Washoe County's Leadership Instructors' Cadre. A wide variety of workshops are offered, ranging from a five-part series for aspiring administrators to a doctoral cohort for advanced leadership through the University of Nevada. National conferences are part of the academy leadership to encourage principals to look beyond their backyard for inspiration and innovations. All new administrators participate in a two-year seminar that covers topics such as teacher evaluation, academic standards, instruction, and assessment. Sessions are held in the early mornings, afternoons, and evenings to meet leaders' needs.

3. Facilitating Change

Obvious leadership challenges will confront you as you move forward, mostly the traditional ones of designing, implementing, and assessing programs. But three challenges are not immediately obvious. First is the challenge of understanding the nature of change and what it means in a large institutional setting such as yours. Next is the problem of taking your staff and teachers where you find them and helping them make the leap of faith required to move forward. Finally, you'll find the imperative of bringing the public along and reassuring parents. You won't get far unless you attend to both your internal and your external publics. This section takes up these issues.

A. Nature of the Change Process

Gene E. Hall
Richard C. Wallace, Jr.

We know enough now about the change process from repeated observations that some major themes, indeed principles of change, can be established. We can state with some confidence that these principles will hold true in all cases. You as a superintendent can count on these things. And that's important, because often the only thing that seems to hold true in the midst of change is that all hell is breaking loose. It may be. But these are the principles with which you can ride out the heat. For those of you who like to see these things whole, the twelve principles are laid out succinctly in the following:

Principles of Change

1. Change is a process, not an event.

2. There are significant differences between what's involved in developing an innovation and implementing it.

3. An organization does not change until the individuals within it change.

4. Innovations come in different sizes.

5. Interventions are the actions and events that are key to the success of the change process.

6. Although both top-down and bottom-up approaches can work, a horizontal perspective is best.

7. Administrator leadership is essential to long-term and successful change.

8. Mandates can work.

9. The school is the primary unit for change.

10. Facilitating change is a team effort.

11. Appropriate interventions reduce the challenges of change.

12. The context of the school influences the process of change.

SOURCE: *Implementing Change: Patterns, Principles, and Potholes,* by Gene E. Hall and Shirley M. Hord (Boston: Allyn and Bacon, 2001).

We may not need to state the obvious, but here it is anyway. Each principle is not mutually exclusive. At first reading, some may seem inconsistent with others. That's because they address selected aspects of the change process—and the principles change as the process develops. And it should be obvious, too, that change is highly complex, multifaceted, and dynamic. If it weren't so complicated, you wouldn't have so much fun with it.

> *It is often noted that the implementation of change itself is the Achilles' Heel of educational improvements. A useful book that puts legs under reforms is Gene E. Hall and Shirley M. Hord's* Implementing Change: Patterns, Principles, and Potholes *(Boston: Allyn and Bacon, 2001).*

Change Principle 1: Change is a process, not an event. This should be obvious. Change isn't accomplished by having some leader make an announcement, or the district requiring some drive-by professional development. Change isn't even the implementation of a new curriculum. Instead, change is a process through which people and organizations move as they gradually come to *understand, and become skilled and competent, in the use of new ways.* If change is an event, implementation is tactical in nature. That explains why you may hear your assistant complain at a meeting: "What do you mean, they need more training? We bought them the books. Can't they read?"

You need to think about change over the long haul as process, not as a press release in the short run or an event.

Change Principle 2: Developing and implementing an innovation are different things. Think about it, and this should be obvious too. But it's amazing how many people don't get it. Development and implementation are different sides of the same coin. But whereas development involves everything required to create the innovation, implementation involves everything needed to establish the innovation onsite. On the development side, we find this to be a high-profile activity, are generous with the time allotted to it, and take a large and visionary perspective because, as developers, we are alert and savvy, and we possess the political skills required to understand timing and public relations. Implementation is almost the reverse. There's little glory, it takes time, people often lack patience, and it requires a sort of technical and clinical skill allied to patience, humor, and creativity.

What does that have to do with you as a superintendent? Here's just one possibility: understand that the style of the facilitator required on each side of this equation is different. It's unlikely your developer can implement his or her innovation—or is even very much interested in doing so.

Change Principle 3: An organization does not change until individuals within it do. Ah, there's the rub! Successful change begins and ends with human beings. An entire organization does not change until every individual within it changes. Some people will grasp the change immediately (and buy into it). Others will need additional time. And a few will avoid the change for a very long time.

But everyone sooner or later has to get on board. There's a lot of truth to the old adage about one bad apple spoiling the barrel. The cynic in the faculty lounge is terribly important. Any opposition is important. It has to be dealt with and respected, not ignored in the hope it will go away.

See the Hall Innovation Category Scale (HiC) (Section 3B), an educational Richter Scale for measuring your environment from background noise to educational earthquake.

Change Principle 4: Innovations come in different sizes. Innovations can be products (computers, texts, or assessment techniques) or processes (constructivist teaching, principles of self-esteem in the classroom). Depending on their complexity, innovations can require more resources and more time. A new edition of a standard curriculum text can be implemented routinely. That's a small-scale innovation. But a new reading curriculum, with entirely new texts, complex variations in how material is introduced and sequenced, and the need for broad teacher training is a large-scale innovation. It's much harder to implement. Now think about something like systemic reform—we're talking about mega-change here, and you shouldn't underestimate what's required to implement it.

Change Principle 5: Interventions are the actions and events that are key to the success of the change process. Leaders tend to be consumed with the innovation and its use. They often don't think of the *interventions,* the actions that they and others take to influence the process. Everyone thinks of training as an important intervention. And it is. But equally important are the "one-legged interviews" you can conduct about the innovation and how it's developing. If you run into a teacher between classes as you leave a school, you can ignore him or her or chat briefly. (Most teachers have more important things to do than waste their time talking with us. So it's quick. That's why it's "one-legged," because most of us can't stand on one leg for long.) In chatting, therefore, you've already intervened in this teacher's life.

Now let's assume you use that chat to ask how the new reading curriculum is going in the teacher's class. Any problems he has with it? Any things she likes about it? Asked as a way of obtaining information—and with a genuine interest in the response—you have a good chance of cementing that teacher's commitment to the innovation.

Change Principle 6: Top-down and bottom-up are fine, but horizontal is best. Everyone understands the hierarchy of a bureaucracy. In schools, you, as superintendent, are on top and teachers and custodians are on the bottom. You might not agree with this, but the public would view the state superintendent as an even superior person, with state legislators and congressional figures on a plane too rarified for most to comprehend. Top-down and bottom-up change can each work, but both are tough. Mandates from on high get horribly mangled by the time they reach the classroom, and most attempts at bottom-up change collapse because the top cannot bear to relinquish control. Think of a horizontal system instead. At the federal, state, district, school, and classroom levels, everyone is on an equal plane. That's the way to encourage change.

Two reports from the Center for the Study of Teaching and Policy, University of Washington, can help principals as they work with teachers—Leading for Learning Sourcebook: Concepts and Examples *and* Leading for Learning: Reflective Tools for School and District Leaders. *These materials can be obtained at* www.ctpweb.org.

When horizontal change is encouraged, it depends on everyone doing his or her own job, trusting that everyone else will do their job as well. Trust is the key to this—the commodity in shortest supply in the school reform discussion.

Change Principle 7: Administrator leadership is essential to long-term change success. If you as superintendent are like most people in education, you tend to genuflect when someone advocates bottom-up change on the grounds that those nearest the action have the best ideas about how to accomplish change. It might not make sense for you to believe that (given your position); still, as Ralph Waldo Emerson once said, "A foolish consistency is the hobgoblin of little minds." Think big. Both leadership and grassroots support is needed for change. Without long-term support from leaders and authority figures, most innovations wither up and die.

This principle is a corollary of Principle 6. Everyone has to do his or her job, and you as a leader have to do yours. One of your tasks as a leader of innovation is to institutionalize the innovation so that it survives when the developers leave—and when you leave too.

Change Principle 8: Mandates can work. No progressive educator wants to believe this for a second. What? Mandates (inevitably *mandates from on high*) work? Oh, yes. They can and do. Not always, but often enough that they cannot be ignored. A mandate is a strategy with a clear priority and the expectation that it will be implemented. Ending Jim Crow schools in the South was a mandate. So too was compensatory education. No one would deny that both were implemented and, although perhaps neither achieved the results it sought, both changed schooling in America more than any innovation developed by the nation's think tanks or academic institutions.

For the most part, mandates get a bad name because they're announced without being backed up with the supports and other innovations needed to make them succeed.

Change Principle 9: The school is the primary unit for change. The key organizational unit for making change is the school. The school's staff and its leaders will make you or break you on any change, whether started from within or without. Obviously the school is not an island. It can do a lot by itself, but it also needs to move in concert with and be supported by the other components of the system.

No single school is likely to have all the expertise it needs to implement the change you request, demand, or implore of it. Once you understand that the school is the primary unit for change, you should also understand why you need to help support it as it goes about making the change.

Change Principle 10: Facilitating change is a team effort. In some ways, this is simply an elaboration of Principles 6, 7, 8, and 9. Change takes leadership. It takes facilitators. It takes principals and teachers. It takes a team.

Understand this: everyone is in this boat together. Whether they pull together, or bail together, or assign some to pull while others bail, getting the boat safely to harbor requires the best efforts of the entire crew.

Change Principle 11: Appropriate interventions reduce the challenges of change. We'll get to this later with "leaps of faith," but for now understand that hard-nosed reformers are wrong when they assert (on the basis of opinion and no evidence) that change is painful and the pain must be endured. Maybe a masochist would pursue change under those conditions, but it's hard to think of anyone else attracted to the idea. Pain is not necessarily the lot of you and your colleagues involved in change. Properly facilitated, *change can be fun.* It should be rewarding and energizing for you, your staff, your teachers, your children, and your parents.

Change Principle 12: The context of the school influences the process of change. Obviously the physical features of the school and the people in it (along with their attitudes, beliefs, and values) can have an important influence on your organization's change efforts. Yet interestingly, a consensus is developing among scholars of schools and corporations about organizational culture and how it relates to the successful implementation of change. When the staff (or corporate officials) collectively reflects with students (or employees) on its work, both staff and officials get a better understanding of what *they* must do to help their students (and employees) become more successful.

In the corporate sector, this requires a shared and supportive leadership. And that's what's required in schools, too.

B. The Hall Innovation Category (HiC) Scale

Gene E. Hall

Do you need help gauging where you are in your change process? The Hall Innovation Category (HiC) Scale, shown in Table 6.4, lets you get a handle on how far along you are and how many people are on board.

Table 6.4   The Hall Innovation Category (HiC) Scale

Level	Name	Example
	Talking	
0	Cruise Control	Teacher in same classroom for many years
1	Whisper	Commission reports
2	Tell	New rules and more regulation of old practices
3	Yell	Prescriptive policy mandates
	Tinkering	
4	Shake	Revise curriculum
5	Rattle	Change principal
6	Roll	Change teacher's classroom
	Transforming	
7	Redesign	Integrated curriculum
8	Restructure	Differentiated staffing
9	Mutation	Changing role of school board
10	Reconstitution	Local constitutional convention

C. The Leap of Faith

James Harvey

Gene Hall describes the gap separating where we are in education today and the Promised Land as a yawning chasm. Under most policy prescriptions, a "leap of faith" is required to get

Figure 6.2   Leap of Faith

SOURCE: *Implementing Change: Patterns, Principles, and Pothole,* by Gene H. Hall and Shirley M. Hord (Boston: Allyn and Bacon, 2001).

from what are described as today's ugly realities to tomorrow's beautiful possibilities (see Figure 6.2). What explains the resistance to most school reforms is the practical reality that most people aren't willing to make that leap of faith. They may like you. They may even think you're a wonderful person. And if you want to leap out over that chasm and crash and burn, you will make the leap with their best wishes. But only a few will be inclined to jump off the cliff with you. The next few sections will help you bridge this chasm.

D. Stages of Concern

Gene T. Hall
James Harvey

Researchers at the RAND Corporation, a government-sponsored think tank, sometimes talk about the "17% solution" in education. By that they mean that no matter what innovation is proposed, somewhere around 17% of all teachers will sign up, practically right away.

That's useful information to you, as a superintendent. It almost doesn't matter what you suggest—school-site budgeting, standards and assessment, reading programs, a new approach to math—17% of teachers will buy in immediately, some because they want to be cooperative and others because they are firmly convinced that the schools in which they teach can be improved. You can count on enthusiastic support right away. Close to one-fifth of your teaching staff will make the leap of faith with you.

Still, don't mistake the approbation from the people who talk to you for general approval of your plans. Even with 17% of the teachers on your side, 83% are unaccounted for. Some of these people are disinterested. Others haven't thought about it and don't know much. Some are anxious about what the changes will mean for them. Still others aren't convinced that what you are proposing is the best thing for the children who appear in their classrooms every day. And some, of course, reflexively dig in to oppose any change in the existing order of things. Your challenge becomes how to bring the other 83% along. How do you get them to join you in the leap of faith?

Actually, you don't. That won't work. It's unlikely that these people will make the leap. What you have to do is span the chasm for them—provide a bridge across the gap so that leaping is unnecessary.

First, some information about what motivates people in the face of change and what kinds of resistance you might expect. In 1970, Frances Fuller at the University of Texas at Austin found that 97 out of 100 students in her educational psychology course rated her course as "irrelevant" or a "waste of time." Faced with these findings, most of us would look for a hole in which to hide our mortification and feelings of inadequacy. Not Fuller. To her, the interesting question was: "What turned on those three smart students?" (All, no doubt, superior people of refinement and good judgment.)

For more information on this study about stages of concern, see Frances F. Fuller, Personalized Education for Teachers: An Introduction for Teacher Educators *(Austin: University of Texas, Research and Development Center for Teacher Education, 1970).*

This was a breakthrough question. It turned out that each of the three students had prior experience with children—either as parents or teachers of a church class. So they enjoyed some background and experience with which to understand and appreciate an introductory course on educational psychology. To them it was neither "irrelevant" nor a "waste of time" but bore directly on their experience and was a useful way to spend time on a subject in which they were already engaged. Establishing the hypothesis that *concerns* are a function of experience, Fuller conducted an in-depth study of student teachers. She settled on three stages of concern among student teachers:

- *Self-concerns* do not revolve around teaching or learning, but more around personal issues. ("Can I get a ticket to the U2 concert?") Beginning teachers with such self-concerns will worry about where to park their car.

- *Task concerns* show up after students have entered student teaching. Now teaching enters the picture. ("I didn't expect to spend all night grading papers.") The issues are still largely teacher oriented, not student centered.

- *Impact concerns* are the ultimate goal. Here student teachers (and teachers and administrators, and even you as superintendent) begin to focus on what is happening with students and how to improve student results. Now the comments center on: "My kids understand what I'm trying to do." Or, "I'm taking Saturday's workshop on involving the parents of special needs kids, because I think that's a win-win situation for everyone."

In her research, Fuller found that more than two-thirds of the concerns of preservice teachers were in the self and task areas, while two-thirds of the concerns of experienced teachers were in the task and impact areas.

Building on this foundation, University of Texas at Austin researchers have developed a seven-stage typology of "Stages of Concern." From the lowest levels of awareness to the highest levels of concern, these stages are outlined in the following:

Seven Stages of Concern

0. *Awareness.* Little concern about or involvement with the innovation.

Self Concerns

1. *Informational.* A general awareness of the innovation and interest in learning more about it. These people seem unworried about themselves in relation to the innovation. They are interested in substantive aspects of the change, such as general characteristics, effects, and requirements for use.

2. *Personal.* Individuals are uncertain about the demands of the innovation or inadequacy to meet those demands. Anxiety exists about role in innovation, including relation to the organization's reward structure and decision making. Financial and status implications of the innovation for self and colleagues may be an issue.

Task Concerns

3. *Management.* Attention focused on processes and tasks of using the innovation and the best use of information and resources. Issues related to efficiency, organizing, managing, scheduling, and time demands are at the forefront.

Impact Concerns

4. *Consequence.* Attention is directed at impact of information on immediate clients or students. Outward-looking concern; the focus is on relevance of innovation for students before teachers, evaluation of outcome related to performance and student competencies, and changes needed to increase student success.

5. *Collaboration.* The focus is on coordination and cooperation with others regarding use of the innovation.

6. *Refocusing.* The focus is on exploring the more universal benefits of the innovation, including the possibility of major changes or replacement with a more powerful alternative. Individuals have definite ideas about the existing form of the innovation and about alternatives that might be proposed.

SOURCE: *Implementing Change: Patterns, Principles, and Potholes,* by Gene H. Hall and Shirley M. Hord (Boston: Allyn and Bacon, 2001).

Now, here's what you need to understand. Although as a superintendent you may expect most of your staff to support you because they are already lined up in stages 4, 5, and 6, many of them will still be stuck in stages 0 through 3.

That is, you have a bit of a dilemma before you. You expect your teachers and administrators to make the leap of faith with you, because they are already considering consequences for their students and entertaining ideas about modes of collaboration and how to refocus and improve your plans. The reality is that many of your people are actually disinterested or only mildly curious about what you propose, and some of them are quite worried, if not frightened, by it.

To get them to make the leap of faith, you are going to have to meet them on their own ground. In fact, except for the people already part of the "17% solution" (probably at levels 5 and 6), most of your staff won't make a leap at all. You're going to have to build bridges (see Section 3E) to get them from where they are in today's ugly reality to where you want them to be in tomorrow's beautiful possibility.

E. Bridging the Leap of Faith

Gene T. Hall
James Harvey

If you want people to make the leap of faith, you will have to span the chasm for them. The best way to bridge the gap is to start where your people are and lead them from there (see Figure 6.3).

Figure 6.3   Bridging the Gap

Today's
Ugly
Reality

Tomorrow's
Beautiful
Possibility

6 - Refocuses and explores innovation to make it more powerful. Needs to be cheered.

5 - Collaborative, interested in cooperation.   Needs support and encouragement.

4 - Interested in impact on students.   Needs data on performance and competencies.

3 - Worried about processes/tasks.   Needs information on efficiency, management, time demands.

2 - Concerned, anxious about innovation.   Needs financial and status information.

1 - General awareness of innovation.   Needs substantive information.

0 - Little awareness of innovation.   Needs general information.

4. Questions for Reflective Practice

Here are some key questions for reflection and for consideration as you develop your principals.

What do you expect principals to know about the principles of learning? Have you identified the specific responsibilities principals have for student learning? Have your actions established student learning as the main priority of the school district?

Do you know how much time principals spend on activities related to student learning? Are principals' performance appraisals related to student learning?

Where do you stand on the question of whether intelligence is inherited, compensated for by hard work, or "socialized"? What about your teachers and administrators?

How well do you support your principals? Take each of the 10 tasks that were identified as part of your role in supporting principals in this part and rate yourself on those tasks. Give yourself two points if you're on target, one if you're making some progress, and zero if you've ignored the task. Are you happy with your score?

How well does your administrative team support principals? Think about your "cabinet" or whatever you call your top administrators. Go through the same assessment with the team. How happy are you with these results?

Does the change process described here make sense to you? Or do you think change can be imposed? How do your principals view change? Have you engaged principals in conversations about the change process?

Let's assume you're ready to make the leap of faith. How many people will leap with you? Have you sympathetically thought about the concerns they might have, so that you can work to address those concerns?

Are you confident that you have a good strategy for engaging parents and the public about student learning? Are you able to state succinctly what you hope the students in your district will know and be able to do? Are principals and teachers able to do the same thing? What about parents? Would the answers support each other or conflict?

Part VII
Collaborating
With Your
Allies

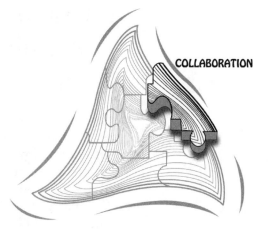

COLLABORATION

C oncerned parents and others across the United States were dismayed to read, in October 2003, about the ordeal a two-year-old Florida child had endured. The girl was forced to fend for herself for nearly three weeks while her mother spent time in jail for assault and petty theft.

Child neglect . . . juvenile violence . . . breakdowns in child protective services . . . inadequate foster-care systems . . . homelessness . . . lack of access to preventive health care . . . all of these things influence your ability to do your job. They are not your responsibility, but increasingly these challenges spill over onto your campuses.

This part of *The Superintendent's Fieldbook* discusses the need for collaborative structures with other government agencies, describes how to build them, and shares with you the stories of some successful collaborations around early care and education.

Why should you worry about any of this? Because children from very troubled backgrounds are showing up in your classrooms, and you cannot educate them effectively unless your community addresses their needs.

1. Orientation: What Is Collaboration?

James Harvey

Why aren't the children in your community learning more? Why are so many young people in trouble in so many different ways—experimenting with drugs and alcohol, dropping out, becoming parents while scarcely more than children themselves, or running afoul of the juvenile justice system?

A big part of the answer to these questions is that many American families are in trouble. They are in trouble everywhere, but in many inner cities they are in crisis. Another part of the answer is less obvious but equally significant: the service delivery system itself is shattered. The human service delivery system has become so fragmented and diffuse, cumbersome, inefficient, and underfunded, that it's hard to make it work. It often fails to meet the needs for which it was designed. Much of the good work you struggle with in your schools can be undone in an hour by a careless caseworker reviewing a family file or a parent finding himself suddenly cut off from access to health care and medicine. Inevitably, failures in these other systems wind up creating problems in your schools.

What Is Collaboration?

Collaboration is more than cooperation. Cooperation implies agencies sharing information with other units of government. Collaboration implies agencies working together. It is an organized and conscious effort to break down the silo walls separating different agencies serving families. Collaboration is intended to make sure that children don't fall between the cracks and that vulnerable families receive—efficiently and with dignity—the services they need. Typically the services involve maternal and child health care, child welfare and protection, parental employment and income support, housing, early care and education, elementary and secondary education, job training and youth employment, and delinquency and juvenile justice.

That's an awfully broad area of responsibility. You may specialize in one particular aspect of it, but you need some familiarity with it all. Outside the safety of school walls, a lot of young people are in danger of sinking. The difficult and tedious work of collaboration may be the best lifeline you can throw them.

This section of the fieldbook introduces you to the concepts of collaboration, explores what is required to make it work, and describes successful collaborative models around early care and education.

2. What Does Collaboration Require?

Just as leading learning demands new images and mental models from you, so too does collaboration require a profound conceptual shift. This section defines that conceptual shift and suggests that thinking of young people's assets instead of their deficits may be a key to improving service delivery to vulnerable families.

A. Build Boats, Not Houses

James Harvey

"When most of us start thinking about building new institutional structures," a former Reagan administration official told us, "we unconsciously think the way a home-builder does—with separate functional structures for different needs." But, said Martin Gerry, once deputy secretary of the U.S. Department of Health and Human Services, "When you think about human services, you need to think about building boats, not houses. If you are building a house and you leave a plank out, the house is basically all right. But if you leave a plank out of a boat, it sinks." "Build boats, not houses" is Gerry's advice. That is, think comprehensively and systematically about government systems, not narrowly and haphazardly about government programs.

It has been estimated that the United States spends more than $500 billion annually on children's services, nearly one-quarter of which (22%) is lost in administration.

The financial consequences of the walls separating the many government programs are incredible. One consequence of these walls and program silos is that most educators are unaware of other funding possibilities and rarely know how to take advantage of them. State programs, like most federal programs, are not programs at all but funding streams, administered for the most part outside the state and local education establishment. Most school systems and administrators do not know how to access these monies. Meanwhile, welfare reform and growing numbers of single-parent and two-income families promise to exert increasing demand on child care resources. You need to think about how to help your community deal with these challenges.

At the heart of the conceptual shift discussed at the outset of this section is the idea of thinking and acting systemically. It involves

Kentucky set the pace with integrated services around schools. As part of the 1990 Kentucky Education Reform Act, the state established 375 FRYSCES (Family Resource Youth Service Centers) around the state. These provide services in most of Kentucky's 1,000 low-income schools. Operating on an average annual grant of $60,000, they hire their own directors, most of whom are not educators. FRYSCES have to provide child care and they are permitted to charge for their services. Most also provide parental education for new and expectant parents, parent-child education and counseling, and health services. See Peter Schrag, Final Test: The Battle for Adequacy in America's Schools (New York: The New Press, 2003).

moving from isolated, individual services to comprehensive and coordinated efforts on behalf of families with their many different needs. It requires moving from tightly defined, often rigid, programs and categorical funding to efforts that are much more flexible and provide greater discretion at the local level. It means that leaders consciously think about, and take advantage of, the connections and relationships between and among different systems in order to concentrate public programs for the greatest effect. Finally, it depends on planning and evaluation as effective tools for improving system operations in place of ad hoc efforts put in place with good intentions while hoping for the best.

Adopt Collaboration as a Way of Life

Collaboration is much more than just cooperation. Collaboration implies shared budgets; joint accountability for results; integrated professional-development activities; and the development of new relationships across branches of government, among government agencies, and between state and local units of government. It has both vertical and horizontal dimensions. The most effective collaboration is grounded in this question: "What can we together do for the people we are supposed to serve?"

Collaboration is not a panacea. It is a difficult, often painful and time-consuming process that can delay decision making. Time spent developing trust and cooperation at the outset, however, can be made up many times over later, down the line, in more effective and efficient delivery of services. Still, the potential benefits and savings are impressive. According to one of the most comprehensive cost-benefit evaluations of early learning (High/Scope Perry Preschool Study; see Section 3C):

- Preventing low birth weight in babies can be accomplished in one year for almost nothing and is likely to save as much as $100,000 in intensive neonatal services for each low-birth-weight infant.

- It is likely to take five years to reduce community reliance on foster care—but the long-term savings are huge, since the correlation between foster care in one's early years and involvement in the criminal justice system later is extremely high.

- It will probably take 10 to 15 years to see the full savings from delaying the arrival of a second child to a young woman who bears her first at the age of 16. But if the community can help delay that second arrival until the woman becomes 21, it is likely to save as much as $500,000 in public assistance and medical expenses.

The true benefits of these programs to society are like the true costs—they don't appear until years later.

B. A New Way of Thinking

James Harvey

Whatever the cause or causes, over the years fragmented policy making at the state and local levels has led to fragmented policy and programs. Most states now have many disconnected program and funding streams with a cumulative impact that is much less powerful than it should be. The results are predictable. During a program review some years ago, for example, Florida officials identified one family that, in a single 30-month period, experienced

- 40 referrals to different community providers
- 17 separate evaluations
- 13 different case managers
- 10 independent treatment plans, including three family support plans, a foster care plan, and a protective services plan

A similar tale was recounted by a Pennsylvania woman. Over several weeks, she had to endure 55 different interviews with social workers from 30 different agencies, all demanding a separate case history that they refused to share with each other because of concerns about confidentiality. Recalling her efforts to maintain a consistent account for each of these caseworkers, the woman commented: "You know, you have to be smart in Philadelphia to be poor."

A New Way of Thinking

To change these dynamics, what is required is a new way of thinking about how social systems function. Although the philosophical basis for change is sometimes lost in the midst of battles about turf and budgets, a clear need exists to develop new mental models for agency collaboration. We need to improve our understanding of what lies beneath the surface of the iceberg of human service delivery failure.

It is increasingly clear that a major reorientation of policy thinking is required to improve the delivery of education and human services. In the main, the shift encourages state and local agencies and personnel to become more entrepreneurial, active, and flexible (see Table 7.1).

According to one former Reagan administration official, our approach to correcting social problems is off-kilter. Says Martin Gerry, "We believe if we can improve education a bit, things will be a little better. We can reform incrementally, by addition. That is absolutely not true. The system is multiplicative, not additive, so that if any of the factors is zero, the product is zero. No matter how good the education provided to a youngster on crack, that young person will not learn. We can say the same thing about child abuse and neglect. These traumas are so severe they stunt learning."

C. Picturing a New Way of Thinking

Beverly Parsons
Sharon Brumbaugh

Table 7.1 maps out how thinking about service delivery is evolving. State officials are being asked to shift from a model that emphasizes crisis intervention, state direction, and the ad hoc delivery of discrete, isolated (and largely undocumented) services to one that focuses on prevention, cooperation, and coordination and that is locally driven, results-oriented, and grounded in data.

Table 7.1   Elements of a New Way of Thinking About Service Delivery

From		To
Crisis intervention	⟶	Preventing, recognizing, and developing the capabilities of youth
Little attention to documenting the impact of changes	⟶	Documentation of changes in results for children, youth, and families
Isolated services	⟶	Coordinated services for children and families with multiple needs
Public assistance	⟶	Emphases on workforce, community, and economic development
State decisions	⟶	State works with communities as equal partners
State directives	⟶	Emphasis on empowering communities to identify needs and design systems to meet community-specific needs
Defined programs	⟶	Broad initiatives designed to provide flexibility at local level
Activities detached from results	⟶	Results-oriented decision making and budgeting
Categorized funds	⟶	Decategorization and flexibility of state and federal funds

SOURCE: *The Policymakers Program: The First Five Years* (St. Louis: The Danforth Foundation, 1999).

D. Engage the Public in Terms It Can Understand

Beverly Parsons
Sharon Brumbaugh
James Harvey

"I was not always a good mother," a poor, single parent of three children (aged 3, 8, and 12) told a roomful of state legislators a few years ago. With impressive self-possession, she described her family's history to a roomful of strangers. "Once, I lost custody of my children. I lost more than custody; I came to understand I had lost a part of my life."

In the face of such experiences, routine professional and bureaucratic language is woefully inadequate. Phrases that flow effortlessly off the tongue at professional meetings—creating developmentally appropriate curriculum . . . instituting staff development oriented around the learning styles of minority children . . . reaching out for multicultural curriculum, while monitoring and evaluating progress . . . building a collaborative planning team for coordinated services—scarcely begin to connect with such human pain.

Fortunately, this young woman got her life back together, with the help of a comprehensive array of programs for child care, transportation, drug abuse treatment, and job counseling and referral. One of the most important parts of that effort was made up of strong, clear communications, both within and across agencies and between government agencies and the public. Engaging the public on its own terms—communications as "public engagement"—is vital to the service reform agenda. It can become a method of involving the public in designing system change.

According to nationally known public opinion analyst Daniel Yankelovich, founder of the Public Agenda Foundation, the process by which the public comes to judgment on difficult public issues is complicated and lengthy. The length and complexity of the process must be respected by leaders who want to bring about long-lasting, deep-rooted, comprehensive system change. The conventional communications model engages an uninformed public through a one-way process emphasizing single-step transmission of simple information. It is time to move from that point of view to "public engagement," a new, two-way model that emphasizes ongoing dialogue about important values while respecting the public's expertise in certain areas.

See Part VIII for more detail on public engagement as it relates specifically to school agendas.

See "The Rainmakers," Chapter XVI of Peter Senge, Nelda Cambron-McCabe, Timothy Lucas, Bryan Smith, Janis Dutton, and Art Kleiner, Schools That Learn: A Fifth Discipline Fieldbook for Educators, Parents, and Everyone Who Cares About Education (New York: Doubleday, 2000), for a detailed account of how the Rainmakers program developed at Feinberg-Fisher.

Genuine engagement with the public can lead public agencies into new and different territory. It is unlikely, for example, that Florida International University (FIU) would have gone into the lice-eradication business on behalf of the parents at Feinberg-Fisher Elementary School in South Miami if it had not engaged in a dialogue with local parents. School leaders complained that parents were uninvolved and disengaged—uninterested in attending school meetings.

What FIU learned was that parents wanted to be consulted. A group of parents started what eventually became known as the Rainmakers program, a parent-run effort to bring the community's concerns to the schools. The first thing the program turned to was the issue of head lice, a problem in every school in the country, but a virtual infestation at Feinberg-Fisher. Through the "LiceBusters" program, lice became old news at Feinberg-Fisher.

Vermont took the public-engagement approach statewide, according to Con Hogan, former state human services director (and a 2002 candidate for Vermont governor). State officials began a "road show" that visited every county in the state and practically every significant community to preach the benefits of agency collaboration and to receive community advice on how to proceed.

Engage Communities Around Solutions, Not Needs

Needs analysis is fine as far as it goes, according to consultants Sharon Edwards and Susan Philliber, who created a new "Community Engagement Process" precisely to address the gap between agency language and public needs. But poor children need everything. As superintendent, you may be committed to the idea of No Child Left Behind. The vision sounds wonderful. But traditional needs analysis may be insufficient because it simply tells you what should be there, not what is there or whether the clients are attracted to it or are able to take advantage of it.

What developed into the Community Engagement Process (CEP) began with that simple insight. Working in Savannah, Georgia, where teenage pregnancy was a huge problem, Edwards and Philliber realized that services were available for young people who did not take advantage of them. "So we started sending youngsters in for services and simply asking them what happened and how they reacted to how they were treated," reports Philliber.

They discovered something fascinating. Most of the time, professionals decide what to do, based on what they think will work. Community input? Who needs it? Philliber concluded that communities are distinct. She and Edwards decided that more needs assessments were not required. What was needed were "solutions assessments."

Work With Local People

Community mapping is a distinct process, according to these experts. They actually sit around a table with parents and other residents to define problems. Then these local people help select local data-collection assistants. Philliber and Edwards train the data collectors to go out and directly administer the questionnaire. The questionnaire is not something developed and administered researcher to researcher—it is a neighbor-to-neighbor proposition.

"Dissemination is a critical result of the process," according to Edwards. "Most people distrust data imposed on them by experts or interpreted for them by experts. But here we have data actually developed and interpreted by neighbors. That makes it very hard for people to say what they often say to researchers, 'That's not true in my experience.'"

"Many professional researchers and analysts would *never* do what we are doing," said Philliber without apology. "We involve real people. Some of them abuse drugs. Some may have records. Some may barely be able to read. We need both men and women on these teams—and we need diverse interviewers in terms of language and age. We don't just want women talking to women or old men sharing war stories with old men."

The CEP process consists of three phases: (1) define the community; (2) map it; and (3) disseminate information. (See Section 3H for a detailed account of the value of this process in St. Martin Parish, Louisiana.)

Philliber and Edwards deploy their teams first thing in the morning and bring them back in to have lunch and collect their interview sheets. They discovered quickly that food is an important part of the process. Meals help break the ice and cheer the local leaders on. "Some interviewers bring in the entire family for breakfast with us!" marvels Edwards.

Despite their modest technical backgrounds, interviewers become very worried about the quality of their data. As they collect their information and fret about its adequacy, they begin to bond with each other as a team, reports Edwards. Communities vary, and the strategies have to vary. "In some places, the best time to find people at home is in the evenings or on Saturday or Sunday. In others, we find the exact reverse. Whatever we have to do, we do—and what happens is fascinating," Edwards says. What they have put in place in small areas, perhaps a few city blocks square, are 500 conversations about what the community wants for its children. "The interviewers are seen as advocates, and the interviewees become advocates," notes Edwards.

"It is amazing what people will tell you when they trust you," says Philliber, "even in a highly charged area such as teenage sexuality." There is normally a lot of denial about this topic on the part of parents—and parents become much more concerned about this set of issues when their children pass the age of 10. "But people will tell you anything if they understand who wants to know, why you want it, and whether or not you are trustworthy," says Philliber. To put the last point a different way—respondents unconsciously ask themselves, "What will this cost if you betray me?"

"Whatever the topic—early childhood education, school reform, or teenage pregnancy—we have never encountered a community that did not learn something surprising about itself," notes Philliber. "And the interviewing teams become budding leaders in the community. In one of our communities, the team we left behind set itself up in business to do all interviews and polling in the neighborhood."

Sharon Edwards sums it up with a challenge to ask the right questions. "When this process ends, you will have answers to a lot of questions, but more important, you'll have a better set of questions. Most of the questions we are asking today are the wrong questions. We are trying to assess needs, when we should be assessing what the community thinks the solutions ought to be."

In short, engage your local communities in ways that they will understand, ideally through their own neighbors.

E. Tool: Key Elements of Collaboration

Beverly Parsons
Sharon Brumbaugh

Several elements seem to be required to make collaboration work. Here's an action checklist:

A Checklist of Key Elements

Start with numbers. You need to build data into your plans to monitor the condition of children and families, and you need to tie data to specific benchmarks of achievement.

Think systems, not programs. Build boats, not houses.

Adopt collaboration as a way of life. Collaboration implies shared budgets, joint accountability, integrated professional development activities, and the creation of new vertical and horizontal relations with other government agencies.

Engage the public on its own terms. Don't give the public governmentspeak. Develop strong, clear, two-way communications strategies.

Develop capacity. Horizontal linkages with your agency peers are one thing. Vertical linkages up and down your different agencies are something else again, and much harder.

Create a critical mass of people who care. You have to find the right people and invest in them. When you move on, you want this new way of thinking to survive.

Beg, borrow, and steal effective ideas. Everything in public life is in the public domain. You're free to steal it. Do so shamelessly if you see something working.

Follow the money. Talk about system reform is cheap and easy. Make sure that real budget resources are put behind the rhetoric.

Insist on results. This is tough work. If you're going to get into it, you have to be serious. Insist on results, assess progress, and report to the public.

Give ownership away. There's truth to the axiom that if we don't care who gets the credit, there's no limit to what we can accomplish. Give the credit away, and it will all come back to you.

Model the behavior you seek. You can't expect your people to cooperate with other agencies if you refuse to give the time of day to your peers in local government.

Be a practical visionary. Visionaries have to be practical, too. You have to have your feet on the ground. Develop an effective plan that provides some demonstrable results in a year or two.

SOURCE: *The Policymakers Program: The First Five Years* (St. Louis: The Danforth Foundation, 1999).

F. Tool: Identify Core Community Values

Beverly Parsons
Sharon Brumbaugh

Some localities have found it useful to identify core community values as part of community revitalization work. Here's a 10-part process developed by Seattle consultant Sherry Wong.

Identify Stakeholders	Who should participate? List should include formal organizations (e.g., schools, religious groups, businesses) and a diverse group of local residents.
Determine Process	How will stakeholder advice be sought? Determine the process for soliciting input on core values, including guidelines for facilitating discussions.
Establish Timeline	Process without a schedule is counterproductive and potentially endless. Create a timeline for soliciting stakeholder comments.
Locate Responsibility	Who will compile the results? Identify the individual or group responsible for compiling the results.
Agree on Process	Who will define the final list and how? Decide on how the final list of core values will be selected (by whom, using which process, and how many core values), and select the final list.
Communications Plan	How will the list be communicated to the community? Develop a communications plan to introduce core values into all areas of community, using key stakeholders to carry the message.
Encourage Use	Encourage all stakeholders (schools, families, churches, coaches, businesses) to use core values to develop and communicate clear expectations about behavior, as well as consistent and appropriate consequences for meeting (or not meeting) expectations.
Provide Assistance	Help parents, teachers, coaches, service providers, and others apply behavioral standards through training and support.
Identify Barriers	What stands in the way of meeting the values standards? Are such things as neighborhood transience or parental substance abuse blocking progress? Develop and implement plans to overcome barriers.
Celebrate Success	Actively seek out and celebrate examples of youth and adults living the standards in all areas of community life.

SOURCE: *Strong Families in Healthy Communities* (St. Louis: The Danforth Foundation, 2002).

G. Think Assets, Not Deficits

James Harvey

For many years, public school educators have understood that it makes much more sense to concentrate on children's strengths than on their weaknesses. Children can be very resilient. If you as superintendent can help the community tap into the children's assets, you will have much more success.

External Assets

1. *Support,* mostly from adults

2. *Empowerment,* from the community

3. *Boundaries and Expectations,* primarily from family and school.

4. *Constructive Use of Time,* including community youth programs

Internal Assets

5. *Commitment to Learning,* including school engagement and motivation.

6. *Positive Values,* such as compassion, integrity, and civic concern.

7. *Social Competencies,* involving planning and interpersonal and cultural competence.

8. *Positive Identity* in the form of self-esteem and sense of purpose.

SOURCE: The Search Institute, Minneapolis, Minnesota.

In recent years, emerging research from the Search Institute in Minneapolis, based on data involving 10,000 students from grades 6 to 12 in some 213 communities across the United States, has developed a much better picture of essential assets. The Institute has identified 40 internal and external assets that are important to young people as they face the many challenges they experience outside school. Many have to cope with crumbling local social infrastructures, adults who are disengaged from their lives, parents with less time for parenting, and an age-segregated society that denies them access to the wisdom and experience of the elderly.

According to this research, the best predictor of a child's success in later life is whether the child comes from a healthy, strong, supportive family. The second best predictor is bonding with school. Moreover, a combination of assets is much more important than any individual asset. Most people can draw on close to 20 assets as they grow up. The more assets they have, the better their chances of avoiding destructive behaviors. The entire list of assets was described earlier, in Part V; here, we want to remind you that the 40 assets come in eight distinct categories:

Work with your community partners to develop these assets and you will provide a real service to your community. You will find that empowering youth with more assets will reduce the likelihood of their engaging in high-risk behavior involving alcohol, drugs, violence, and sexual activity.

3. Collaboration in the Field: Early Care and Education

Increasingly, K–12 educators are looking at school readiness as a key issue in helping young children meet higher standards. But the worlds of Head Start, preschools, and fee-based day-care are strange and unusual territory for most superintendents. In this section, you are introduced to this strange new world while learning how several superintendents, in very different kinds of districts, used collaboratives designed around early care and education to great effect.

A. Orientation

James Harvey

In December 1971, President Nixon vetoed an early childhood education bill passed by Congress. The legislation threatened to undermine the American family, the president claimed in his veto message. In fact, said syndicated columnist James J. Kilpatrick, it might "Sovietize" American children.

Yet within 15 years, business groups such as the Committee for Economic Development were calling for early childhood programs as an "investment" in the American future. Within

20 years, President George H. W. Bush and the nation's governors had agreed on a national education goal that children should start school "ready to learn." And within 25 years, Congress and President Clinton had cooperated to enact welfare reform legislation requiring single mothers of infants and children to leave the home for work and expanding early childhood programs to ease mothers' transition to work.

Over one generation, in short, attitudes about the need for preschool programs had been almost completely transformed. This part of the fieldbook explores what we know about brain development in infants and young children, and it describes the value of a unique seven-year effort to expand early care and education programs funded by the Danforth Foundation in the 1990s.

B. Where Learning Begins: The Remarkable Human Brain

James Harvey

"The world of education really centers on the human brain and curiosity," asserts John Medina, a molecular biologist, formerly associated with the University of Washington's medical school and now CEO of the Talaris Research Institute in Seattle. New brain research, he believes, has changed our perception of reality and it can change our perceptions of how we should understand learning (and hence teaching).

"The brain is a remarkable instrument," enthuses Medina. Its total power is perhaps six volts; many flashlights have more energy. Yet it sends messages to each toe about 177,000 times a second and oversees a nervous system that could circle the globe 20,000 times over. The word "remarkable" scarcely begins to do it justice. The brain with its six volts is the raw power behind the prodigious development of individuals and society.

Medina likes to point to research on stroke victims and infants. This work is beginning to unlock the brain's secrets. Because some stroke victims can interpret graphics or perhaps vowels, but not text or consonants, it has become clear that different parts of the brain are responsible for perceiving different things. One part of the brain discerns text, another graphics, and still others pick out vowels and consonants. Scientists who have transferred neurons from quails to chicks have created chicks that "trill" like quails. All of this is work at the frontiers of human knowledge. Research on artificial intelligence, for example, opens up the

A popular paragraph making the rounds of the Internet in the summer of 2003 made the point that the human brain imposes meaning on what it sees. It turns out that the correct spelling of words isn't that important to people's understanding of written text. What's important is placing the first and last letters in the correct place. Then, human perception corrects for spelling errors. Here's the paragraph:

Aoccdrnig to a rscheearch at an Elingsh uinervtisy, it deosn't mttaer in waht oredr the ltteers in a wrod are, the olny iprmoetnt tihng is taht frist and lsat ltteer is at the rghit pclae. The rset can be a toatl mses and you can sitll raed it wouthit a porbelm. Tihs is bcuseae we do not raed ervey lteter by it slef but the wrod as a wlohe.

Psychologist Abraham Maslow identified five basic needs that he called a "hierarchy of needs." The most basic needs are physiological, that is, for food, air, and water. Next, people look for safety and security. Once that need is met, human beings desire affiliation and belonging, and they look for supportive relationships. With those fundamental needs taken care of, people's needs become more complicated. First, they seek what Maslow labeled "esteem," that is, respect, both from others (i.e., recognition) and from themselves (i.e., confidence and competence). They want to feel their contributions are appreciated. The highest need of human beings is: self-actualization. All of us want to feel that our contributions are having a significant impact.

possibility of creating a silicon chip capable of human thought because human neurons can be located within it.

Meanwhile, says Medina, "At the cellular level, we're learning how neurons process and use information and how babies learn." At six months, infants know how to categorize sounds; by eight months they can learn to categorize some sounds that they won't be able to categorize if the sound is presented to them at 12 months. "The brain can rewire itself around language between birth and age five," he notes.

Science, reports Medina, has completely turned our understanding of reality on its head. Aristotle thought large objects fell to the ground faster than smaller ones. And it used to be thought that men had fewer ribs than women. We now know that neither of those things is true. "Critical, abstract thinking was a luxury before the twentieth century," says Medina. "It is now an absolute necessity." It is at the top of Abraham Maslow's pyramid of human needs.

We need to worry about Maslow's basic needs for security, food, shelter, and love and attention, says Medina. Curiosity is fragile, yet critical to human development. Curiosity is fragile in your schools as well. As superintendent you need to nourish it.

Early Childhood Learning and Neuroscience

It doesn't require a brain surgeon to figure out that learning and development in the child's earliest years are important. It's an incredible, "sponge-like" age for children, a period when children are curious about everything.

Katherine Bick, an internationally known neurobiologist, echoes Medina. She compares the development of the human brain to something that earlier generations might recall, transforming "Heath Kits" into working radios. "Our parents received this package of parts in the mail, which they assembled," she recalls. "They put the parts together and didn't know if the radio would work until they turned it on." She argues that "a healthy child is primed to learn, and the brain should work when you switch it on." Citing "spectacular" advances in understanding of the brain in the past decade, Bick offers the following insights:

- We are born with all the brain cells we'll ever have. The first great wave of cell creation takes place about six weeks after conception; the second, about 10 weeks later.

- Many more cells are created than survive. In a critical process known as "pruning" (which we might also think of as cell learning), each of 3 billion brain cells makes an average of 15,000 connections with other brain cells, nerve endings, or muscles. Nature expects brain cells that don't make connections to die—and they do.

- Remarkably, half of this pruning is already complete by birth. It proceeds rapidly through age 3; reaches maturity around adolescence; and continues, to some extent, throughout life.

- In the past 15 years, we have identified through PET scans (Positron Emissions Topography involving radio-active material) the centers of the brain that govern hearing, seeing, speaking, generating language, and intentional behavior.

- Likewise, MRI (Magnetic Resonance Imaging) has helped us understand the brain changes involved with learning mathematics and reading in 4-, 6-, and 10-year-olds, as well as the brain centers that govern language, memory, and control of impulsivity in children aged 6 to 10.

The benefit of collaborative services for children is enormous, according to Con Hogan, former human services director in Vermont and a 2002 candidate for governor. "Every dollar spent on the front end getting children off to a good start in life and school reduces Vermont's downstream expenditures by five dollars. All the dollars ploughed into trying to correct problems in young people after they're in trouble are much more expensive. Doesn't it make more sense to get kids off to the right start?"

Studies indicate, reports Bick, that in solving maze problems over four trials, many parts of the brain are used in the first trial, indicating that the brain is trying to use a lot of different problem-solving strategies. By the fourth trial, however, much less of the brain is involved since "improvements in learning efficiency let us become more efficient in using our brains."

What does all of this have to do with educational policy? Everything. We need to pay attention to the "ready phases" for learning; the periods of greatest learning efficiency, by subject, in babies and children. Babies and children are learning machines. "They learn effortlessly when they're ready," reports Bick. Among the ready phases:

- Babies can recognize new and old scenes at four months old; they can understand something about numeracy at 10 months; and, everywhere in the world, they appear to start picking up language by 18 months.

- Children are primed for easy second-language development between the ages of 3 and 5. Every child born in the world is capable of learning every spoken language. If you're wondering why you're having trouble with those Chinese vowels, it's because you passed up the chance to pick them up effortlessly in childhood.

- Although neural wiring is fairly complete by age 5, wiring of the prefrontal lobe (the "executive function" that governs intentionality, planning, and understanding consequences) is not complete until preadolescence. "If you've ever wondered why your young teenager doesn't worry about tomorrow, that's why," smiles Bick.

- About 80% of preschool children are "phonemenologically" aware—they can recognize phonemes (letters and sounds); about 20% can't recognize them and will experience difficulty learning to read—and some of them may never read.

Edwin Zigler, Natia Finn-Stevenson, and Nancy Wilson Hall draw on the latest research and explore its implications for policy development in The First Three Years and Beyond: Brain Development and Social Policy *(New Haven, CT: Yale University Press, 2003).*

- Look-say systems of teaching reading rely on brute-force memory and are probably a pretty inefficient and tiring way for most children to learn. The phoneme approach, on the other hand, is probably pretty efficient. Different interventions are required for different students.

- Preschool children who have difficulty with rhyming games are likely to have trouble with phonemes later in school and may experience reading difficulty.

- Having trouble with music as a child? You may also experience problems with mathematics later on.

The solutions to early learning challenges, stresses Bick, don't lie in Washington or the state capitals. They lie in local communities and day-care centers and schools. And the solutions aren't high tech. They're much simpler than that. They start with good prenatal care. They continue through high-quality child care. And they require paying attention to individual differences in the early school years. Above all, they involve being "loved, cuddled, played with, and read to." In short, they involve the first four foundations of Maslow's hierarchy.

C. The Need and Value of Early Learning Programs

James Harvey

If the United States is to meet the promise it makes to every child—that he or she will have a chance to prosper—a powerful preschool experience, either in the home or elsewhere, is absolutely essential, according to Steven Barnett from the Center for Policy Studies at Rutgers University. It's really that simple. In addition, early learning programs provide big-time returns down the line, says Barnett, an expert on the economic benefits of early care and education.

Drawing on findings from a number of different studies, Barnett presents data demonstrating startling advantages available to children born to professional and upper-income families in the first 36 months of life (see Table 7.2). At the simplest level of verbal stimulation, a child from a professional family receives twice as much verbal attention as a child from a working-class family. The child from an upper-income home receives four times as much verbal attention as a child in a family on public assistance. Upper-income children also obtain a huge head start over their working-class and public-assistance contemporaries in vocabulary, the basic building block of language and learning. Moreover, says Barnett, "Upper-income children receive many more incidents of encouragement than discouragement within their homes, whereas, for children in welfare families, the reverse is true."

Table 7.2   Selected Data on Children's Experiences, by Family, Through 36 Months

Indicator at 36 Months	Child From Professional Family	Child From Working-Class Family	Child From Welfare Family
Cumulative Words Addressed to Child	35,000,000	20,000,000	10,000,000
Child's Cumulative Vocabulary	1,100	750	500
Incidents in Which Adult Encourages Child	500,000	200,000	100,000
Incidents in Which Adult Discourages Child	80,000	100,000	200,000

SOURCE: Betty Hart and Todd R. Risley, *Meaningful Differences in the Everyday Experiences of Young American Children* (Baltimore, MD: Brookes Publishing, 1995).

In short, by the age of 3, the child of affluence has mastered a sophisticated and complex vocabulary and has been led to believe that great things lie ahead. The child of poverty, on the other hand, has mastered barely enough words to get by, accompanied by the implicit message that the future is bleak.

From a policy standpoint, the issue is, can early childhood education do anything about these disparities. They are apparent, after all, long before the child appears in your classrooms, indeed long before many parents have any idea their child has already fallen behind. Barnett's answer is an unqualified "yes." The short-term effects of early childhood education programs are well established, he says. Moreover, "we now have literally dozens of studies demonstrating significant benefits that last through school and are sustained over time in terms of student achievement."

The Benefits of Early Care and Education

Barnett's conclusions are the latest arguments supporting the value of high-quality preschool programs. The High/Scope Perry Preschool Study was the first, a landmark evaluation establishing the human and financial potential of high-quality early childhood education programs.

The Perry Preschool Study involved a longitudinal 30-year follow-up study of 123 African American children—all living in poverty and at risk of school failure—who participated in a comprehensive study of the effectiveness of preschool programs provided to 3- and 4-year-olds during the 1970s.

A problem that society has never fully addressed in both preschool and K–12 education is that we have imposed a template on the diversity in the way children learn, according to the late David Weikert, former president of the High/Scope Foundation. The Perry Preschool program emphasized active learning; a supportive curriculum; assessment by observation; and extensive outreach to parents—including home visits to encourage learning support. The "program group" was made up of 58 children randomly assigned to a preschool program; 65 children who did not participate in the program were included to help determine the program's effects.

For additional information on the High/Scope Perry Preschool research, see Lawrence Schweinhart, H. Barnes, and David Weikert, Significant Benefits: The High/Scope Perry Preschool Study Through Age 27 (Ypsilanti, MI: High/Scope Press, 1993). Further information is available at www.highscope.org.

When these participants were followed through age 27, the results were little less than extraordinary (see Table 7.3). When compared with those who did not participate in the program, participants earned more, were much more likely to have finished high school, and were much less likely to have been arrested several times. Even the proportion owning their own homes favored students who had been in the program. In short, in the areas where positive effects from program participation might be found, graduates displayed them; in the areas where negative effects might be avoided, graduates avoided them. The Perry findings provide robust evidence of the educational, economic, and social value of high-quality preschool programs.

The findings are unambiguous. Children in these programs do better across the board. Because they do better in class, they are less likely to need remedial work. And because they do better in school, they are less likely to drop out or require expensive social services later in life.

Weikert estimated that, for a cost of $12,356 per child on preschool education, society could receive a return of $88,433 in the form of savings on welfare, the criminal justice system, remedial education, and foregone taxes. "This works out to be a public return of $7.16 for every dollar spent," he concluded.

Table 7.3   Key Findings of the High/Scope Perry Preschool Study Through Age 27

Indicator	Program	No Program
Completed 12th Grade		
All	71%	54%
Male	61%	67%
Female	84%	35%
Monthly Earnings		
All	$1,219	$766
Male	$1,368	$830
Female	$1,047	$651
Home Ownership		
All	36%	13%
Male	52%	21%
Female	16%	0%
Married		
All	—	—
Male	26%	26%
Female	40%	8%
Received Social Services		
All	59%	80%
Male	52%	77%
Female	66%	85%
Five or More Arrests		
All	7%	35%
Male	12%	49%
Female	0%	16%

SOURCE: Lawrence Schweinhart, H. Barnes, and David Weikert, *Significant Benefits: The High/Scope Perry Preschool Study Through Age 27* (Ypsilanti, MI: High/Scope Press, 1993).

"The only choice we have is between spending an average of $12,000 on low-income children or spending $88,000 later—we do not have a choice of spending nothing."

The kinds of returns discussed by Barnett and Weikert would generate headlines in the *Wall Street Journal* if reported by a mutual fund, but they have been largely ignored around early childhood programs. Still, it seems as true in early childhood programs as elsewhere: an ounce of prevention is worth a pound of cure.

D. A Seven-District Collaboration Around Early Learning

Nelda Cambron-McCabe
Luvern L. Cunningham

Preschool programs may seem to you, as superintendent, to be an interesting academic matter best handled by state policymakers. You have enough on your plate. Why add this? But the fallout of not engaging this issue affects your job every day. Can you afford to wait for the state to act? You'd be well advised to start agitating for state action. Failing that, you may need to get the ball rolling. Some superintendents have done that. Here are their stories.

Convinced by evidence such as that just presented, the Danforth Forum supported seven districts in a seven-year effort to improve local early care and learning opportunities in their communities. What did these districts look like? Are they broadly representative of American communities? Or so unusual that most American educators can learn little from them? Are they places in which the typical child's success is practically guaranteed? Or are they communities in which families struggle to meet life's necessities?

As the following thumbnail sketches indicate, these districts—Bozeman, Montana; Hartford, Connecticut; Memphis, Tennessee; St. Martin Parish, Louisiana; University City, Missouri; Washoe County, Nevada; and Webster County, West Virginia—are a cross section of America. They are broadly representative of many low- and middle-income communities across the country—urban, rural, and suburban.

Bozeman, Montana

The history of the Bozeman area is the history of the American West. Barely an hour's drive from Three Forks, where Lewis and Clark in 1805 found three rivers coming together to form the headwaters of the Missouri, the railroad town of Bozeman was a terminus of the great cattle drives from Texas in the nineteenth century.

Bozeman's participation in this program produced the first communitywide directory of service agencies in the Bozeman area. It also encouraged a statewide initiative to promote early care and learning.

The Bozeman area is largely a white, low- and low-middle-income community of more than 30,000 residents. Data indicate that about one-half the community (mostly parents of schoolchildren) had incomes under $35,000 per year, including 25% with incomes below $20,000. About nine out of ten are Caucasian, with a Native American population of about 5%, and a minuscule population of African American and Asian residents. Affordable housing has become a genuine problem as wealthy West Coast entrepreneurs and entertainment figures have bid up attractive properties.

Hartford, Connecticut

Contradictions abound in Hartford. Long recognized as a substantial manufacturing center located in a state with one of the highest per capita incomes in the United States, the city itself recently ranked seventh nationally in the percentage of children living in poverty. Hartford's visibility as an eastern economic center and the "insurance capital" of the nation obscures a population that is becoming younger, poorer, and increasingly minority.

With a population of about 140,000, Hartford is culturally diverse with 17 distinct neighborhoods. The city's racial composition is about evenly divided among white, African American, and Hispanic residents; but the school enrollment of 27,000 is 92% minority, with Latino students composing the largest group. More than half of the young children enrolled at the 26 elementary schools are eligible for Title I assistance. Many students have been ill prepared to begin school—only 25% of those eligible for Head Start were served. Approximately 25% of children repeated kindergarten as the Danforth effort began.

In Hartford, despite a chaotic situation in the superintendent's office over several years (including annual turnover among incumbents), the program focused on early care, formed a partnership with other community groups, and sought support from local foundations.

Memphis, Tennessee

Memphis is more than just one of the great distribution and transportation hubs of the South, a tradition it continues today as the headquarters of Federal Express. It is also the birthplace of the blues, which developed and still flourish in the nightclubs of world-famous Beale Avenue. The Memphis City School District is the largest system in the State of Tennessee, and the nineteenth largest in the country. It enrolls more than 109,000 students in 102 elementary schools, 11 middle schools, 9 junior high schools, 28 high schools, and 2 special education centers. The district has a disproportionate and growing number of disadvantaged and underachieving students, many of them, according to school officials, disaffected and alienated from their communities and schools. All of these students are at risk of failure in school and, ultimately, of failure in life. Memphis students are predominantly African American (more than 80%), and nearly two-thirds of them (62%) participate in free or reduced-price meal programs. The dropout rate for grades 9 through 12 exceeds one-third of enrollment.

Memphis built on an existing districtwide strategic-planning process by incorporating Philliber and Edwards's "Community Engagement Process" (see Section 2D) to determine community preferences in three neighborhoods (Binghamton, Douglass, and Orange Mound) served by four schools. In these neighborhoods, the effort focused on building advocacy for children, preparing them for school, and strengthening collaboration with other service providers.

St. Martin Parish, Louisiana

St. Martin Parish is a rural, farm-based economy that is known for its foods, dancing, and *joie de vivre*. The children's heritage lies in a unique blend of the Creole and Cajun cultures. When the French-speaking Acadians migrated from Nova Scotia

St. Martin used this program to complete a Community Engagement Survey, launch a school-based health clinic, initiate a "Dads Make a Difference" campaign, secure Medicaid reimbursement for health services, and create before- and afterschool care programs. "Think about what you'd want for our own kids and try to provide that in the community," says former superintendent Roland Chevalier simply. "You won't make too many mistakes."

to Louisiana in the mid-1700s, they settled in St. Martinville, making this land of bayous, swamps, and bottomland their home. The largest wilderness swamp in the world lies within the Parish's boundaries, where craw fishermen, trappers, and rice and sugarcane farmers coexist with blue-collar workers. Unemployment is high; one-third of Parish children live below the poverty level; more than 25% of parents have not gone beyond ninth grade. Children here face significant barriers.

University City, Missouri

University City, adjoining St. Louis, Missouri, is a six-square-mile suburb in transition. Historically, the community of 40,000 has been middle to upper middle class and expressed significant pride in its racial and ethnic diversity and its excellent schools. University City now faces new diversity. A growing number of low-income families reside in the community, which finds itself at a crossroads.

University City focused on school readiness, backing a bond issue for a new early childhood center and opening the new center with 27,000 square feet and 12 classrooms. At the close of its first year, more than a dozen programs for early learners were housed in the new center.

Washoe County, Nevada

When one thinks of Washoe County and Reno, Nevada, famous resorts, gambling, recreation, and breathtaking desert scenery may come to mind. These images, however, fail to capture the character of nearby Sun Valley, with most of its 15,000 residents living in poverty. Most of the Sun Valley residents live in mobile homes, some manufactured in the 1940s. Substandard living conditions abound. Rates of child and spousal abuse are high, and severe health problems are common. Most residents live on minimum-wage jobs or public assistance. The highest per capita concentration of ex-felons in the nation lives in Sun Valley.

Former Washoe County superintendent Mary Nebgen opened a new health-screening facility for Sun Valley residents in a centrally located trailer. The facility was made possible by the generosity of a local developer who volunteered to run water and electricity to it. Nebgen's replacement, James Hager, enthusiastically supported the effort within days of taking office.

Webster County, West Virginia

Located in a thinly populated state, Webster County is considered one of the most sparsely populated and remote counties in West Virginia. Access is severely limited by rugged terrain and poor highways. The litany of rural problems that appear elsewhere seem to be exacerbated by the remoteness of the location.

Nearly half of the county's adults have completed less than 12 years of school; current dropout rates average 22%; unemployment approaches 20%; and more than one quarter of the residents receive public assistance. With an average per capita income of $6,108, resources to support children are severely limited, and an exodus of recent school graduates seeking work elsewhere is a chronic reality in the county.

Typical School Districts

While each of these districts is unique, there is nothing particularly novel about them as a group. Not one of them is wealthy, but not all of them are poor. Whether the district is found in an aging East Coast city, an isolated rural county, a bustling Southern distribution center, or the great plains and deserts of the West, each of these communities faces substantial challenges in early care and education. They seem, in short, to be fairly representative of school districts across the nation, both in geography and demographics and in their capacity to meet the needs of young children. The message is clear. If these districts can make significant progress on early childhood issues, most districts can.

Webster County citizens don't always welcome change and are frequently suspicious of government programs. Many services already exist, but people don't know about them or can't reach them. Webster County used foundation support to create a directory of services and to seek grant money to open health clinics in two schools.

For resources on early childhood education, visit the Web site of the National Association for the Education of Young Children (www. naeyc.org).

E. First Steps: Getting Started

Luvern L. Cunningham

Getting started can be intimidating. Here are some ideas to keep in mind.

1. *Keep it local.* Although the problem is conceptually the same everywhere, whether the district is urban, rural, or suburban, the strategic response probably differs district by district.

2. *It's more about mindset than policy.* New district policies may be required, but perhaps not. Policies and legalities intimidate people. The real problem is one of changing views, attitudes, and mindsets and developing commitment.

3. *Bring the board along.* Your board needs to back you. It doesn't need detailed involvement, but you need to brief it, put experts before the board, and draw on the board as a resource and ally, when needed. The board also needs to make a commitment to you if you are to succeed.

4. *Build on local talent.* Outside experts are nice, but the homegrown variety is always better. Draw on local expertise from Head Start programs, children's hospitals, social service agencies, and universities.

5. *Reach beyond the usual suspects.* To get started, make your first calls to local power brokers—business leaders, editorial boards, and professional or business leaders. If you can bring them on board, getting the backing of others within the system will be easier.

F. Parental Involvement

Ethel Seiderman

Parents, families, and schools have to work and play together. Here are seven key principles for parental involvement.

1. *Parents are the most important persons to the child.* To ensure the health and well-being of children, assure the well-being of their parents.

2. *Parents are your partners.* Parents are partners in the work on behalf of the child. The relationship with them is predicated on equality and respect. The first priority is to establish and nurture this relationship as a support network that is mutually beneficial to all.

3. *Parents are their own best advocates.* They are decision makers on a collaborative team. Programs should be nonprescriptive so that parents can make their own choices about what services they want.

4. *Parents are assets.* Parents aren't your problem. They're not a barrier to be worked around or overcome. They are assets to you. Programs should build on parents' strengths by promoting their excellence and fostering their belief in themselves.

5. *Make programs relevant and community based.* Programs should be grounded in the community and relevant to the ethnic groups in the community. Each community should define its own reality, according to what its members agree is good for them.

6. *Voluntary is good.* Programs and services should be voluntary. Compelling participation accomplishes little. Parents, students, and community members seeking services should be understood as a sign of strength.

7. *Make it fun, not drudgery.* Self-esteem, joy, hopefulness, confidence, and optimism are important elements of strong families. Social support networks are a crucial element in the happiness, health, and productivity of people.

G. Parents and Steps to Success for Children

Lynn Beckwith, Jr.

Parental involvement was a hallmark of early learning programs in University City, Missouri. The following guidelines—10 steps to success for children—were developed by parents for parents and disseminated via a remarkable educational innovation, the refrigerator magnet. They became a sort of child-rearing bible for the parents in our community; they can serve the same role in yours, too.

---

1. Time.

2. Communication.

3. Reading.

4. Taking your children places.

5. Plan time for study in a structured environment.

6. Play games with your children.

7. Do not compare or label your children.

8. Set standards for your children's academic success.

9. Seek out support and expect to get it!

10. Become involved with your children's ongoing learning processes as they prepare for standardized tests.

H. Engaging Community in St. Martin Parish

Roland Chevalier

Here is a story describing a method for tackling community problems that has worked numerous times in practice. School leaders can use it to help develop an entire community's ability to learn. Parents survey each other, but this is not your typical community survey; it brings people together to learn together. This technique helped St. Martin Parish address a pernicious problem with early childhood reading, but it also gave the people of the parish a sense of identity they never had before, with a raft of significant effects.

Adapted with permission from Schools That Learn *by Senge and colleagues (New York: Doubleday, 2000).*

Around 1993, we identified a serious problem in our district: in some elementary schools, 30% of the students were being held back a year. That atrocious record was the *good* news. The bad news was, many parents, teachers, and principals thought we were doing the right thing, especially for our slow learners in reading, by giving them an "extra shot" of second- or third-grade medicine. They didn't know that when children are retained in the early grades even once, their chances of graduating from high school are cut in half. Retain them twice and you might as well write them off right there; almost none of those students graduate, either in our district or anywhere. By holding back the late developers at the end of second grade, you send the message, "We don't think you can do it," and you disconnect them from their age-group.

Phase I: Defining the Community and Assembling the Core Group

Step 1: Preliminary meetings are held to define precisely what is meant by "community" and to design a strategy for interviewing individuals most easily.

The first step was to find volunteers from the community in the areas that most needed help. We listed all the kids who had been retained, from grades K through 8, found their home addresses, and stuck pins in a map accordingly. Wherever the pins clustered, we looked for key volunteers—people who would join our core group and make a long-term commitment to us. Fortunately, I grew up here and knew some parts of the parish very well.

We started with a core committee of six volunteers, all key stakeholders who had credibility and knew the community's needs. It was vital to make sure that not all of them were from the school district administration. Some, like the local director of Head Start and a private day-care center owner, had been traditionally seen as our rivals. (In fact, the Head Start director knew much of the parish I didn't know; his involvement was key to starting off on the right track.) We also had the personnel director of Fruit of the Loom, our biggest employer in the district; someone from social services in Child Protection; some principals of primary schools; and someone from the sheriff's office. This group became our advisory council, and they organized the process.

We needed the community to bare its soul and talk about its needs—which meant talking about shortcomings and weaknesses. That's why it was so critical for community people, not school officials or outside consultants, to create our survey. We brought together about 40 people from every segment of the population, all invited by word of mouth, for a one-day session to create a questionnaire. We included business leaders, elected officials, and people in the sheriff's department.

We brought them together in a room for several hours and asked, "What do you want to know from the community?" Consultants Sharon Edwards and Susan Philliber facilitated the meeting and then took the questions and refined them. They brought the refined questions back to us so the group of 40 could approve the final draft.

The result was several pages of questions about the things people cared about, in their community and in their schools. What kinds of support did they need for their children? What did they think about homework? What did they want for their children's futures? What were they afraid might happen to their kids? What were they afraid their kids would do? We didn't restrict the content to education; we included a page of their questions about safety at home and on the streets, written by the sheriff's department. This ultimately led to a lot of innovations in community policing, including the placement of "school resource deputies" in our three high schools. Even before we got any answers, the questions themselves were eye-openers for me and other community leaders; we would not have thought to ask many of them.

Phase II: Community Mapping

The "question design" group then suggested another 50 or so people as "foot soldiers"—to be trained in the interview process and go door-to-door, like the Census Bureau. They would interview their neighbors, or conduct coffee get-togethers in their houses. We avoided using teachers or

Step 2: A discussion is held with a committee of community residents to determine the nature and content of the survey instrument and how best to recruit interviewers.

Step 3: The researcher/evaluator drafts the survey instrument from committee responses.

Step 4: The community group reviews the questionnaire and makes recommendations for the final version.

Step 5: The community group recruits interviewers and introduces them to the objectives and purposes of CEP.

Step 6: The researcher/evaluator trains the interviewers and supervises the survey work.

Step 7: At the completion of the surveying, a focus group is held with the interviewing team to discuss what they heard.

students for this. If a teacher holds the key to your child's future, you will say what you think he or she wants to hear. You're more apt to tell a neighbor how you really feel. Some of our parent-to-parent interviewers had never graduated from high school. Many of them weren't very confident at first, until we trained them: "This is how you introduce yourself," and so on. The sheriff, who was getting more and more involved, provided food for the training session.

Finally, we conducted a companion survey, with questions on the same themes, for the teachers and administrators. This brought us into dangerous territory. It turned out that teachers and parents disagreed on several key issues. Parents, for example, had much higher expectations for their children than their teachers did. Many teachers believed that parents didn't care much about schools, or didn't want to get involved. But 98 to 99% of the parents wanted to be involved. They felt shut out.

One question asked: "Do you believe all children can learn?" Most of the parents said yes. Sixty-two teachers said no. That was eye-opening for me; I wouldn't want my own child in the class of a teacher who doesn't believe all kids can learn. That raised some issues in terms of staff-development needs for our faculty. The damning part was that parents correctly understood the teachers' attitudes; they knew that the teachers did not expect their children to graduate. In all of our planning sessions, we had never considered this.

Phase III: Engaging the Community

Step 8: The researcher/evaluator prepares a computer database from the questionnaires and develops a report for the community drawing from the questionnaires and the interviewers' perceptions.

Sharon and Susan, the consultants, analyzed the data and wrote up a report. We were supposed to hold a focus group for the "foot soldiers," and we made it part of a celebration. Once again, the sheriff provided food. We gave them copies of the report, because it was their report. We had awards for the youngest interviewer, the oldest interviewer (Mrs. Potkin, a lady in her 70s), and the person with the most interviews. And we talked about what we had found and what we might do about it.

Step 9: The researcher/evaluator reconvenes the group to review the data and report.

One of the biggest complaints was a lack of quality child care at 5:00 A.M. for people who work factory shifts. People on late shifts had no one to help their kids with homework. Hearing about this, people volunteered solutions. One guy, who was retired, started a homework club in one of the subsidized low-income housing projects. All the kids ended up in a common room in the building after school, with older kids helping younger kids, and parents, on a rotating basis, supervising. The school had nothing to do with organizing it; the child care professionals had never imagined it. All of that came out of the residents' sense of efficacy: they could do something significant and make a difference.

The interaction with the community expanded our focus and direction. It made us really take a hard look at what the community expected of us; our task was much more complex than we had realized. We expanded our health services for children; there are now three school-based health clinics, serving 16 of our 17 schools. We addressed the issue of teenage pregnancy, with a facility where students could have a child, finish their education, get day care, learn parenting and nursing skills, and eventually pay back the costs by working at the center themselves.

> *Step 10: The community team plans the dissemination process and the strategies for engaging all stakeholders in dialogue.*

Other benefits of community engagement went far beyond our original intent. A group of people from the low-income housing project, trained in our method, contracted to conduct surveys for other towns and corporations in the area. They started a tutoring program. We had offered tutoring at school; nobody came. This project was so successful it needed help from our teachers. Catholic and Baptist ministers who had never been in the same room with each other began to meet with us around monthly lunches. The sheriff's office and mine looked into joint programs and collaborated to build a gymnasium and classrooms in a detention facility. Benefits emerged that we had never expected.

Making It Work in Your Community

Can this work in your community? Of course it can. It worked in ours. It was difficult for me at first, because I had to learn to listen and not speak. I had to learn to be open to suggestions and prepared for criticism, because the community might not necessarily think that *my* answer would be the right answer. And I had to realize that I could not be the one to do everything. As with the day-care center, which has been successfully managed by Head Start, sometimes I had to learn to support projects that other people were running.

Give it a try. You have nothing to lose. And if you're lucky, you'll hear what I heard from Fay Tucker, the local personnel director at our Fruit of the Loom plant. At one of our Community Engagement meetings five years ago, she said, "You know, I like these meetings. This is the first group I've worked with that actually gets something done." How often do you hear that in your office!

4. Questions for Reflective Practice

Collaboration—making sure that essential services are delivered effectively and on time—may be a key to your success. Here are some issues you should be exploring.

Have troubling incidents of child or spousal abuse received prominent attention in your community? Have you tried to get a conversation started about how this relates to school performance?

Are you routinely involved with local leaders in thinking through community challenges? Are you a member of Kiwanis or the local chamber of commerce, for example? Could you put issues of collaboration on the table here?

What kind of data do you have about patterns of social problems within your district's boundaries? Incidence of substance abuse? Involvement with the criminal or juvenile justice systems? Rates of family poverty? Proportion of adults who have dropped out of high school? What do these imply for your educational mission?

Who, in your community or state, is potentially a natural ally on the question of improving service delivery for families and children? Who's going to oppose you? How can you support the former and neutralize the latter?

Are your elementary principals and teachers satisfied that the children arriving at their schools are ready to learn? If not, what steps have you taken?

Can you document early care and learning opportunities in your community? How many children are enrolled in Head Start–like programs? In proprietary day-care centers? How many are served in home day-care settings? Are day-care providers well credentialed? Can you quantify the number of families seeking day-care or preschool programs who cannot find them?

Has anyone in your community or state quantified how an investment in early care and education might return dividends down the line?

Where is your board on the question of early learning opportunities? Intrigued? Uninterested? Willing to leave it up to you?

If you wanted to get started, who are the first people you would call together to begin the discussion? What's stopping you?

Part VIII
Engaging Your
Community

I t's not clear that there ever really were any "good old days" in
American schools, but one of the things that many remember
with nostalgia was a sense that school leaders defined the schools'
agenda. Those days are over. Today, the public expects to be
involved in determining the future of its schools. As superintendent, you need to understand that and learn how to engage your
diverse "publics."

1. Orientation

Bertha Pendleton
Richard Benjamin

Rapid national and global change ... greater racial and ethnic
diversity ... terrorism and the threat of more terrorism ...
violence and rampant abuse of powerful drugs ... traditional
families coming apart at the seams—how are schools to cope?
And how, amid demands for better performance, can you
as superintendent build and sustain community support for
important educational work?

Those two questions frame the concept of public engagement.

> *When the Columbine tragedy developed in Colorado, it sent a shudder through my district. That could happen in any of our communities.*
>
> Carol Choye,
> Superintendent,
> Scotch
> Plains–Fanwood
> Public Schools,
> New Jersey

The Central Idea

The central idea behind public engagement is not public relations but getting the public to "own" its own schools. You may be tempted to think of the schools as "yours." They're not. In the final analysis, they belong to the public. If local citizens don't feel that deep in their bones, you will not be able to count on public support when you need it. It's important, therefore, that you get your local community thoroughly engaged, connected, and deeply committed to its schools.

Throughout this part you will find the people and other resources that can help support this effort. Daniel Yankelovich's work with the Public Agenda Foundation provides a broad framework for understanding the concept of public engagement. Kathleen Hall Jamieson of the Annenberg School for Communication, University of Pennsylvania, teaches you how to negotiate and survive the world of mass media. Will Friedman, formerly of the Public Agenda Foundation, and Adam Kernan-Schloss of KSA-Plus Communications, teach you how to "do" public engagement.

2. Public Engagement

Public engagement is really a two-way deal between you and your local community. It's basically a conversation in which the agreement is: I will listen respectfully to what you have to say as long as you hear me out. Public engagement involves seven distinct stages, and you can use it most effectively if you take advantage of several tools and guidelines outlined in this section.

A. Moving From Public Relations to Public Engagement

Bertha Pendleton
Richard Benjamin

Your challenge in public engagement involves a significant change in mindset. Public engagement is not public relations. True public engagement requires developing strategies that involve all sectors of a community in ongoing deliberations that build common ground for effective solutions. In your district, it will require developing collaboration to sustain the serious work of school reform.

Public engagement is a shift in culture from authoritarian directives to greater self-governance. (We know you don't have to make that shift! But the people reading over your shoulder might.) It is also a shift in perspective from seeing the children solely in schools to seeing them as part of a community committed to the proposition that educating the young is important.

You will find that effective public engagement grows out of several questions: "What do we want for our children? How can we collaborate to help them achieve as students and as citizens? How do we increase student learning and raise student achievement for all the district's children? What do we have to do to sustain American democracy?"

These are not easy questions. If we're honest, most of us will admit we weren't trained to deal with them. In today's environment, however, you and your staff must cope with them. Because the simple truth is that we, as educators, no longer enjoy the luxury of doing things without the public's permission. You and your staff need to develop the skills involved with gathering and presenting information about these questions and listening thoughtfully to what the public has to say about them.

Building Capacity and Sustainability

We understand. Your time is precious. In the face of other priorities, why spend any of it on public engagement? The short answer is that it might help you "see around corners." No, public engagement won't turn you into a Super Hero. Yet it may alert you to changes in the force field around schools that will permit you to anticipate and respond before you are blindsided by something you didn't expect. So for you personally and professionally, public engagement has a lot to offer.

The longer answer is equally important. Public engagement is an investment in your district and community. It will provide you and your citizens with huge benefits over the long haul. Despite the behavior of some people, when members of the public ask you to jump, they don't necessarily expect you to say "how high?" They don't always insist that you do what they ask you to do. What they do expect is that you'll listen to their concerns. Sometimes that's all they want, a sense that they've been heard. Listening to what people have to say—and helping your citizens have a meaningful conversation about the children of their community—builds local capacity to support and sustain viable schools over time.

You'll find another benefit, too. Properly conducted, public engagement can shield schools from the whims of the market and the shallowness and rancor of much political discourse. You'll be surprised at who will come to your defense once they understand what you're trying to do. They'll support you because they're really defending what they've had a chance to shape.

Think of public engagement in Gareth Morgan's terms. What's the image? It's akin to helping an organism grow. It's like gardening. The effort you put into it—tilling the ground, watering the seeds, and keeping the weeds at bay—is time well spent. The product of your garden will be an informed and engaged citizenry. Your fruit will be the assurance that, when battles develop around your schools, you won't fight them alone.

B. Listening to Your Public

James Harvey

The first thing you need to understand about public engagement is that we are living in difficult times, according to internationally known pollster Daniel Yankelovich.

You can learn a lot about listening to the public in Daniel Yankelovich's Coming to Public Judgment: Making Democracy Work in a Complex World *(Syracuse, NY: Syracuse University Press, 1991).*

The public is anxious, and educators have to pay attention to that anxiety. This is a period of American life that is "strange, frustrating, and anxious," says Yankelovich. The frustration has been building for years. "Most Americans are deeply troubled. They feel something is wrong, but they don't know what it is." The breadth of the public's discomfort with the rapid rate of change is not restricted to education. "There is a serious decline in levels of confidence in all walks of life," he notes, citing a decline in public confidence in medicine from 70 to 22% in the last generation. Large proportions of Americans consider government to be incompetent, he reports, and in the 1990s, three times as many people thought American education was getting worse as believed it was getting better.

You may be worried about how to finance local afterschool care programs, and your local community may, in fact, embrace your program. But the underlying anxieties affecting Americans often have little to do with day-to-day events in your community, and people may vote against your proposal based on general anxiety about the future. Worry about terrorism . . . globalization . . . the lop-sided nature of the domestic economy . . . a sense that America has lost its moral bearings . . . concerns about violence, crime, and their manifestations in the disorder in our schools—all of these things and others are on the public mind.

Public Engagement in Crossett, Arkansas

Crossett, carved out of the pine forests of southeast Arkansas, is a typical small town in a rural area. Through a public-engagement effort, we spent four years strengthening ties with the business, professional, and political communities and with civic organizations, faith-based groups, parents, and members of the general public.

Shifts in attitudes and behaviors, increasing communication, and deeper conversations are not easily measurable. Yet positive results are still evident from the decline of discipline problems in schools to the way people are included in community conversations.

If schools want the community to know what they are all about—the problems they are struggling with and the vision they have—they don't necessarily have to create new programs or send out more newsletters. Becoming more involved in organizations that already exist and building on successful programs they already have is the best place to start.

In Crossett, public engagement has become a priority. When I retired, the board began searching for a new superintendent. One of the first questions: "What do you know about public engagement?"

—Barbara Gates, Superintendent

It's in this context that you need to listen carefully to your citizens' concerns about schools. "People are worried that they may lose their jobs," says Yankelovich. They are worried about their access to health care. They are on the treadmill of two incomes. They are anxious that they may not be able to afford to send their kids to college. As Alexis de Tocqueville, said, "the minds of men wander in confusion and obscurity."

Confusion and obscurity. That's where we are today, in some ways. Events are inexplicable to the man on the street. Groping for solutions, your parents and members of the community are often forced to deal with issues they would rather avoid. It is within this tough climate that policymakers ask this question: How do the American people feel about their schools and what do they want from them?

David Mathews, president of the Kettering Foundation, argues that public attitudes toward schools have changed dramatically. See his book, Is There a Public for Public Schools? *(Dayton, OH: Kettering Foundation, 1997).*

Much of the standards conversation is "a dialogue of the deaf," Yankelovich believes. Based on research at the Public Agenda Foundation, American leaders (politicians, journalists, and corporate and academic chiefs) are preoccupied with raising standards so that American students can compete in a global economy. But the public has blocked this out with a "Yes, but . . ." attitude, he notes. The public, says Yankelovich, is worried that attention to the basics and to order and discipline in the schools has been sacrificed in order to protect the rights of what it thinks of as troublemakers. To the public, "Ignoring the basics is like encouraging students to run before they can walk."

One result, says Yankelovich, is that "the public feels that schools are no longer 'their' schools. They are not public schools in a real way. They are 'teachers' schools,' or 'the union's schools' or the 'professionals' schools.' But they are no longer 'our schools.'"

To respond, he suggested, school leaders need to work with citizens through seven distinct stages as they come to public judgment. The seven steps are made up of (1) Awareness; (2) Sense of Urgency; (3) Grasping for Answers; (4) Resistance; (5) Choice Work; (6) Cognitive Acceptance; and (7) Moral and Emotional Resolution. If it's easier to think of the steps as simply three stages, then think of them as consciousness, deliberation, and decision.

The remainder of this section describes these seven stages. It includes tools and exercises that you can use to learn how to "do" public engagement. In a sense, the first step is easy: stop talking and start listening.

C. A Seven-Stage Model of Engagement

Will Friedman

Daniel Yankelovich's seven-stage model provides a powerful tool for you as superintendent. With this tool, you can begin to understand how the citizens in your community behave around public issues. Once you understand these seven stages, you will be in a better position to track how raw, unstable opinion evolves toward stable and responsible "public judgment." Ideally, public judgment will mean that your community has deliberated on an issue sufficiently to produce a working consensus that will allow you to move forward.

Communications in Nye County, Nevada

To a newcomer, the sheer scale and scope of Nye County, Nevada, is hard to take in. With a land area of 11 million acres, it's bigger than Massachusetts, Rhode Island, New Jersey, and Delaware combined. The Nye County School District (NCSD) covers this vast area (the largest school district in Nevada in terms of geography) and a wide cultural expanse as well. Student population in the district had been increasing at over 1% *per month*, with the district seeing as much as 15% growth in some recent years.

We spent most of our energy focusing on two things. First, listening to and developing internal voices for change—teachers, educational support staff, and administrators. Second, helping teachers and principals make specific changes in classroom practices that would increase student learning and meet the unique needs of each student.

The formal process of public engagement began with rounds of intensive surveying and questioning of staff. The purpose was to determine what they knew about their work and school reform, what they believed about school improvement (and what they distrusted or discounted), and whether they truly believed that changing practices (e.g., using data-based documentation and decision making) would improve student learning. Our focus:

1. What do we want kids to know and be able to do when they leave our system?

2. What is our vision of a successful graduate of the NCSD?

3. What concrete changes in learning standards, assessments, and methodology must occur to allow us to produce such graduates?

4. What is the status of today's classroom?

5. What changes must we make to what we are doing now?

The jury is still out on the impact. But this is clear: attention to internal audiences improved communication with district stakeholders and built support for our schools.

—Geraldine Harge

Take the issue of women in the workplace. At one time, the fact that women pursued careers outside of professions like teaching and nursing was a highly controversial matter. While prejudices remain, the basic idea that a woman has the right to pursue virtually any career she wants is now broadly accepted. Or take school segregation. Many of the minority members of the Danforth Forum recall attending segregated Southern schools in an era when it was inconceivable to white Southerners that their children would attend schools with African Americans. No responsible person takes such views seriously anymore. On issues such as these and others, what had been widely accepted public judgments have been completely transformed.

Public attitudes are in the midst of enormous flux. Some communities may still harbor racist attitudes. Some individuals may still think that a woman's place is in the home. Undoubtedly, many people are convinced that recent court cases about sexual orientation are profoundly misguided. But, on balance, broader public judgments are not sympathetic to these views. As a community leader, you cannot make the mistake of thinking you know what your local community thinks about controversial matters such as these. You need to know what it thinks. If you come from a conservative and traditional background, you should not assume that everyone shares your views. And if you are ready to storm the barricades to advance new social, ethical, or environmental views through the classrooms you oversee, you should not be surprised to find that some members of your community will object. The point is you need a better understanding of where your community is.

In school reform, the public is wrestling with many important questions. What is the proper role of standardized tests in helping students succeed? Should schools place a greater emphasis on moral education? If so, how? How can we keep our schools safe? Understanding where your community stands on these issues often depends on where it is with regard to the stages of public judgment. The seven stages can be clustered into three major phases (see the following box). What you do as a superintendent will vary depending on where your community is in terms of the phases. If your citizens are barely aware of the issue, then you shouldn't be asking them to make hard choices. This is adaptive work, in Ron Heifetz's terms, not technical. Your job is to bring the problem (whatever it is) to their attention. On the other hand, if they've worked through a number of alternatives over several weeks or months (or even years), you may be close to a technical problem of how to get their solution implemented. Here, it's probably not a good idea to suggest that local citizens don't know what they're talking about.

As superintendent, you may also find some of these ideas useful in figuring out how to encourage teachers and administrators to believe that commitment to standards and assessment will advance learning. As you saw in Part VI, getting from where we are today in terms of student achievement to the Promised Land of equal outcomes for all requires a "leap of faith." You're going to have to take some of your teachers and administrators where they are and build bridges for them to span the chasm. The seven stages described here may build the bridges you need for teachers and administrators.

Seven Stages of Coming to Public Judgment

Consciousness-Raising Stages

1. Awareness

2. Urgency

Working-Through Stages

3. Looking for answers

4. Resistance

5. "Choicework"

Integration Stages

6. Initial, intellectual acceptance

7. Moral commitment

Awareness and Urgency: The Consciousness-Raising Stages

The journey toward public judgment begins with a dawning *awareness* that something is at issue, often as the result of media coverage or the efforts of advocacy groups. But simple awareness

Interested in a long-range campaign for public support? Look into how the Pritchard Committee, in Kentucky, operated. See Robert Sexton's Mobilizing Citizens for Better Schools *(New York: Teachers College Press, 2004).*

isn't enough to drive the hard work of forming public judgment. There must be a sense of *urgency* that sets it apart from the many issues clamoring for attention. Realistically, your public has "room" for only a handful of issues at any one time. If your parents are anxious about terrorism, loved ones overseas on military missions, or a local assault on a child, they may have little time to spend worrying about high-stakes testing. In fact, it's conceivable that the worst time to bring up complex issues such as these is when the community is upset and alarmed about life-threatening issues. Citizens may ignore you or provide you with ill-considered and angry responses. For the most part, too, people are unaware of the complexity of the problems before them. You have an expert's understanding. At best, they have a layman's grasp. Sometimes, your local constituents don't even know what they don't know. These consciousness-raising stages are critical foundations for coming to public judgment.

Looking for Answers, Resistance, Obstacles, and "Choicework": Working-Through Stages

During stage 3, people are "looking for answers." Naturally enough, they prefer the easy answers at first. Often, political leaders and advocates for various solutions sense opportunity in the public's growing concern and offer solutions. Just as often, people gravitate to the first attractive solution they encounter. Why struggle with painful tradeoffs, giving up "x" to gain "y," before it has been established that the pain can't be escaped?

Wishful thinking describes the many types of resistance that mark stage 4. Premature closure . . . denying the existence of trade-offs ("we won't have to raise taxes or cut programs, we just need to cut waste") . . . excessive cynicism ("there's so much corruption there's no point in even getting involved") . . . and scapegoating ("if not for *them* this wouldn't even be an issue") . . . are all types of wishful thinking and resistance. (Heifetz describes a similar phenomenon, which he calls "work avoidance.") This phase is where your leadership will be most sorely tested. It is tempting to throw up one's hands in the face of such obstacles.

"Choicework" (stage 5) is where people seriously consider alternative solutions, discover how they relate to their values and experience, weigh the tradeoffs of different paths, and begin to make hard choices.

Intellectual Acceptance and Moral Commitment: The Integration Stages

Finally, the model describes two stages involved in reaching a working consensus and integrating it into the life of the schools. First is accepting an idea or direction in theory, that is, *intellectually accepting* it. At this point, your people have decided in principle. But they have yet to make a moral commitment to a new position, meaning changing their practices and behavior. Recycling makes sense to most people, but that doesn't mean everyone does it. So you may hear, "I don't doubt the high school needs new fields, more modern wiring, and rehabilitation of the South Wing, but I can't afford to vote for a levy."

When your community reaches the stage of *moral acceptance*, it has completed the seven-stage journey to public judgment. And the good news is, you can now begin to plan the bond campaign needed to overhaul the high school. Your community is ready to pay for it.

This doesn't mean everyone is in perfect agreement. The issue has not been closed to further consideration. Still, enough stable acceptance of a course of action has been established that you as a community leader can move ahead, confident that local citizens will not change their position on a whim.

Implications for Educational Leadership

In education, research by Public Agenda and others has shown that the nation, in general, has gone a long way toward reaching public judgment on a number of important school issues. Individual communities, of course, have their variations. Still, the vast majority of Americans view school safety and order, student mastery of the academic basics, and high standards as important priorities for schools.

You also need to understand that *how* to achieve those priorities is less firmly established. If these goals are poorly implemented, the public is likely to react badly. That these goals are essential, however, is widely accepted.

Your "public," of course, will not progress through these seven stages in a lockstep progression. Different individuals and groups are at different stages. Some may fall back or jump ahead in response to events and information. As an overall guide, however, these are the stages your community will go through as it engages an issue and works out a response. The seven-stage model can become a powerful tool for you. If it does nothing else, it reminds you that there are no shortcuts in coming to public judgment.

D. Tool: Tips on the Seven Stages

Will Friedman

Need help? Different stages have different challenges and require different strategies. Table 8.1 offers some general rules of the road.

Table 8.1   Tips on the Seven Stages

Consciousness Raising	
Awareness	• Media and traditional PR strategies help bring issues to public attention.
Urgency	• Boring and complex issues can be challenging. If a complex issue connects to a strong public concern, that helps (e.g., how does the budget relate to school safety?).
	• Remember the "first things first" principle: people must know you understand their priorities if you want them to pay attention to yours.
Working Through	
Looking for Answers	• Be wary of poll results regarding public preferences before the public has had a chance to deliberate in depth.
Resistance	• Resistance to the hard work of deliberation and decision making is a natural part of the process. As a leader, your job is to understand resistance and help the public get past it. Sometimes providing the right piece of information does the trick; sometimes confronting people's wishful thinking is required.
Choicework	• Avoid forcing a single solution on people—particularly your preferred one. Help people understand the pros and cons of different approaches. That provides an opportunity to develop mature views.
	• Nonpartisan, user-friendly issue guides can help people deliberate effectively, as can "public journalism" strategies that provide nonpartisan, in-depth, user-friendly treatments of issues.
	• Community conversations are an excellent strategy for helping significant cross sections of the community work through their thinking (see Sections 2H and 2I, on Community Conversations).
Integration	
Intellectual Acceptance	• People need time to really integrate new ideas and solutions. Don't mistake initial acceptance as whole-hearted commitment.
Moral Commitment	• Give people opportunities to play an active role as solutions develop. Include the community in implementing and devising solutions. This deepens the sense of ownership and helps ensure success as all community assets are brought to bear on the problem.

E. Essential Tools: Focus Groups and Surveys

Will Friedman

Properly done, focus groups and surveys are an excellent way to improve your understanding of the views, priorities, and concerns of your community. What do people in "If You Have to Ask, You Can't Afford It" estates think about the new tax levy? What about the folks in the trailer park across the tracks? You probably have many different "publics" in your community. You need to understand what each group thinks.

Focus groups are a qualitative way for you to explore views in depth. They help you probe the motivations underlying people's responses. Focus group interviews are especially useful in exploring issues that people haven't really given much thought to, because time can be taken during the interview to present background information. Focus groups are often the essential first step in survey design.

Opinion surveys, conducted by telephone or mail (and occasionally in person), expand on focus group research. They provide a more detailed and quantitative look at public attitudes. Obviously they have to be properly done. Loaded questions will provide loaded answers. To the extent possible, questions should be as neutral and nonjudgmental as possible. How you ask the question has a lot to do with the answers you get.

There is no doubt about the following: if you launch a well-conceived survey, you will receive extremely valuable information. It will be information to which you will return again and again. And it will help you plumb the thinking of your community. You will also gain something else: there is nothing like the results of a survey to concentrate media attention on the issues that concern you.

The Limits and Uses of Opinion Research

We want to stress that you need to understand that focus groups and surveys are tools, not public engagement itself. Both tools can be powerful assets in a public engagement effort, but they are not a substitute for the effort, much less public engagement. You shouldn't mistake the tools for the process.

These tools provide a reading of what's on your people's minds, but these tools do not, by themselves, help your citizens develop their thinking. They illuminate confusion but do not provide the communication to fix it.

The terms "focus groups" and "focus group interviews" mean the same thing. The technique was developed decades ago at the University of Minnesota and called, at the time, "focused interviews." The "interview" aspect of the focus group is important. If you employ this technique, what you want to know is what your focus group participants think. You want to interview them. You are not conducting this exercise to persuade them of your views, but to discover theirs.

A questionnaire directed at employers might ask: "When I employ the graduates of Anytown High, I find them (1) well equipped to begin work immediately; (2) moderately well equipped to begin work, with some training; or (3) poorly equipped to begin work, no matter what we do." On balance, that's a fairly neutral question and the choices seem reasonable. But the question might begin with a variation of the following: "Considering recent reports from the state indicating that the graduates of Anytown High are too stupid to brush their own teeth, would you say that when they come to work in your community they are. . . ." Even if offered the same three choices, there's no doubt that respondents are being asked to check off (3).

They distinguish issues your constituents are willing to delegate to professionals from those issues they want a voice in, but they do not necessarily give your people much of a say. They can clarify differences in priority among various stakeholders, but they will not help your community work through those differences. In brief, they are the beginning, not the end.

Tulsa's Experience

Oklahoma, of course, was "Indian Territory" until it opened up in the great land rush after the Civil War. Even then, Tulsa was just a backwater until the oil boom that started a century ago turned Tulsa into the "oil capital of the United States." It's a conservative, oil-bound culture that had turned down three bond levies in a row. Communications were essential to turning that around. Here's what we learned:

Do Research on Your Community
Understand your community's demographics and research your constituents to generate specific information about their attitudes and perceptions.

Identify Your Voters
Make no mistake, bond issues are political campaigns. Identify "yes," "no," and "maybe" voters. Then ignore the "no's" and concentrate on the "maybe's."

Establish Goals and Objectives
Begin with goals and objectives. Add objectives that are specific to the campaign. Tie goals and objectives into what the community already knows it wants to do.

Select a Child-Centered Theme Such as "Do It For the Kids!"
President Bush's "Leave No Child Behind" slogan is an example at the national level. When you focus on children, voters have a difficult time justifying a "no" vote.

Create Messages for Both Internal and External Audiences
List the various internal and external publics or stakeholder groups. The more targeted the publics, the better the plan. Direct messages to specific groups.

Remember: The Campaign Continues After the Election
The announcement that we would be back for another campaign sent a signal to the community and our supporters that we weren't finished. These campaigns never end. As superintendent, you have to hold the community together in support of schools.

—John Thompson, Superintendent

As part of a larger engagement effort, focus groups and surveys can be useful tools for steering you and other local leaders in productive directions. Prior to community conversations, media campaigns, or the production of informational materials, public opinion research can help answer such questions as these

- What are the main concerns and priorities of the people in our community? Which issues emerge spontaneously and provoke lively debate? How do people view the importance of this particular issue in comparison to that one?

- On which issues do our people especially want a voice? On which are they comfortable relying on the direction of our elected and appointed officials? Do they insist on addressing aspects of particular issues?

- Where does our community start out on particular issues (e.g., closing the achievement gap or consolidating schools)? Is a problem that is high on the leaders' agenda even on the public's radar screen? Are our people aware of a range of potential solutions? Or are they stuck on a single train of thought?

- Have people given much thought to the issue, or is it pretty new to them? If the former, is there much common ground? Or do people see powerful divisions in the community? If the latter, how willing are people to engage the issue, and what kinds of information do they need? In other words, where do you locate our public (and its various subpublics) on the seven stages of public judgment?

- What language do people in our community typically use when talking about a particular issue? Are there "blinking words" (see Part II, Section 4) that we should avoid? What are people's first questions and concerns? What is the most useful way to frame issues so that we can have a productive public conversation?

- Are these topics easy to explain? Or do they invite confusion? How much contextual information do our people need to engage effectively with these issues? What other hurdles are likely to be come up? Are there, for example, misperceptions, hot-button issues, or alienated groups that need addressing?

As your public engagement campaign unfolds, focus groups and surveys can help assess how well things are going and help you fine-tune your efforts.

F. Guidelines on Opinion Research

Will Friedman

Several straightforward questions and commonsense caution should guide you as you approach public opinion research.

First, the Questions

1. *What do you want to know?* The previous section listed several lines of inquiry you might want to explore. There may be others. Generally speaking, it's the job of superintendents and their leadership teams (including, one hopes, local citizens) to decide on the areas of inquiry needing attention. It's the researcher's job to translate those decisions into specific questions.

2. *Who do you want to ask?* Are you interested in the general population? Parents? Teachers? Students? Homeowners? Older residents? Business leaders? What about religious, racial/ethnic, or income groups? How about "all of the above"? These groups also reflect the small, breakout groups in the Public Conversations method (see Section 2H, on Community Conversations), thus providing a lab for testing materials before going public with them.

3. *What's the best way to obtain answers?* Do you want to do focus groups, surveys, or both? The main factors coming into play here are purpose and costs. If you want a cost-effective preliminary exploration, focus groups will do the job. More detailed and reliable results probably require a survey and considerable additional time and expense. You need a survey if

- You want to confirm or expand on your focus group results.
- You want to go public with the results and stimulate press and public attention.
- You want to be able to track changing results over time.

Now the Cautions

1. *Quality counts.* Poor research is not better than nothing. It can steer you in the wrong direction. Do it right the first time because you might not get another chance.

2. *The media is a wild card.* Public opinion results are natural media hooks. This can be a huge asset. On the other hand, if the press focuses on bad news, you may be on your way out the door.

3. *Remember why you are doing it.* Many good reasons exist for adding public opinion research into your public engagement efforts. You need to know what your citizens think. But it is a mistake to use this research for political purposes, to manipulate

the community, or to look for emotionally charged buzzwords supporting short-term, and illusory, consensus. Don't go there. Remember the seven stages. You can't short- circuit them without engendering cynicism and mistrust.

G. Community Conversations in San Jose

Linda Murray
Thomas S. Poetter

The San Jose described years ago by John Steinbeck bears little resemblance to the image of the capital of Silicon Valley carried around in most people's heads today. Still, the inheritance of the former and the reality of the latter frame the educational task facing our schools in San Jose.

Steinbeck wrote powerfully about the migrant workers, food processors, and cannery employees who took their living from the fertile fruit fields in the region. Yet, by the 1970s, the demands of burgeoning aerospace and high-tech industries in the area were such that, over the next 20 years, San Jose's population exploded by 70%. With that explosion came a call for a more highly skilled labor force. Clearly our schools were expected to develop it.

Against the backdrop of those complex economic and social dynamics, we set out in the late 1990s to engage the community in a conversation about what it wanted from its schools.

San Jose Unified School District has a student population of 33,000 in 42 schools. The district stretches 24 miles long, but it is only 4 miles wide. The northern portion of the district is predominately Latino, with many students qualifying for free- and reduced-price lunch programs. The southern area of the district is predominately Anglo and Asian. This affluent area has little demand for reduced-price meals.

Desegregation and distrust have been major issues in our district. In the fall of 1982, the district began a voluntary desegregation program by establishing several magnet elementary, middle, and high schools. In 1985, a court-ordered desegregation plan directed the district to rely heavily on the use of magnet schools to encourage voluntary transfers for the purpose of desegregation. Historic feelings of mistrust and instability among constituencies also had to be addressed. In part, this dynamic stemmed from numerous changes in leadership,

San Jose in Brief

Students: 33,000

Schools: 42

Geography: A strip of Silicon Valley measuring 24 miles long and 4 miles wide.

Demographics: North, primarily Latino and poor; South, primarily Anglo, Asian, and affluent strikes, bankruptcy, and a perceived lack of interest on the part of the district in the community's input.

Laying the Groundwork

Before initiating local community conversations, we held our first public forum in the spring of 1995. During the meeting, we convened a cross section of community members to address issues of trust and communication.

The participants in those first sessions identified three primary issues: (1) increasing student achievement, (2) educating parents, and (3) including neighborhoods and communities. The participants felt these issues should be part of any long-range public engagement road map.

See Section 4, Communications Planning, for a description of communications audits.

Next, we conducted a communications audit that polled principals, teachers, students, parents, and community leaders. Five questions framed a discussion of the data gathered in the communications audit: (1) Which audiences do we need to reach? (2) What do we want these publics to do? (3) What is feasible for them to do (given our resources)? (4) What will success look like? (5) How will we know?

At the conclusion of the audit, analyses of the data yielded a consensus on five broad areas the district should take up: strategic communications planning; focus group research; communicating about standards and assessment; one-on-one group communications training; and parent education and outreach.

The results were fascinating. In all focus groups, people generally agreed that schools in the northern and southern portions of the district were uneven in quality. We were pleased to see broad agreement that something needed to be done about this. There was also widespread agreement across groups on the following:

- Parental and community involvement are important factors that account for uneven quality.
- Academic expectations should be raised.
- Students should receive a broad, balanced education.
- Schools across the district should be equal in quality and in the emphasis placed on different subjects.

Much agreement could be found, therefore, even among our very diverse parent populations in San Jose Unified. What about differences?

A major distinction between groups revolved around support for diversity. Non-English-speaking Latino parents valued diversity in schools. One woman noted, "I like diversity—races, different cultures—because that really nourishes children's souls. Students get to know about everyone."

The English-speaking focus groups, however, voiced little support for policies aimed at increasing diversity. They generally felt that schools should focus on academics and not "social issues beyond their control." Schools should also reinforce social values, they thought, although the core of moral teaching should take place at home through the family.

The members of the non-English-speaking parent focus groups split between those who favored consistent, high academic standards for all students, and those who felt that students needed to be treated more individually. The focus groups reached a consensus that higher expectations and clearer, more consistent standards will lead to higher student achievement. Parents asked for very clear and frequent feedback on how their children were doing in school.

Responding to this advice, our school board adopted a policy that increased student graduation requirements to include an additional year of math, science, and foreign language, and it implemented a community service requirement for every entering high-school freshman. At about the same time, 74% of the district's residents voted to pass a $165 million bond measure. We were making progress.

> *Latina Parent:*
>
> *"I like diversity . . . students get to know almost everyone."*
>
> *Anglo Parent:*
>
> *"Schools should focus on academics and not 'social issues beyond their control'."*

Community Task Force

Our community conversation did not stop with focus groups. Working with the Public Agenda Foundation, we launched a task force to plan a community conversation around student achievement, standards, and what students needed in order to succeed. We wanted an open, respectful, and honest discussion.

On a rainy Saturday morning in January 1998, 140 community members convened in downtown San Jose to discuss standards and expectations. We received a number of recommendations:

- Expand community conversations and take them into schools.
- Develop an action plan for increasing community involvement.

- Develop strategies to help parents become more effectively engaged in helping their children meet expectations.
- Define and clearly communicate standards and expectations to parents and community.
- Improve articulation/communication between and among levels of schooling and schools.
- Involve parents and community to support teachers in meeting the challenge of helping students achieve.
- Communicate about the community conversation.

Holding Community Conversations

We went deeper. The district hosted a series of six community conversations for each of the high-school attendance areas in 1999. These community conversations *involved more than 1,000 people*—parents, students, businesses, and community members—from every district school.

The Nuts-and-Bolts of Community Conversations

1. Stress respectful conversations.

2. Provide trained facilitators.

3. Keep school administrators in the background, or else they become the conversation.

4. Start with informed outside observations—academic, community activist, or corporate views of the schools—to get the conversation rolling. Videos can be ideal.

5. Work through a brief structured list of questions.

6. Make sure everyone participates, paying special attention to the shy and the insecure.

7. Provide visual evidence that comments are being heard by having someone from the community take down key points on poster boards.

District personnel learned facilitation skills for these conversations from trained district facilitators. This team then trained a team of facilitators at each school. The facilitation team included parents and a neutral facilitator from the school community. Although principals attended the training, they played the role of observers, not participants, in the conversations.

Each conversation began with a brief video presentation featuring representatives from local businesses and the community describing their expectations for what district graduates should be able to do to qualify for higher education in Silicon Valley. The video described student-performance data and addressed expectations for student performance.

Facilitators asked participants: "What skills and competencies do students need to perform well on the job?" and "What should we be doing in our schools so that our students can meet your expectations?" A breakout session, focused on the needs of individual school communities, addressed the following question: "How can families, schools, and the broader community work together to help students achieve academically?"

What We Learned

The challenge of this effort was to create an internal culture that actively engaged the public around school issues. The old culture was grounded in the belief that, if legal requirements obligated the district to talk to the community, it would, of course, do so. We wanted the public to know that we were interested in changing schools and community expectations of the schools—and we wanted it to know that, regardless of our legal obligations.

We were reminded of something in this process. Too frequently we forget it: every member of the community cares deeply about children and their educational progress. Parents and community members from all walks of life continue to hold the success of children in school as a central value. Our parents and citizens certainly do— and so do yours.

Every member of the community cares deeply about children and their educational progress.

Trust us: if you can find the courage to listen to your community, you have everything to gain and nothing to lose.

H. Community Conversations: A Tool for Public Engagement

Will Friedman

Sponsorship Should Be Nonpartisan and Broad Based

When districts are the lone organizers and hosts of community conversations, they attract the usual suspects—those already active in school affairs. A broad-based leadership coalition is more likely to draw fresh faces, both because it includes leaders that more people relate to and because it communicates openness to new views.

Who Should Attend?

Anyone who wants to. Beyond that, anyone with interesting perspectives on kids and schooling. Ask yourself: who do we rarely hear from? You want them. Among important participants are the following:

- Parents of students in public and private schools
- Students (especially juniors and seniors) and recent graduates
- Nonparent taxpayers from the community and employers of young people
- Educators (but their participation should be limited so they do not dominate)
- Representatives from higher education, such as admissions officers and freshman professors
- Community leaders including public officials, activists, and religious and law-enforcement leaders
- Experts on specific topics on the agenda; for example, law enforcement if the topic is school safety

Participants should reflect the community's diversity.

How Do We Get Them There?

People have a lot of ways to spend their time. Here are ways to encourage participation:

- Personal outreach is best. Senior citizens will generally have more success recruiting peers, business leaders more success recruiting employers, and so on.

- Hold the conversations in safe, accessible, and neutral sites. A community center or library may be better than a school (more neutral).

- Recruit those who don't think of themselves as parts of the school community, such as senior citizens. Address the needs of more marginalized segments of the community by considering language, transportation, and child-care needs.

- Community conversations should be more engaging and meaningful than typical public meetings. They should expect a lively, participative session, where hearing from "regular folks" is the heart of the effort. This is a forum where everyone needs to work together if the right decision is to be reached.

- Just as important, people should know there will be a social dimension. Food is always a good idea. Perhaps you can persuade the local school jazz band to give a brief performance. You should advertise these elements to draw a robust and diverse participation. (Free food, music, and the chance to give the superintendent an earful! What more could anyone want?)

> *Community conversations must be "real," not empty gestures creating an illusion of participation.*

- Finally, it is crucial that the specific topic of conversation is one that most people care strongly about and want to weigh in on.

Choose the Issue to Be Discussed With Care

People's time and energy for public engagement is limited. It shouldn't be wasted. Here are some guiding principles:

- An issue is likely to be seen as relevant and legitimate if it is chosen by a broad steering committee.

- In selecting an issue, separate the educational priorities of the district from those of the community. Those that overlap will be ripe for discussion.

- The topic must be one you and the public care about, and about which you are open. If your mind is made up, or legal issues drive your options, this isn't the place for a community conversation. Community conversations must be "real," not empty gestures creating an illusion of participation.

> *Visit Public Agenda's Web site at www .publicagenda .org for a range of print and video materials (often in English and Spanish) to help guide you in your efforts to engage your community.*

- Also, highly technical issues, or highly technical *dimensions* of issues, aren't appropriate. Questions about basic values and general directions are. The role of standardized tests in schooling is a question the public can engage. Detail about question design and format is best left to experts.

- It is usually a good idea to tackle truly important but not nearly intractable issues. You might want to discuss "Bullying and Discipline," or "Testing for Graduation," for example, but you may want to hold off on "Race Relations in Our Schools" until you've had more practice.

I. Tool: Framing Community Conversations

Will Friedman

Issues must be carefully framed in a community conversation, as shown in Table 8.2.

Table 8.2   Framing Community Conversations

Don't	Do
Ask people to:	Instead:
• Brainstorm solutions out of thin air (an approach more suited to professional meetings where it can be assumed people have a deep knowledge base). • Critique a single approach (which makes people passive and deprives them of comparative leverage). • Present material in a "cross-fire" style (which leads to predictable, simplistic antagonistic debate).	• Provide people with several choices to weigh. • Reflect a spectrum of views. • Spell out pros and cons.
Use hypercharged buzzwords.	Make the connection to people's deeply felt values and concerns.
Use professional jargon and stiff, formal language.	Use plain, straightforward language and visuals that everyone can readily understand.
Create inappropriately large groups.	Bring together large groups, but break them down to smaller work groups of about 12 participants.
Imagine that anyone can lead this work.	Understand you need well-trained, nonpartisan moderators and recorders to ensure success and that no single view dominates.
Go home and forget the conversation.	Plan strategic follow-up so that people see their ideas were taken seriously.

3. Working With Your News and Media Outlets

Does your stomach sink when your administrative assistant announces a local reporter is on the phone and is holding for you? Are you worried about stepping off the media cliff? What's the first thing you should do on hearing a student was shot outside the high school? How do you handle persistent skepticism during a television or radio interview? Answers to these and other questions are found in this section. Public engagement is proactive; media relations is too frequently reactive. Learn how the pros, from presidential candidates to the best local do-gooders, find their message, stay with it, and work with newspapers and radio and television reporters.

A. Reframe . . . Inoculate . . . Communicate

James Harvey

"I can give you a framework for a good answer to any question ever put to you in public," says Kathleen Hall Jamieson, an expert on communications who worked in the U.S. House of Representatives before becoming dean of the Annenberg School for Communication at the University of Pennsylvania. "First, you tell them about your own local success." (For example, Johnny, deaf since the age of four, recently graduated as a Merit Scholar, and Mary, a blind student, has been offered voice scholarships from several prestigious universities.) "Then tell them how that fits into the national success." (American public schools are serving more than 4 million students with disabilities.) "Then illustrate what that means for real kids." (The career choices of students like Johnny and Mary aren't limited anymore; now they can pursue their dreams as contributing members of society, as researchers, teachers, managers, and musicians.)

Educators who permit outsiders to put them on the defensive are one of Jamieson's main peeves. Don't let them do that to you, she says. She's right. You shouldn't let journalists define you; you shouldn't let them pigeonhole you; and under no circumstances should you permit them to set the terms of the discussion. To avoid these traps, you always need to know who you're talking to, where they're coming from, and, perhaps more important, what *you* want to get across.

"Remember," admonishes Jamieson, "audiences invest communication with meaning. Communications experts call that an *enthymeme*—the idea that the audience is as responsible for creating meaning as the speaker." Jamieson offers another three-part structure as a scaffolding for understanding communicating with the public. Point #1: Reframe issues—don't let other people define you. You define yourself. Point #2: Inoculate yourself—acknowledge criticisms you know are coming and define them in your terms. And point #3: Communicate—don't hide from the public. Get out and tell your story.

See Part II for mental models.

Enthymemes. In one sense, the Aristotelian concept of enthymemes is like the modern wag's definition of a communications problem: I know you believe you understand what you think I said, but I'm not sure you comprehend that what you heard is not what I meant! People have their own belief structures; you have to work within and around them.

To be aware of enthymemes, says Jamieson, you have to understand the typical critique of schools and be prepared to both acknowledge and attack it. The standard critique might be outlined in five parts: our teachers aren't very good; teachers are overpaid and underperform; money doesn't make any difference in improving performance; American students lag behind their peers in other countries; and our schools have too few teachers and too many bureaucrats. (Doesn't that cover most of it?) That's the enthymeme many members of the public carry around in their heads, says Jamieson. As superintendent, you have to be aware of it, but you don't need to confirm any of it.

Reframe. When people argue that teachers are overpaid, your question needs to be: compared to what? In comparison with other professionals with advanced degrees, teachers are notoriously underpaid. It's not even unusual for skilled tradesmen to make more than teachers. The point isn't that you want to cut other people's pay; it's that, as Jamieson puts it, "the people who teach our children shouldn't be paid less than computer technicians or carpenters."

Teachers don't work hard? What planet are you on? Who do you think corrects those papers on evenings and weekends? Our teachers average a 50-hour workweek. Money may not make a difference, but tell that to people forking over $20,000 a year and more for private schools. Look at what the wealthy pay on their kids' education. That should be a hint.

Inoculate. And, says Jamieson, it's important to inoculate yourself and your profession against many of these criticisms. "It's a very important principle because it means, just as it does in medicine, that you infect yourself with a weaker strain of the virus in order to develop immunity to it." Take up some of the criticisms that you know are out there, even if they're not openly expressed. Don't be afraid, for example, to tackle the issue of bureaucrats. Say openly, "I know some people believe we have too many people on central payroll." Then, says Jamieson, ask, "Surely you don't mean bus drivers, nurses, counselors, and librarians are little more than bureaucrats? These are the people who get your kids to school safely and take care of them when they're ill."

That's how you reframe an issue. Nobody likes bureaucrats. (Deep down in our souls, most of us don't like bureaucrats, either.) But you lead a system that's full of nurses, librarians, and teacher's aides, not bureaucrats. And while you're reframing this issue, you're doing one of the essential jobs of leadership: you're defending the institution you lead.

Communicate. You need some public-relations savvy too, according to Jamieson. One needs to be tactful in telling members of the media, or the public, that they have their facts wrong. But the truth is, often they don't know what they're talking about. Reframing is often a matter of trying to get your audience to pay attention to something that it already knows. In addition, you need to be able to answer Jamieson's "Twenty Questions" (see Section 3B). These are basic facts and figures about local schools that any citizen expects the superintendent to have at his or her fingertips. It's often surprising, notes Jamieson, how many professionals in a variety of fields just don't have command of the basic facts. We know your budget people are on top of these numbers. Your assistants (if you have them) can probably come up with most of them or run them down quickly. To communicate effectively, however, you need to be able to toss out these figures effortlessly, on demand, and even when nobody's asking.

Media Engagement in Arlington

Many Americans know Arlington, Texas, as the home of the Texas Rangers and the Six Flags Over Texas theme park. It is also one of the nation's largest school districts, home to nearly 60,000 students, with a budget approaching a quarter of a billion annually. In this complex environment, the Arlington Independent School District has campaigned successfully through the media for public support in six bond and two tax-cap elections since 1986. This is how we did it.

Know Your Voters. We study district demographics. Then we survey voters to find out what's on their minds. The assumption in many quarters (sometimes stated, mostly unspoken) is that schools are loaded with deadwood teachers who are failing the community's children. Well-written survey questions will tell you about your community and how to approach it.

Educate the Press and the Media. Work with local journalists in the press and media. Because of the relationship you develop with reporters and editors, they'll trust you to help them get the information they need to write about your referendum. You become, in essence, co-dependent. Most reporters are generalists. You have to educate reporters about your issues.

Stage Events. We tipped off the media that the superintendent would be walking neighborhoods one Saturday morning to talk to citizens about an upcoming bond election. A blizzard hit the city on the night before. Undeterred, the stalwart superintendent continued as planned, and the media jumped all over this great story. The superintendent walked only a few blocks in the bitter cold, but even months after the event columnists referred approvingly to this "pseudo event" that humanized the district.

Inoculate the District. When announcing Arlington's 2000 tax-cap election, the superintendent submitted a guest column to both newspapers that outlined the need for an increase in the tax cap and also presented the opposition's stance. It then countered the criticisms with facts. Inoculation forewarns the public and casts suspicion on the opposition's credibility.

—"Mac" Bernd, Superintendent
(Assisted by Charlene Robertson)

Rules of Engagement for the Media

Your secretary tells you she's not sure what it's all about, but Mr. Making Mountains out of Molehills from the local *Gazette* is on the line. You should pick up right away, correct? Nonsense! You're a busy person. Nobody will be surprised to hear you're tied up in a meeting. Have your secretary get back to Mr. Making Mountains, explaining to him that you're busy, asking what it's about, and telling him you'll be in touch. That way, you'll know if you're dealing with a routine inquiry about a budget number or a hot rumor about your state-championship football coach leaving. (You may also spare yourself the embarrassment of learning from the journalist that the coach is leaving.) You don't want to start answering questions about a serious school brawl without knowing what happened. That's perhaps the most important rule about dealing with the media: you need to scope out the lay of the land ahead of time, as much as possible.

Before you give an interview, advises Jamieson, have someone call the newspaper or the television station and find out what it's all about. "You shouldn't be taken by surprise," she says. "You have a right to know what they're interested in. You may, in fact, be the wrong person to talk to about this issue. Besides, you're a busy person; you have other things to do, and you may need time to collect the data they want. You don't have to agree to do an interview immediately unless it's a genuine crisis—then you need to do it right away."

Next, bracket the time for the interview. "Fifteen minutes is normally about the right amount of time. That way you can extend it if it's going well or you can get out of the situation without being defensive—sorry, I told you I had to go."

In interviews or elsewhere, Jamieson recommends being inclusive and being specific. Always talk about "all of our children" and not "these children." With a pithy tool (see Table 8.6), Jamieson offers a checklist for communicating through newsworthy statements—ways of saying things that are likely to be covered, as opposed to ways of saying things that will elicit a yawn or, worse, invite ridicule.

All professions have their own language, Jamieson notes. But the public doesn't understand "educationese" any more than it understands business mumbo jumbo or legal jargon. As she notes, in discussing all of our children, all of our people are "entitled to clear, jargon-free English."

One final point: pay attention to who's answering your telephone. They can make or break you with journalists. Your assistants need to be your first line of defense, not an excuse for undermining you. You can't afford an administrative assistant who does the following:

- Tells a reporter you'll be right with him and puts the call through without a clue about its purpose.
- Responds at 9:45 A.M. that you're not in yet (which is true but overlooks your 7:00 A.M. breakfast with the local chamber and your Walkthrough at Jefferson Elementary).
- Gets excited if a journalist calls, conceivably ratcheting up tension in high-pressure situations.

This isn't about blaming your support staff. It's about your obligation to provide the right training to your people so that they don't get you into trouble. It's also about finding the right people for the job. What you want is the unflappable assistant who can respond coolly and smoothly under fire with, "Dr. Smith isn't available right now. Can I tell her what this is about and have her get back to you later today?"

The District Under Crisis

OK. You've got the main possibilities for problems contained. Your staff is trained and knows how to take a call from a reporter on deadline. You're rarely put in the position of handling a surprise question from a journalist. You can quote facts and figures with the best of them. And, when called on for interviews, you come across with the aplomb and polish of a professional diplomat (see Section D).

But now a genuine emergency strikes. We've all seen the headlines. You may be faced with them too. A boy is shot outside the high school . . . a boiler explodes just after the children arrive at one of the elementary schools . . . a truly ugly and violent incident of race or gay bashing develops after one of the high school basketball games.

People will look to you with their own metaphor in mind. If you are able to deliver, you can be a genuine leader. The public's metaphor here will not be the superintendent as mechanic or gardener. The public is looking for someone to reassure it. The metaphor it has in mind (and toward which you might reach) is protector of the community's children. Incidents such as these genuinely frighten people. Parents want to be reassured that their children are safe.

Think of Rudy Giuliani, mayor of New York City, in the immediate aftermath of the atrocity of September 11, 2001. Giuliani responded instinctively with precisely the set of attributes any public official should demonstrate amid crisis, says Jamieson. It was a masterful and instinctive performance. Here's what he did (and what you should do with district-size crises):

- He empathized with a shocked community by demonstrating that he shared its sense of horror at the enormity of the great tragedy that had struck the city.
- He communicated clearly about what emergency services were doing in the immediate aftermath of the attacks on the World Trade Center and what the city was doing to prevent further problems.
- He reassured his constituents that New York would emerge stronger and better.
- He gave out information as it came to him, knocked down rumors as nothing more than rumors, and refused to exaggerate the extent of death and destruction until he had a better sense of what was going on.
- He provided phone numbers where anxious citizens could call to learn about fatalities and injuries in the attacks.
- He visited the families of the bereaved, consoling them and sharing their grief.

In short, a man who, on September 10, had been a media laughingstock (because of the collapse of his political ambitions, problems in his personal life that forced him to leave the mayor's mansion, and rumors of an explosive temper) was transformed into a national hero. All this on the basis of his extraordinary public performance on September 11 and the days immediately following.

Here's how Giuliani's performance might play out for you in, say, the incident of the boiler exploding. You issue the following statement (in person before radio and television reporters and in writing for the print press):

All of us are shocked at this terrible explosion that frightened the children in Eden Elementary. [You care about the children and the emotional impact it had on them.] We understand there was a loud explosion as a boiler blew out. As far as we know, no children or staff were hurt. [Give people the facts. Remember that teachers' wives, husbands, parents, and children are worried too.] In accordance with our emergency procedures, the principal and faculty led the children down the street to St. James Episcopal Church, where they were met by a crisis counseling team. [We're well prepared and have an emergency plan for every school.] Parents can pick up their children at St. James, which is located at Pine and 11th. [You don't want parents arriving at your office looking for their kids.] We will keep the children there and feed them until parents pick them up. [We're not bureaucrats; we take care of your children.] We have set up an emergency number at 333-555-1234. [You don't want your switchboard overloaded with calls, either.] I have directed our engineers to check the heating, cooling, electrical, and plumbing systems in all 11 schools in the district to make sure our children are safe. I've asked them to report back to me this afternoon. [Every parent in the district is upset and wants to know you're worrying about their kids as well.] We will not reopen Eden until the fire marshal tells me it's safe to do so. [I will seek competent, disinterested advice on this.] If need be, Eden children will be distributed to Adam and Eve elementary schools on a temporary basis. [Here is what we are going to do if we can't reopen the school in the short run.] Parents can learn more about this from the emergency number. I am heading over to St. James right now to see the children, thank our staff, and see what else needs to be done. [I care about your children's safety. I'm on top of this and I'm going to stay on top of it.]

You will experience a near-irresistible urge to remind people that the boiler in Eden Elementary would have been replaced if the bond issue had passed two years ago. Resist the temptation. Nobody cares today, and it is petty to bring it up. Tomorrow (when the finger-pointing starts), you can depend on the press to make this point for you.

You can be assured your statement will be playing on the car radio as you head for St. James. That number will be flashing on local television screens. This statement may not put you in Giuliani's league, but it could help make you a local hero.

B. Tool: 20 Questions

Kathleen Hall Jamieson

Every superintendent should have answers to the following 20 questions at their fingertips.

District Profile: Information
Every Superintendent Needs to Know

- What is the expenditure per pupil in your district?
- How much has that figure increased or decreased in the last decade?
- What is the average teacher salary?
- How much has the average teacher salary increased or decreased in the last decade?
- What is the district graduation rate?
- How much has the graduation rate increased or decreased in the last decade?
- What proportion of students go on to college?
- What proportion of students are classified as special-needs students?
- What proportion of students use English as a second language?
- What proportion of students qualify for help under the Americans With Disabilities Act?
- What are district test scores (local and comparison with national data)? What are five-year comparisons with national and local scores?
- What is the total district budget? How much has the budget increased or decreased in the last decade? Compare that with the city budget? The county budget?
- What proportion of students come from homes defined as in poverty?
- What is the ethnic/minority composition of the student body?
- What proportion do not speak English at home?
- What proportion of students are mainstreamed? Have a serious disability?
- What is the average salary of workers in your community? What has been their proportionate salary increase over the last five years?
- List members of your state legislature who have a public school education. What proportion were educated in public versus private schools?
- Are any legislators alumni of your district/schools?
- List members of the press who have a public school education. Are any of them alumni of your district/schools?

C. Tool: Creating a Newsworthy Statement

Kathleen Hall Jamieson

Want the press to pay attention to your news? Make it easy for them by following the easy checklist in Table 8.3.

Table 8.3   A Checklist for Creating Newsworthy Statements Likely to Be Covered and Published

To Be	Or . . . Not to Be
A single coherent statement clearly summarizing the issue in jargon-free English	A rambling statement skirting the issue in gobbledygook
Available before deadline at a convenient place for news gatherers	Available at midnight near the North Pole
Requiring no additional information	Requiring at least five appendices to clarify the point
Written to be understood on first hearing or reading	Written to be figured out by a cryptographer
Which can be delivered clearly and dramatically in less than 14 seconds	Which could not be delivered effectively by Laurence Olivier in less than 35 minutes
Delivered in a symbolic setting	Delivered in a setting with no apparent relationship to the statement
By a person who dramatizes the issue	By a mumbler
In a manner not subject to parody	In a manner that brings joy to the hearts of comedians everywhere, who encourage the speaker to run for office

D. Tool: Tackling the Media Interview

Kathleen Hall Jamieson

So, a journalist wants to interview you? You need to come across as professional and competent. Table 8.4 shows some guidelines for making a good impression and staying on message.

Table 8.4   Tackling the Media Interview

Interviewer Takes Seriously Someone Who:	*Interviewer Takes With a Grain of Salt Someone Who:*
Is professionally dressed (decent tie and coat for men; jacket for women)	Is inappropriately dressed (men in sweaty golf shirt and shorts; women competing with Britney Spears)
Is professionally groomed	Is unshaven or tattooed
Understands what the interview is about	Is curious about what interviewer wants
Is on top of district facts	Is at sea on critical points
Reframes, inoculates, and communicates	Wanders all over the map
Hands you a district fact-sheet (understanding that the interviewer just came from reporting on car prices)	Expects interviewer to understand the district population and geographic boundaries
Offers a business card with clearly spelled name and title	Trusts the television producer will spell the district's name properly
Follows up on promised information	Forgets the interviewer the moment she leaves the office

4. Communications Planning

Just as your administrative assistant can leave you open to criticism in dealing with the media, so too can your district's publications. You cannot afford to have the message you are communicating—a dedication to high standards and a commitment to leaving no child behind—contradicted by district publications or surly receptionists. Communications planning is a critical component of public engagement. In this section, you'll learn about internal and external communications, communications planning, and how to use communications audits to improve your district's performance.

A. Communications: Internal and External

James Harvey

Recently, a former school principal, now a teacher and the father of a middle-school boy, discovered that he needed to pay a fee to allow his son to participate in the school band and orchestra. The written instructions were a bit confusing. It was unclear if one fee would be sufficient, or if one was required for the band and another for the orchestra. Eager to get his son signed up, he set out to get some clarification.

Picking up the phone to talk with the school, this experienced school administrator soon discovered himself hopelessly lost in the school's voice mail system. Irritated, he stopped by the school to seek an answer and, following the posted instructions, reported to the school office. There, he found an imposing barrier walling him off from the office itself, behind which a receptionist was talking animatedly on the phone. She glanced at the father fleetingly, before turning her back to continue what seemed to be a private conversation. About five minutes later, she finished her conversation, hung up, and, turning to her visitor, said, without interest, "What do you want?"

Your efforts as a superintendent to create an open, inclusive district that welcomes visitors can be wrecked in five minutes by the receptionist whose attitude says: "Get lost." When you think of communications, you need to think of both external and internal audiences. And you also need to be sure that everyone in your organization is acting on the same set of assumptions.

This section of the fieldbook guides you through some of these land mines.

B. Tool: A Communications Audit

Adam Kernan-Schloss
Sylvia Soholt

How do you get started in assessing your communications? A communications audit is one way. You should interview a broad cross section of the district and its citizens. Interview each group separately. In diverse districts, it is often helpful to subdivide the parent groups by race and ethnicity. A neutral source, not a district employee, should conduct these interviews, using the same questions with each group and guaranteeing confidentiality. The audit report should be divided into Findings and Recommendations and should include both short- and long-term recommendations. (Short-term recommendations are to be implemented within a month or two as a demonstration that the district acts on the feedback it receives.) Share the report with participants to build trust. Here are the questions you need to begin with.

- What comes to mind when you think of _____ school district?
- How would you describe the district to someone not familiar with it? (Strengths? Weaknesses?)
- What are the most important issues (goals) in your schools?
- *Follow with:* Are you currently receiving information about these issues? *Or:* Do you feel you're being informed about progress on these issues on a regular basis?
- How do you learn about what's going on in the school district? Are the communications activities very effective, in your view? Or does the district use tools or activities that don't work very well?
- *For parents and other community members:* What kind of information do you need to be able to talk to your neighbors about what's going on in the district? *For school employees:* What information do you need to be successful in your job?
- *For both:* How would you like to receive this information?
- Do barriers stand in the way of communication in the school district? (What keeps communication from happening?)
- Tell me one thing that would make communications better in _____ schools.
- How does the public judge the success of _____ school district? What measures does the district use? What would you use?
- What would it take for people to know that _____ schools were getting better?
- Is there anything else you would like me to know?

C. Tool: Vital Signs of Public Engagement

Adam Kernan-Schloss

Here are some vital signs of public engagement:

- *Are you doing a lot of listening?* Do you have a clear idea of the concerns of various segments of the public? Do you have public opinion research about the concerns? Are you regularly surveying staff, parents, students, and the general public?

- *Are you responding to what you want to hear?* Do you change policies and practices based on what you're hearing?

- *Are you inclusive?* Do you communicate clearly with non-English-speaking constituents in your district?

- *Is everyone focused on learning?* That includes staff, students, parents, and community. Do all policies lead to this goal? Are your communications activities directly linked to this goal?

- *Does everyone understand the standards?* Are you confident that principals, teachers, and parents could all give a fairly good answer to the question of what students in fourth, seventh, and eleventh grades are expected to know and be able to do?

- *Have you taken care of the basics?* Do you see welcoming receptionists, clean grounds, sufficient textbooks, timely pay-checks, and all the rest of what goes into a respectful environment?

- *Are your messages free of jargon?* Whether written in English, Spanish, or other languages, can people understand what you're saying?

- *Do you have a strategic engagement plan with measurable goals and objectives?* "We want to increase public support" is not sufficient. Something like: "We want to involve 15% more parents in school activities" would be.

- *Are you explaining standards clearly to everyone?* That includes staff, teachers, students, and parents. Are you reporting results honestly?

- *Do you have a calendar of key events and opportunities?* This can help you get ahead of the curve to communicate your main messages.

- *Do you have a sounding board?* Have you formed a group of key communicators as a listening post? Key allies, staff and non-staff, can serve as a feedback loop and outreach tool.

- *Can you point to specific examples of success?* What can you identify in terms of student work, classrooms, schools, and the district?

D. Tool: How User-Friendly Is Your School?

Sylvia Soholt

Effective communication and engagement isn't just the superintendent's job. Here's a tool for school principals.

An Inventory of User-Friendliness

School _____

First Impressions

1. What do people see when they come to our school? To our classrooms?
2. What visible evidence do visitors find that demonstrates our focus on learning and student achievement?
3. How are people greeted on the phone and in person by staff? What kind of encounters do they have with students?
4. What kind of materials do we give them to provide a picture of what goes on at our school?
5. What information do we prepare to inform parents (and community) about student learning?

____ Standards or curriculum guides for parents

____ Brochure

____ Calendar

____ Newsletter

____ Student newsletter

____ Student portfolios

____ Report cards

____ Web site

____ Video

____ Cable TV

____ School radio

_____ Homework hotlines

_____ Other

6. What messages about student learning and achievement will readers find in our materials (about student learning, how it's measured, or how parents can help their children)?

7. What activities do we offer that provide opportunities for parents to have person-to-person conversations about learning? (For example, parent conferences, response to calls, home visits, and the like. Set target percentage rates for each.)

8. What are we doing to ensure a high rate of participation in the activities we provide?

9. What volunteer opportunities do we offer for parents and others to promote student achievement? (For example, tutoring, mentoring, or classroom assistance. Set target participation rates for each.)

10. What assistance do we provide parents so they can help their children learn?

11. How do we identify the parents who need person-to-person support in helping their children learn? What parenting support do we provide families?

12. How are we providing access to information about our school through the Internet?

13. Are our teachers using the school Web sites or national sites (such as *School Notes.com*) to provide parents with information about classroom progress, materials, options for enrichment, and homework?

E. Tool: A Matrix for Public Engagement

Adam Kernan-Schloss
Sylvia Soholt

"How are we doing?" is a question you need to ask everyone not just once in a while but practically every week. The matrix in Table 8.5 can help you ask and track your responses to that question. This one-page outline summarizes a more extensive 26-page document developed for the Forum by KSA-Plus Communications and the Public Agenda Foundation.

Table 8.5   Matrix: Public Engagement at a Glance

Activity	Level 1	Level 2	Level 3	Level 4
Infrastructure				
1. Planning	Planning to plan	Plan focuses on ad-hoc mix of materials/ messages/events	Plan, based on an audit, focuses on priorities	Plan, built with community involvement, focuses on student achievement
2. Staff Training	Printed materials only	Limited customer-service training for administrators and support staff	Broad communications training, including media training, for all staff	Broad communications training for all staff, focused on district priorities
3. Resources (Budget, Staff, Technology)	Resources for emergencies only	Minimal resources and tools; part-time staff; no e-mail or Web	Moderate resources; full-time staff; some e-mail and Web	Funded public engagement office; extensive e-mail and Web
Activities				
4. Listening/ Research	Listening only when initiated by public	Infrequent efforts to listen	Regular listening with mix of tools	Feedback actively sought—and acted on
5. Welcoming Environment	Visitors usually feel welcome	Visitors feel welcome	District proactively reaches out to bring community into the schools	Customer-service ethic embedded in schools; community use of schools increases; district meets community on its turf
6. Two-Way Communications	Two-way is still mostly one-way	Minimal attempt to promote conversations, mainly with involved parents	Regular opportunities for conversations are planned, with outreach to nontraditional audiences	Systematic effort to promote conversation, focused on student achievement, engage publics to develop mutual understanding about how to improve schools
7. School- Community Partnerships	Partners limited to PTA	District controls partnerships	Partners share decision making with district	District and partners focus benchmarks on achievement
8. Publications	Basic information only	Materials are reader friendly and match readers' interests	Materials improved with citizen and student input	Greater focus on achievement, more opportunities for users to customize information
9. Media Relations	The priority is damage control	Ongoing relationship with media is built on trust	Media efforts focused on district goals, student achievement, public engagement	Media help promote student achievement and public engagement

The complete matrix can be obtained at the Danforth Forum's Web site, www.muohio .edu/forumscp/ *under the public engagement section.*

In brief, it helps you address questions such as: What does good practice look like? How are we doing? What specifically can we do to improve our efforts to communicate effectively and to engage our community's many stakeholders in the work of the school district? Questions such as these are routine among superintendents, school board members, and others charged with public relations, community relations, public engagement, customer service, and similar responsibilities.

The matrix (and each of the sections in the more fully developed scheme) is organized into four levels. Level 1 (far left) covers the most basic, bare-bones work. The work in Levels 2 and 3 tends to be progressively more sophisticated and complex—involving more face-to-face interactions, and some recognition of the importance of partnerships and two-way communications with your stakeholders. The work described under Level 4 in each section represents best practice; these activities focus heavily on student achievement and all work is regularly evaluated and improved, based on feedback from staff and community.

The levels and activities are not perfectly linear. Superintendents should not feel they have to check off all the activities in Level 1 before moving on to Level 2 and so on. Nor should this guide be considered a performance rubric—the intent is to describe activities that are worth doing in each level, not to define *how well* they should be done.

5. Reflective Practice

How do we make sense out of all this material? We asked several superintendents who had been engaged in serious efforts at public engagement to share their thoughts with us. After reviewing their reflections, use the list of Reflective Practice questions to guide your work in public engagement.

A. Which Page Are You On? Superintendents Speak

Nelda Cambron-McCabe

Several superintendents shared their thoughts about public engagement with other school leaders embarking on this journey. Here's what they had to say.

*With everything else on the superintendent's
shoulders, why do you think it's important
to immerse yourself in public engagement?*

Barbara Gates (Crossett, Arkansas): Public engagement provides a way to focus our leadership work. We've constantly reminded each other to stay focused on the main thing—student achievement. We may be trying to pass a bond issue, but it is not for physical facilities but for student learning. Public engagement keeps achievement up front for the district and community.

Cloyde "Mac" Bernd (Arlington, Texas): I agree completely that focus is paramount. We really do know how to improve student learning. The problem is keeping the district focused enough to be able to do it. Our ability to do that is affected tremendously by the public's support and attitude toward the district.

Linda Murray (San Jose, California): It's about creating better schools and working with the community. We cannot make the mistake of thinking public engagement is an end in itself. It's not.

Richard Benjamin (Cobb County, Georgia): Creating better schools is a critical point. It's not about defending or ensuring the survival of our present schools. I took on public engagement as a way of building new and better learning opportunities for kids. It also models our democratic values for students, showing the public how to shape the outcomes for schools.

*What does a superintendent need
to know before initiating public engagement?*

Benjamin: The most critical aspect may be an understanding of the differences among public engagement, public relations, and marketing. They all come into play, but the purpose and nature of each is quite different. I've noticed that a lot of school systems are now using the term "public engagement." They don't have a clue what it is. They are still focusing on one-way communication.

John Thompson (Pittsburgh, Pennsylvania): It's the same all over. A problem comes up and we rush out and bring a group of people together, calling it public engagement. But public engagement is systemic. You work on it always. When a problem occurs, convening the public is not a crisis response because they are part of the ongoing deliberations about what kinds of schools we want.

Murray: Educational leaders must recognize up front that there is a real discipline with this work. It's not just opening the doors and saying, "you all come on in and tell me what you think." Capacity building may be the most important background task. . . . We weren't taught public engagement in Leadership 101, and it may be our most essential work.

Cliff Janey (Rochester, New York): Leaders must realize that engagement is not about simply using the tools and processes that we share here. The real work is a shift in thinking about the schools' relationship with the community.

Benjamin: For me, this shift in mental models occurred with the question, Whose schools are these? When I stopped thinking of them as my schools and started thinking about them as belonging to the community, involvement of the public then became a necessity. You see your role differently.

Gerry Harge (Nye County, Nevada): I thought a particularly successful shift in mental models for our group is that schools don't do it by themselves. That caused us to include a lot of people in the process.

Thompson: School administrators must know their community and their environment before they start a public engagement initiative. You must be able to identify your public first. For instance, in Pittsburgh we have 47 school districts in Allegheny County. So who's my public? Thirty-five percent of the people do not have kids in the school district. Who's my public?

Murray: Bottom line—public engagement is hard work. People know when you're just touching the surface and simply doing it for public relations as opposed to real engagement. Engagement is everyone's responsibility, especially the superintendent's.

Bernd: It's also important to remember that public engagement and public relations are not mutually exclusive. A piece of this work is public relations.

What do you point to as your most significant learning?

Murray: The process of developing the format for community conversations, facilitating them, drawing people in, making it worth people's time to participate, and following up. In such a diverse community as San Jose, we discovered so much common ground in our various communities. All these individuals really want the best for their children and for their children's education and they feel so frustrated about not knowing how to really make that happen. Over and over we heard, "What's my role? How do I sign on?"

Harge: Without a doubt, my greatest learning occurred with the recognition that I could not do public engagement without first doing internal engagement with the school district staff and school board. We could not begin to engage the public until the staff had the capacity to work through these issues.

Benjamin: I came to appreciate the importance of focusing on parents first, helping parents see their contributions to student achievement. Through public engagement, we focused on building different relationships with parents—more active involvement at home and greater participation in the schools.

Bernd: An important insight for me is that the unimaginable can come from the engagement process. Two teachers in one of our high schools were disenchanted with the fact that so many kids were just lost in the shuffle. So they decided to start a charter school. My initial reaction was, "No way! Fix it inside." But we began a civic discourse and now have this wonderful school in the community. . . . I turned from a skeptic to a strong believer that this school has a place and belongs.

What are the implications of public engagement for your work with other public officials in the community?

Janey: What I've seen so often is that everyone is waiting for someone to convene the groups. The courts are waiting; the social services are waiting. Public engagement showed us that we could take on that role. Many of us convened the initial conversations and other people took off with it. Public engagement is a way to build better communities, not just better schools.

Thompson: We found that we not only had some common interests and problems but we also had some commons skills and things to share. This led to joint workshops where frontline employees began to work together and increased their ability to share and communicate data that affected all organizations.

The conversations cannot simply take place at the top among superintendents, mayors, police chiefs, and commissioners.

Gates: So much of the relationship comes through sitting down with other public officials and realizing that the person pointing his finger at you really wants the same thing you do. When we can have open conversations, we break down those barriers.

Where does the media fit into your work?

Bernd: We cannot overemphasize the importance of the super-intendent's working relationship with the media. In many of our school systems, the public forms its opinion of the schools based on the media message. I'm in a community of 300,000 people. I have people come up to me all the time who think they know me and the schools on the basis of what they have read in the newspaper. You can never forget this. Too often we learn how to work with the media through the mistakes we make.

Harge: The lessons from Kathleen Hall Jamieson stay in my mind. You must be proactive by setting the stage yourself. Public engagement certainly can shape that stage.

Are there other considerations that you think are important to succeed in this effort?

Janey: Networking with other superintendents may be the key to this work. It's hard to do it alone. You need someone to listen to you and critique your ideas. It helps to watch others. You can learn together.

Thompson: Other superintendents starting this work must be ready to make a long-term commitment to see success.

Harge: It's essential to identify individuals who can provide the training to do the work. The capacity does not reside in most school systems.

Murray: The engagement must be systemic. The focus cannot be simply on the community but also must include the school district staff, from the school board office to the school level. In the face of high mobility among superintendents, this becomes essential to sustain the effort.

B. Questions for Reflective Practice

Public engagement, sending messages through the media, making sure you're communicating effectively . . . it's a big challenge. Here are some questions that may hold the key to your success.

How would you define the difference between public engagement and public relations? Do key staff members, including those in public affairs, share your understanding?

How many different kinds of publics do you serve in your district? Do they all share the same perceptions, or do variations exist? What, if any, differences exist between how you and the other elites in your community view the world and the perceptions of your publics?

Where do you and your key people stand on the seven-stage continuum of coming to public judgment? Where do the leaders of your community stand? What about citizens and parents?

Define the issues that might frame a community conversation in your district. Think about how you could hold such a conversation. How would you start? Where would you hold the meetings? Who would you invite? How could you ensure expert and neutral facilitation?

Are you confident that your administrative assistant possesses the poise and savvy to act in your best interests when the phones light up during a crisis?

Are emergency procedures available in your schools to cover unexpected events and disasters? Does everyone understand them? Are you confident of that?

Can you answer Kathleen Hall Jamieson's 20 questions? If not, why not? How do you know what's going on in your district?

Can your board members answer the same questions? If not, why not? How do they know what's going on in their district?

Are you relaxed and confident during media interviews? Don't worry if you are not. These situations are stressful for everyone. Can you find some coaching to improve your performance and reduce the level of stress?

How "user friendly" are your schools? Is there a welcoming atmosphere? Are communications clear and in jargon-free English? Are clear, jargon-free communications available in any second languages spoken in your community?

Have you thought about a "communications audit" or "communications matrix" to improve your relationship with your publics?

Part IX
So What Does
All This Mean?

We can't blame you if your head is spinning. We've asked you to keep your eye on several moving targets (the seven commonplaces) from a platform that moves from one image or metaphor to another. This concluding part pulls these disparate strands together. First, it asks how each of the commonplaces would play itself out in your district depending on which metaphor of the district you (and your colleagues) have in mind. How would you expect your district to behave if driven by an image of the district as a political entity? What would it look like if the image were a brain functioning as a learning organization? And what does each of these images mean for each of the commonplaces?

Next, we try to illustrate the material more clearly by working around a graphic that ties together much of the discussion of images, adaptive work, and learning organizations. This helps you revisit your leadership role against a simple template. This template asks two questions. How complicated is the challenge you are addressing? And how confident are you that you know how to respond? We suggest four leadership styles you might adopt depending on your answers to those questions.

1. Reconciling
Commonplaces and Images

What does all of this mean, in practical terms, for the way your district functions? Theory's fine. It's as true in this part as it was when we mentioned it in Part II: there's nothing as practical as a good theory.

But amid all the data and theory presented here, how are you as a superintendent or aspiring district leader to make sense out of what's happening around you? We don't pretend that's easy. We've covered a lot of ground with you. Let's review it. First, recall each of the commonplaces of leadership explored in this fieldbook: leadership, governance, standards and assessment, race and class, school principals, collaboration, and community engagement. Now try to imagine how each of these commonplaces might play itself out in districts functioning under different images. To keep this as straightforward as possible, we've laid out many of the possibilities you'd expect in Table 9.1.

We're going to lead you through the table but, first, just take a look at it. Anything jump out at you? What seems clear is that as different images interact with the commonplaces within your district, they are likely to elicit different behaviors, either on your part or the part of others. A district functioning under the "machine" image, for example, is likely to react to issues of race and class by insisting that everyone should be treated alike. But the political image may well involve selective advocacy around race and class—on behalf of either minority or majority groups. Glance at the table again. The interrelationship between the images and the commonplaces potentially explains a lot of the behavior you see in your district.

The second thing that jumps out of the table is that most of the behavior elicited by the old images is tough and hard-nosed, whichever image is involved. This is Mars talking. And Mars speaks single-loop language. These are images that appeal to the status quo or the status quo ante. They encourage behaviors that narrow our aspirations for human possibilities. Most of these images are likely to take for granted that the problems you encounter are technical in nature. The expectation is that you should be able to "fix" them with technical approaches. These images emphasize playing by the rules, following bureaucratic norms, reinforcing tradition, manipulating data and interest groups, and expecting schools to sort children into winners and losers. If you see unattractive behavior in your district, examine the images people use when speaking and writing to you. You can count on it: most of these will be older, inherited images of the world.

Conversely, the emerging images elicit behaviors that are much more nuanced in their appreciation for the challenges the commonplaces pose. Here, Venus enters the picture. And Venus is a double-loop thinker. These are metaphors that demonstrate

Table 9.1   Understanding How Images Drive the Commonplaces of Leadership

| | Inherited Images | | | |
The Commonplaces	*Machine*	*Political*	*Psychic*	*Domination*
Leadership	Hierarchical and rule driven	Balance group demands	Protect status quo	Autocratic
Governance	Focused on control	Interest driven	Focus on ends	Winners and losers
Standards/Assessment	Ensuring uniform outcomes	Data manipulation	Selective data usage	Expect bell curve
Race and Class	Treat everyone alike	Selective advocacy	Tracking	Blame the victim
Developing Principals	Technical skills	Emphasis on loyalty	"Groupthink"	Demand party line
Collaboration	Limited by rules	Shifting alliances	Narrow and limited	Polarize groups
Engagement	Mechanical	Building coalitions	Reinforce tradition	With selected elites

| | Emerging Images | | | |
The Commonplaces	*Culture*	*Organism*	*Brain*	*Flux/Transformation*
Leadership	Symbolic	Nurturing	Distributed	Transformative
Governance	Focused on values, norms, rituals	Survival	Self-organizing systems	Evolving
Standards/Assessment	Ethnography—story, symbol	Feedback	Integrated information web	Data as "attractor"
Race and Class	All children can learn	Nourishing	Formative and summative	Massive system/social change
Developing Principals	Shape school culture	Emphasize adaptation	Learning to learn	Leaders of "chaos"
Collaboration	Affirm cooperation	Stress cohesion	Systems perspective	Around meaning and purpose
Engagement	Develop shared meaning	Symbiotic	Authentic and continuous	Relational

considerably more respect for the possibilities of human growth and skepticism about the status quo and the status quo ante. These emerging images also are more likely to acknowledge the complexity of what you're facing, to consider emerging challenges to be adaptive in nature, and to require the entire range of skills and talents in the community for their resolution. These are images that emphasize that all children can learn, that collaboration is important, that feedback is essential, and that organizations have meaning and purpose that we shape every day. If you see kinder and gentler behavior in your district or portions of it, you may be sure that what is driving this behavior are images of the district as more of a culture or organism than a machine or political system.

Work your way through these images and commonplaces. Explore them with your staff and members of the board. Bringing the underlying tensions involved in the interaction of these images with the commonplaces might go a long way toward illuminating some of the problems keeping you awake at night. This exercise is unlikely to do much harm. If it does, you shouldn't be in that district anyway. But potentially, it can do you and the children in your district a lot of good. It can do so by bringing greater clarity to what is going on in the district, spotlighting the motivations underlying the behavior you see, and surfacing potential "double-loop" solutions in place of attractive but deceptive quick fixes.

Inherited Images

Clearly, in the terms of Peter Senge, Ron Heifetz, and others, the inherited images presented here do not encourage a learning organization focused on difficult adaptive work. These are images emphasizing power. Many of them assume we already have all the answers. In such a situation, why waste time on questions? We already have the answers. You, and the obdurate people on your payroll, are probably part of the problem. And why should we adapt to the environment around us? The environment should bend to our will.

District as a Machine. This appears to be one of the more benign of the inherited images. Unlike several of the others, it has the attraction of apparent neutrality. Its drawback, of course, is its technocratic (and therefore unrealistic) approach to resolving complicated human problems. The district as machine is a district committed to alignment to such a degree that everybody will be marching to the same drummer, conceivably creating oppressive conditions for the most challenged children. This is a metaphor in which district leadership will be driven by rules and governed by hierarchy. The governance system of which you are (or will be) a part will be organized around maintaining control. Standards and assessment will be central to your district's functioning here (and the state's and the nation's) and oriented around attempting to ensure uniform results for all children. This mode of thinking has crystal-clear implications for race and class, as district officials insist on treating everyone alike. What this metaphor implies for developing principals, collaboration, and public engagement is not promising. Principal development will emphasize mastery of technical skills (since we know what we're doing). Collaboration will be grudging and rule driven, while community engagement, to the extent it exists at all, will be perfunctory, mechanical, and oriented around confirming where the district is already headed.

As superintendent, you will be a mechanic in charge of a bureaucracy, greasing and lubricating the gears that keep the machine functioning, while periodically replacing parts during routine maintenance.

District as Political System. This metaphor describes many school systems, large and small alike. It might describe yours. On the surface, of course, few acknowledge the politics of district leadership, but behind the scenes many districts are all about who is in charge and how the money is spent and jobs allocated. If you find yourself worrying more about procurement and hiring than learning, you're probably in a highly politicized district. This is a district that is driven by the imperative to balance the demands of competing interests. To achieve those ends, it will not hesitate to advocate selectively on the part of key groups (advantaged or disadvantaged) and manipulate data to make itself look as good as possible. It emphasizes principal loyalty; collaboration and public engagement will be seen as coalition building and system maintenance.

As superintendent, you will be a political operative, more attuned to constituency demands than student needs.

District as Psychic Prison. This powerful image describes the people within the district perhaps more than the district itself. This could very easily be the mindset of the inhabitants of any of the eight images presented here. People create their own psychic prisons, whether in a district dominated by a power-driven autocrat in the mayor's office or a flower child leading the board. But in general, if this is your district, it will be one that protects the status quo and sees governance as something oriented around the mission and end of protecting the status quo. It will selectively use data to serve its purposes; it will also be surprised that anyone would think of questioning tracking (or expanding programs for the gifted and talented) as a sound educational strategy. Seeking convergent thinking (groupthink) will drive principal selection and collaboration, while engagement will be narrow, limited, and oriented around reinforcing tradition.

Where do you stand in this district, as superintendent or potential superintendent? The expectation of your role will be clear: you will be there to tend the flame and keep it alive.

District as Instrument of Domination. Practically all of us can recall a boss at some point who was an intimidating autocrat, a bully. But what if an entire district behaves that way? Impossible, you say? How would you describe the existence of "separate but equal" schools in the South until a few generations ago if not as instruments of domination? Vestiges of such behavior undoubtedly remain in some districts. Here, leadership will be autocratic. It's not likely to be your leadership style, but it could be. It could also be the board chair's, or the mayor's, or the local county commissioner's. It will be all about control. Governance will nod approvingly as winners and losers are defined in the classroom, since the bell curve will be taken for granted and failure will be blamed on the students. The ability to hew to the party line will be the major selection criterion for principals. Collaboration will be more akin to polarization and demonizing of weaker groups, while public engagement will be limited largely to local elites.

There's no nice way to say it: as superintendent, you will be a flunkey. If you sense these dynamics at work in your next interview, don't take the job. If you're already there, get out.

Emerging Images

The emerging images described here are much more suited to working through adaptive challenges. These are images of organizations that don't assume leaders and other influential figures have all the answers. Leaders in these organizations don't believe they're smarter than everyone else. People in these districts are likely to be far more modest about their own certainties, more respectful of the knowledge and experience brought to the organization by employees and people outside the district. Districts found in the "emerging images" cluster will heed the wisdom of the great journalist H. L. Mencken to the effect that, "For every problem, no matter how difficult or complicated, there is a solution that is simple, direct and wrong."

District as Culture. Individual public school districts in the United States follow this model, but it is likely to be much more common in associations of like-minded school leaders (e.g., The Coalition for Essential Schools) or in private (frequently religious) school coalitions. This is a system in which leadership often emphasizes symbolism, because symbols carry so much meaning within the community. Governance focuses also on shared values, norms, and rituals. Standards and assessment are as likely to rely on stories and symbols as on tests and data, because universal meanings can be read into individual experience. Districts emphasizing shared culture will always insist that all children can learn and will encourage cooperation and the development of shared meaning because collaboration and engagement are at the heart of the culture.

As superintendent, you will be a very lucky man or woman. You will preside over a district that shares your norms and values. It will also be a district that is much more likely to seek to explain failure by looking for faults within itself than by highlighting your shortcomings or those of your students.

District as an Organism. This district will be another one with a remarkably open environment. If this district is seriously threatened, however, it will, like most organisms, concentrate on survival. And then things might get sticky for you as superintendent. Here, leadership will emphasize nurturing staff, teachers, and students. It will rarely be coercive except, perhaps, when the need to emphasize survival emerges and balancing relationships between the schools and the community comes to the fore. Standards and assessment will be directed at feedback for students, teachers, and parents, not high-stakes decisions or punishment. The district as organism will emphasize nurturing all students as a strategy for closing the achievement gap. And it will also concentrate on encouraging principals who can adapt, while emphasizing community cohesion and close bonding with the community (symbiosis) as strategies for collaboration and engagement.

As superintendent, you will be a gardener, expected to lovingly tend to the needs of the organism for which you're responsible.

District as a Brain. Here we find one of the most complex images. It is also an image that, while appearing highly technocratic, works at creating conscious looping and feedback systems to encourage innovation and growth. It routinely engages in double-loop learning, in the process questioning the appropriateness of its norms and practices. Here, district leadership is distributed. The board is likely to delegate to you a great deal of authority, which you in turn are expected to pass on to school teams. Governance will not be hierarchical, but more self-organizing, with groups and committees springing up to deal with issues as they arrive. Standards and assessment will go far beyond mindless "truth and consequences" to set out to build a truly integrated web of information. Are children in your seventh-grade classroom doing poorly on math tests? This district will be able to point to assessments on these specific children indicating that the blockage lies in "order of operations," not "converting fractions to decimals." The brain will emphasize formative and summative evaluations to deal with challenges of race, class, and the achievement gap. In fact, it will consider the existence of the achievement gap to be a challenge to the system's intelligence. Principals? They must become learners who model learning for others. And collaboration and community engagement will be genuine, authentic, and continuous, both because the brain continuously senses its environment and because it is committed to a systems approach to everything.

As superintendent, you will be a combination of field scientist (presiding over data) and systems designer (ever alert to how changes in one part of the district's nervous system vibrate elsewhere in this complex organism).

District as a Site of Flux and Transformation. Leading this district will provide you with the ultimate experience in dealing with adaptive challenges and developing a learning organization. Educational organizations have been described as "loosely organized anarchies," and the district as a site of flux and transformation is likely to exhibit those tendencies. Leadership here will require you to be transformative. All leaders today say that's what they're interested in, but in this district that is what you'd better be.

Governance in this district will evolve as the district changes. Data will not so much drive change as "attract" attention around which change can be explored. Issues of race and class will call for similar transformation—in this case reaching far beyond the school to encourage massive social transformations. Principals will be developed as people who are comfortable with the ambiguity (or even chaos) of the district. Collaboration and engagement will be important, but only to the extent that they serve the district's interest in evolving. Collaboration will be around meaning and purpose, while public engagement will emphasize relationships that assist the change the district pursues.

What about you? As superintendent, you are likely to be a philosopher, attuned to the "Zen" of change. Even if you're not a philosopher, you'll need to be comfortable with the central contradiction of flux and transformation, the reality that the district might shift direction tomorrow.

Mutually Exclusive?

These metaphors resonate powerfully with much of the current discussion about organizational life in school districts. Are these images and their implications for organizational behavior around the commonplaces mutually exclusive? Of course not. That's the value of the images. You are almost certain to find several of these images (and their associated behaviors) simultaneously at work in your district.

In many ways, each of these metaphors describes a genuine reality in your organizational life. At different times, you will draw on different metaphors to describe what is happening before you—and others within your district will also. Doing justice to the complexity of a school district requires multiple images.

Our argument (and Gareth Morgan's) is not that a single metaphor exists to best explain your district, but that you must become adept at developing a story line to "read" and shape your organization. What is the dominant metaphor that applies in a particular situation (e.g., the machine)? What other images support and shape that dominant metaphor (e.g., organizations as cultures or political systems)? How do different people within your district (for example, the board and the union) "read" what's happening? And what are the implications of what both you and they believe in terms of the seven commonplaces? Your challenge is to move beyond the conflicts that appear in your office with predictable regularity every morning to understand the mindsets and mental models contributing to them. Here, nuance and a subtle touch will be your allies.

2. Four Leadership Styles

In the end, of course, your success as superintendent will come down to leadership. It always does. What does all the detail and complexity we've nearly overwhelmed you with in this book imply for your actions as a leader?

Marc Roberts of the School of Public Health at Harvard University has a take on this that you may find helpful. It pulls together in a useful way a lot of the material presented here. Are you intrigued by the distinctions between adaptive and technical work? Are you trying to use double-loop learning? You can find a way to think about both here. Do the organizational images interest you? You will be able to see them here and find new images to guide your own behavior. What about leading a learning organization? Are you relying too frequently on "quick fixes"? Roberts's intuition can help you with all of these leadership challenges.

What is a learning organization? And how do we create one? The answer to these questions, suggests Roberts, cannot be found in particular models. You need to get your district to understand that its sense of mastery is embedded not in specific technologies or procedures but in its capacity to adapt and change, that is, its capacity to learn. Progress depends on a state of mind that's willing to say "farewell."

Leader as Poet, Prophet, Coach, or Therapist. Metaphors are a form of knowledge, agrees Roberts, an important way for us to understand the realities we experience. There is no ideal leadership model, he argues. Different situations require different ways of looking at leadership. Sometimes it's reasonable to issue ultimatums and orders (if a hurricane is bearing down on the district, for example, you don't want principals wondering whether to close schools). In other situations, exhortation may be the leadership style required (for example, encouraging the local child protective services agency to visit a home one more time).

One way to think of this is to envision a two-part continuum, suggests Roberts (see Figure 9.1). Along the vertical continuum, we find changes ranging from the very big to the relatively modest. That continuum intersects with a horizontal one, where leaders' confidence in what they know about the challenge varies from almost complete ignorance to total mastery. The leadership style appropriate for each of the quadrants this figure creates is quite different.

The leadership style called for in quadrant A (the change required is major and you are confident you know what to do) is that of a prophet. You are determined to close the achievement gap. You are convinced that the way to accomplish that is through standards and assessment, harnessed to powerful consequences for failure. You cannot blow an uncertain trumpet in such a situation. Only Moses will do. To succeed as a leader here, you have to show people the Promised Land while guaranteeing them a road map through the desert. In this role, if you need the seas to part and the sun to stand still to permit you to finish your work, you must assure the public you're up to the task.

Being a prophet is a big job. It's a very satisfying role. The public will stand in awe of you. But make sure you deliver on the prophecy. People very quickly get testy with prophets who disappoint them.

Figure 9.1   Leader as Poet, Prophet, Coach, and Therapist

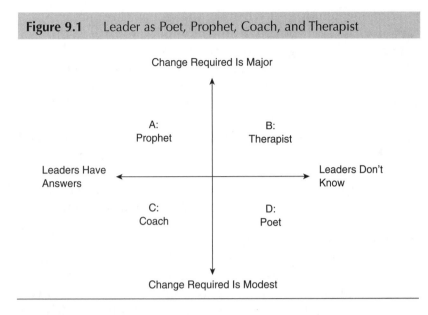

Quadrant B presents a different leadership challenge. Here the required change is massive, but you're not sure what to do. This is the classic adaptive challenge. The leadership style required is that of a therapist. Think of Bob Newhart dealing with the impossible demands of a neurotic on the phone. When things start falling apart, everyone tends to become a bit neurotic, particularly when faced with the loss of something precious.

When a judge hands down a decision about integration that requires substantial realignment of attendance boundaries, your community will tighten up. People in the district will also get excited when population shifts require you to close schools in the South End while building new ones in the North. (Beware of false prophets showing up in this quadrant, promising easy solutions to these challenging problems. Neurotics are likely to be attracted to them.) When it comes to shutting down schools, citizens are going to look around for someone to blame. You could very easily wind up in the firing line. In these situations, you have to do a lot of hand-holding, keeping the community together and listening to its problems as it works them out. This is precisely the role Ron Heifetz suggests you adopt in working through adaptive challenges. In addition to hand-holding, make sure you gather some critical friends around and find some way to get to the balcony. This is very difficult work, requiring double-loop learning. It's not a question of doing things properly, but of doing the proper thing.

Life is much simpler when the changes required are minimal (quadrant C) and you are confident you know what to do. This is technical and single-loop work. You know how to handle it. It's a breeze. Ideally, you could turn the problem over to an assistant and head for the beach. If it's a little more challenging, you can coach your people through what needs to be done. The changes required are probably fairly minor. You don't have to be a prophet or a therapist. People can see what's required and probably won't be angry about it. Here you can visualize yourself as "leader as coach."

A therapist may be required when the changes are enormous and you are unsure, but when relatively modest change is in the air and you are uncertain (quadrant D) you might want to think of yourself as a poet. Here it's important to remind the community of what it stands for, what its "song" is. Even though, in your mind, the change is a relatively modest administrative matter (closing High School A for 12 months, over two school years, to refurbish it, while enrolling the students in High School B), it may loom as enormous and life-shattering for students and parents. You have to help people through this, too. A little hand-holding is probably in order, while reminding the community of its values—passing on excellence in education to the next generation. So you need to be a bit of a bard here. Bards and poets, after all, remind the community of its history and songs; they help preserve the vision and emotions that make the community a community.

The challenge, of course, is knowing when to apply which leadership style to which challenge. On one level, that might require another fieldbook. But for now, revisit the images and commonplaces outlined in this one. They cover a lot of ground and promise to give shape and meaning to your superintendency and your leadership. Good luck.

3. Questions for Reflective Practice

Think about leadership, your style, and your district. Where are you, your colleagues, and your district on these issues?

What images of organization do you hold about your district? Think about this carefully. What's the dominant story line in your mind? What images support that story?

Track recent developments in the district against your images. Do the images still hold up? Or are you kidding yourself about how the district functions?

What images of organization do major players in your district hold? Board members? Unions? Business and community leadership? Are they similar or different?

What are the implications of those images for your work?

How do the images of the various stakeholders affect the "commonplaces"? Are you fairly comfortable with the cross-indexed table presented in this section? If not, how would you change it?

Are you more attracted to the emerging images? Or do the inherited images seem more real to you? Each of these metaphors has some strengths and weaknesses. Can you work through an exercise in which, individually, your board, unions, and central office lay out the pros and cons? Could you then bring the three groups together to compare their perceptions?

Identify three to five issues in your community and relate these issues or developments to the images and commonplaces described in this section. Does your district lean toward quick fixes? Or toward laying the groundwork to pursue fundamental solutions?

If you had to define your job from the many metaphors presented in this part (ranging from prophet to flunkey), what would it be?

Can you describe situations in which you have exercised leadership in a different way depending on your level of knowledge and the complexity of the challenge? When have you been a prophet? When have you felt more like a therapist?

Where is your board on these leadership questions? What about the union and the central office?

What do you stand for? Name the one thing on which you'd be willing to stake your career.

Appendices

The four of us spent 10 years working with fascinating school leaders in The Forum for the American School Superintendent. The Forum was a unique professional learning opportunity generously funded for a decade by the Danforth Foundation. Our experiences with the superintendents in the Forum provided the backbone of this fieldbook. Here, in these appendices, we provide a short description of the Forum and as complete a listing of the membership over the years as we can reconstruct.

Clearly, also, we relied on a lot of help, from both within and outside the Forum, to put this volume together. We want to acknowledge the huge debt we owe to all of our contributors. These appendices tell you who they are.

Appendix A

The Forum for the American School Superintendent

As a school leader, do you smile grimly if someone reminds you that, when you're up to your knees in alligators, it's hard to remember you started out to drain the swamp? You're not alone. That's why the Danforth Foundation set out in 1992 to create a 10-year effort to help practicing school superintendents deal with the leadership challenges they face.

These superintendents, drawn equally from urban, rural, and suburban jurisdictions, were deliberately selected to be as diverse as America itself and to represent districts with high concentrations of students at risk of school failure.

Throughout this work, Forum superintendents challenged themselves to improve learning opportunities for their students. In semiannual meetings and working groups known as "initiatives," in hotel meeting rooms, public gatherings, and school board meetings, the questions they put to themselves were always the same: how can we make sure all children learn? What do we have to do to help young children make the transition from home to school? How can we work with our communities to create schools that are vibrant and strong? Can we lead when difficult problems have no easy answers? Where can we find new ways to strengthen the front line of school administration, the school principal? And, as the number of "minority" Americans becomes a majority, how does this society make good on its promises of equal opportunity?

The people who made up the Forum harbored no illusions that the task of improving American schools was easy. We don't have to tell you that turnover among superintendents is endemic. Chaos within individual Forum members' districts was hardly unknown. Signs of turnover were everywhere around the Forum. Over the life of this effort, approximately 200 superintendents participated in it, but rarely more than 50 at a time. Forty-one superintendents gathered at the inaugural Forum meeting in 1992. Ten years later, just one of them held the same position. The rest had retired or moved on, voluntarily or involuntarily. Several members served in three different superintendencies during the Forum's lifetime, and one of those, in the final year, was "between opportunities." One of the superintendents who participated for the entire 10 years had worked in four different school districts in the first 6 years. Sustaining leadership amid turmoil of this sort is beyond challenge; it's well-nigh impossible. But Forum members took up the burden.

Several basic considerations dominated the Forum's structure and functions:

• First, this was a forum "for" superintendents. This was not an activity to study superintendents or something that was "about" them. It was "for" them. Superintendents themselves determined the agenda.

• Next, it provided a "safe harbor," a place in which superintendents could feel secure discussing their challenges while reflecting on their successes and disappointments.

• Third, Forum membership was made up about equally of leaders of urban, rural, and suburban districts. The nonnegotiable requirement was that at least 50% of the students in each district would be from "at-risk" backgrounds. This Forum served districts with great challenges.

• Apart from geography, what about diversity? The Forum was determined to break the mold of a school leadership structure dominated by white males. Typically, about 60% of Forum participants over the years were women or members of minority groups.

Two Major Thrusts

The Forum operated with a two-pronged program emphasis. First, it convened two intensive, plenary, four-day meetings each year. During these meetings, all Forum members wrestled with the substantive difficulties, programmatic complexities, and political challenges of their public positions.

Between the semiannual meetings, the second emphasis came into play. Selected superintendents, normally 8 to 10, participated in carefully structured leadership development activities organized around special initiatives. Five initiatives were developed by an advisory committee made up of participating superintendents. Each initiative—early childhood education, leadership, public engagement, school principals, and race and class—was designed to last for at least five years.

And so was born a diverse group harnessed to a diverse agenda. Men and women. White superintendents and superintendents from minority backgrounds. Big districts . . . small districts . . . and everything in between. Something greater than the sum of its parts developed. These superintendents realized that what they shared in common was much more powerful than what seemed to set them apart.

Like most people in the world today, educators rarely have the opportunity to stick to one thing for 10 years. This program was a gift to its participants. The great value of the Forum was the extended support it provided to superintendents. The great benefit was delivered to the children and families in these superintendents' districts. And the Forum's great glory was made up of the men and women in it. This fieldbook is dedicated to them.

Appendix B

Members of the
Forum for the American
School Superintendent

Our records haven't been perfect, and the list below may miss a few people, but it includes most of the superintendents who were members of the Forum. Because several participants moved among positions, this list follows the book's general convention: the affiliation listed is the last official position the individual held during the Forum's lifetime. The list also includes members of the Forum's advisory committee.

Antony Amato	Hartford, Connecticut
Raymond Armstrong	Normandy Public Schools, Missouri
Lynn Beckwith, Jr.	University City, Missouri
Alan Beitman	Manchester Public Schools, Connecticut
Arnold Bell	Chaffee R-2 Public Schools, Missouri
Richard Benjamin	Cobb County Schools, Georgia
Stuart D. Berger	Baltimore, Maryland
Cloyde "Mac" Bernd	Arlington Public Schools, Texas
Thomas C. Boysen	Commissioner of Education, Kentucky
Hugh Burkett	Clover Park Schools, Washington

Paula Butterfield	Mercer Island, Washington
Nelda Cambron-McCabe	Miami University, Oxford, Ohio
Benjamin Canada	Portland, Oregon
Gene R. Carter	Association for Supervision and Curricululm Development, Alexandria, Virginia
Rudy M. Castruita	San Diego County, California
Cile Chavez	Littleton, Colorado
Roland Chevalier	St. Martin Parish School District, Louisiana
Carol B. Choye	Scotch Plains–Fanwood Public Schools, New Jersey
Pendery Clark	San Mateo, California
Audrey Clarke	Lynwood, California
Constance Clayton	Philadelphia, Pennsylvania
Dan Colgan	St. Joseph's, Missouri
Paul Copes	Bloomfield, Connecticut
Joe Coto	East Side Union High School District, California
Rudolph F. Crew	New York, New York
Luvern L. Cunningham	(Retired) The Ohio State University, Columbus, Ohio
Beatriz Reyna-Curry	San Elizario, Texas
Patricia Daniel	Hartford, Connecticut
Ray Daniels	Kansas City Public Schools, Kansas
Daniel Daste	Anderson County, Tennessee
Eddie Davis	Manchester, Connecticut
John E. Deasy	Santa Monica–Malibu Unified School District, California
Ronald Epps	Richland County Schools, Columbia, South Carolina
Howard Fuller	Marquette University, Wisconsin
Barbara Gates	Crossett School District, Arkansas
Shirl Gilbert	Indianapolis, Indiana
James Hager	Washoe County, Nevada
T. Josiha Haig	East Orange School District, New Jersey
Beverly Hall	Atlanta, Georgia

Cleveland Hammonds	St. Louis, Missouri
Geraldine Harge	Nye County School District, Nevada
E. Jean Harper	Elyria City Schools, Ohio
Lois Harrison-Jones	Boston, Massachusetts
James Harvey	University of Washington, Seattle, Washington
Robert Henley	University of Missouri, Kansas City, Missouri
Paul T. Hill	University of Washington, Seattle, Washington
N. Gerry House	Memphis, Tennessee
Peter Hutchinson	Minneapolis, Minnesota
Clifford Janey	Rochester City Schools, New York
Robert H. Koff	The Danforth Foundation, St. Louis, Missouri
Joan P. Kowal	Hayward Unified School District, California
Diana Lam	Providence Public Schools, Rhode Island
Mary Leiker	Kentwood Public Schools, Kentwood, Michigan
Wayne Lett	Newport News Public Schools, Newport News, Virginia
David Mahan	St. Louis, Missouri
Mark A. Manchin	Webster County, West Virginia
Floretta McKenzie	The McKenzie Group, Washington, DC
Patsy Menefee	Kendleton, Texas
Richard "Pete" Mesa	Oakland, California
Iris Metts	Christina Schools, Newark, Delaware
Vern Moore	University City, Missouri
Linda Murray	San Jose Unified School District, California
Mary Nebgen	Washoe County, Nevada
Peter Negroni	Springfield Public Schools, Massachusetts
Margaret E. Nichols	Eugene School District 4-J, Oregon

Steven C. Norton	Cache County School District, North Logan, Utah
Les Omotani	West Des Moines Community Schools, Iowa
Sammi Campbell Parrish	Cleveland, Ohio
Bertha Pendleton	San Diego Public Schools, California
Robert Peterkin	Harvard University, Cambridge, Massachusetts
Frank Petruzielo	Broward County, Florida
Michael Redburn	Bozeman Public Schools, Montana
Waldemar Rojas	San Francisco, California
George Russell	Eugene School District 4-J, Oregon
Abelardo Saavedra	Corpus Christi, Texas
Howard Sanders	Hollandale, Mississippi
Neal Schmidt	Santa Monica–Malibu Unified School District, California
Janice Sheets	Tahlequah, Oklahoma
Patricia Sholar	Binger-Oney School District, Oklahoma
Bruce Smith	Normandy Schools, St. Louis, Missouri
Franklin Smith	Washington, DC
Rosa Smith	Columbus Public Schools, Ohio
Ronald Stanfield	Coalville, Utah
William Symons	Charlottesville City Schools, Virginia
Charles Terrett	Fulton County, Kentucky
John Thompson	Pittsburgh Public Schools, Pennsylvania
J. Herbert Torres	Silver Consolidated Schools, Las Cruces, New Mexico
Frank Tota	Dobbs Ferry, New York
Doris Walker	Clover Park Schools, Washington
Richard C. Wallace, Jr.	(Retired) Pittsburgh Public Schools, Pennsylvania
Gary Wegenke	Des Moines, Iowa
Ron White	Cameron, Missouri

Cheryl Wilhoyte	Madison, Wisconsin
Henry P. Williams	Kansas City, Missouri
James Williams	Dayton, Ohio
Ron Williams	Webster County, West Virginia
Charlotte Wright	Weiner, Arkansas
Gary Wright	Cooperating School Districts, St. Louis, Missouri
Saul Yanofsky	White Plains City School District, New York
Arthur Zarrella	Providence, Rhode Island

Appendix C

Contributors

The experience of the contributors to this volume amounts to several hundred years in education. The affiliations listed here are the last held by the contributors during the life of the Forum.

Richard Benjamin	Cobb County Schools, Georgia
Cloyde "Mac" Bernd	Arlington Public Schools, Texas
Mary Beth Celio	University of Washington, Seattle, Washington
Roland Chevalier	St. Martin Parish School District, Louisiana
Janis Dutton	Freelance writer, Oxford, Ohio
Jim Ellsberry	Dewitt Institute for Professional Development, Prince's Lakes, Indiana
Will Friedman	Will Friedman & Associates, Harrison, New York
Howard Fuller	Marquette University, Wisconsin
Barbara Gates	Crossett School District, Arkansas
Michael Goodman	Innovation Associates, Massachusetts
Otto Graf	University of Pittsburgh, Pennsylvania
Gene Hall	University of Nevada, Las Vegas
Geraldine Harge	Nye County School District, Nevada
Constance Iervolino	White Plains City School District, New York
Kathleen Hall Jamieson	University of Pennsylvania, Philadelphia, Pennsylvania

Adam Kernan-Schloss	KSA-Plus Communications, Arlington, Virginia
Art Kleiner	Dialogos, Cambridge, Massachusetts
Diana Lam	Providence Public Schools, Rhode Island
Mary Leiker	Kentwood Public Schools, Kentwood, Michigan
Wayne Lett	Newport News Public Schools, Newport News, Virginia
Linda Murray	San Jose Unified School District, California
Peter Negroni	Springfield Public Schools, Massachusetts
Steven Norton	Cache County School District, North Logan, Utah
Barbara Omotani	Heartland Area Education Agency, Johnston, Iowa
Les Omotani	West Des Moines Community Schools, Iowa
Bertha Pendleton	(Retired) San Diego Public Schools, California
Thomas Poetter	Miami University, Oxford, Ohio
Linda Powell Pruitt	New York University, New York
Charlene Robertson	Arlington Public Schools, Texas
Neal Schmidt	Santa Monica–Malibu Unified School District, California
Rosa Smith	Columbus Public Schools, Ohio
Sylvia Soholt	KSA-Plus Communications, Arlington, Virginia
John Thompson	Pittsburgh Public Schools, Pennsylvania
Richard C. Wallace, Jr.	(Retired) Pittsburgh Public Schools, Pennsylvania
Gary Wegenke	Des Moines, Iowa
Emily White	Bank Street College of Education, New York
Saul Yanofsky	White Plains City School District, New York
Stephen Zsiray, Jr.	Cache County School District, North Logan, Utah

Index

**CORWIN
PRESS**

The Corwin Press logo—a raven striding across an open book—represents the union of courage and learning. Corwin Press is committed to improving education for all learners by publishing books and other professional development resources for those serving the field of K–12 education. By providing practical, hands-on materials, Corwin Press continues to carry out the promise of its motto: **"Helping Educators Do Their Work Better."**

AASA, founded in 1865, is the professional organization for over 13,000 educational leaders across America and in many other countries. AASA's mission is to support and develop effective school system leaders who are dedicated to the highest quality public education for all children.